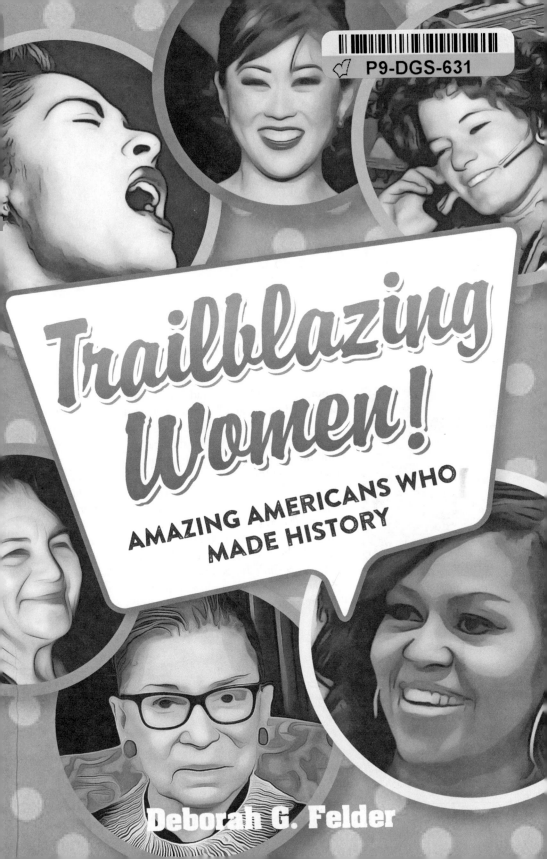

P9-DGS-631

Trailblazing Women!

AMAZING AMERICANS WHO MADE HISTORY

Deborah G. Felder

ABOUT THE AUTHOR

Deborah G. Felder is a graduate of Bard College, where she studied drama and literature. She worked as an editor at Scholastic, Inc., and has been a freelance writer and editor for over thirty years. The author of more than twenty publications, including fiction and nonfiction books and articles for middle grade, young adult, and adult readers, she has published such titles as *The 100 Most Influential Women of All Time: A Ranking Past and Present*; *A Century of Women: The Most Influential Events in Twentieth-Century Women's History*; and *A Bookshelf of Our Own: Works That Changed Women's Lives*. She has also written book reviews for the *New York Times Book Review*, *Kirkus Reviews*, and *Publishers Weekly*. She resides with her husband, Daniel Burt, in South Chatham, Massachusetts.

CONTENTS

Copyright © 2021 by Visible Ink Press®

This publication is a creative work fully protected by all applicable copyright laws, as well as by misappropriation, trade secret, unfair competition, and other applicable laws.

No part of this book may be reproduced in any form without permission in writing from the publisher, except by a reviewer who wishes to quote brief passages in connection with a review written for inclusion in a magazine, newspaper, or website.

All rights to this publication will be vigorously defended.

Visible Ink Press®
43311 Joy Rd., #414
Canton, MI 48187-2075

Visible Ink Press is a registered trademark of Visible Ink Press LLC.

Most Visible Ink Press books are available at special quantity discounts when purchased in bulk by corporations, organizations, or groups. Customized printings, special imprints, messages, and excerpts can be produced to meet your needs. For more information, contact Special Markets Director, Visible Ink Press, www.visibleink.com, or 734-667-3211.

Managing Editor: Kevin S. Hile
Page Design: Sandro Cinelli and Kevin Hile
Cover Design: Graphikitchen, LLC
Typesetting: Marco Divita
Proofreader: Kevin Hile

Cover images: (Billie Holiday) William P. Gottlieb collection, Library of Congress; (Kristi Yamaguch) U.S. Department of Health and Human Services; (Sally Ride) National Archives at College Park; (Michelle Obama) Gage Skidmore; (Ruth Bader Ginsburg) Steve Petteway, Collection of the Supreme Court of the United States; (Dolores Huerta) John Mathew Smith/www.celebrity-photos.com.

ISBN: 978-1-57859-729-1

Cataloging-in-Publication data is on file at the Library of Congress.

Printed in the United States of America.

ALSO FROM VISIBLE INK PRESS

*Black Firsts: 500 Years of Trailblazing
Achievements and Ground-Breaking
Events,* 4th edition
by Jessie Carney Smith, Ph.D.
ISBN: 978-1-57859-688-1

*Freedom Facts and Firsts: 400 Years of the
African American Civil Rights
Experience*
by Jessie Carney Smith, Ph.D. and Linda T. Wynn
ISBN: 978-1-57859-192-3

*The Handy African American History
Answer Book*
by Jessie Carney Smith, Ph.D.
ISBN: 978-1-57859-452-8

The Handy American History Answer Book
by David L. Hudson, Jr.
ISBN: 978-1-57859-471-9

The Handy History Answer Book, 4th edition
by Stephen A. Werner, Ph.D.
ISBN: 978-1-57859-680-5

*The Handy Literature Answer Book: An
Engaging Guide to Unraveling Symbols,
Signs and Meanings in Great Works*
by Daniel S. Burt, Ph.D., and Deborah G. Felder
ISBN: 978-1-57859-635-5

*Native American Almanac: More Than
50,000 Years of the Cultures and
Histories of Indigenous Peoples*
by Yvonne Wakim Dennis, Arlene Hirschfelder
and Shannon Rothenberger Flynn
ISBN: 978-1-57859-507-5

*Native American Landmarks and Festivals:
A Traveler's Guide to Indigenous United
States and Canada*
by Yvonne Wakim Dennis and Arlene Hirschfelder
ISBN: 978-1-57859-641-6

PHOTO SOURCES

American Federation of Government Employees: p. 221. / Associated Publishers, Inc.: p. 9. / George Bergman: p. 215. / Mathew Brady: p. 237. / Bureau of Industrial Service: p. 25. / Camera Craft Studios: p. 21. / Carl Van Vechten Photographs, Library of Congress: pp. 23, 157. / Clifton Waller Barrett Library of American Literature, University of Virginia: p. 181. / Collection of the National Museum of African American History and Culture, Library of Congress: p. 213. / Columbia GSAPP: p. 55. / Columbia University: p. 7. / Dance Magazine: p. 203. / Dutch National Archives (Nationaal Archief): pp. 31, 183. / The Frick Collection/Frick Art Reference Library Archives: p. 37. / George Grantham Bain†collection, Library of Congress: p. 167. / Lynn Gilbert: pp. 39, 49, 57. / Jay Godwin: p. 103. / GSK Heritage Archives: p. 65. / John F. Kennedy Presidential Library and Museum: p. 159. / Steve Jurvetson: p. 83. / Jeff Kern: p. 91. / J. D. Lasica: p. 27. / Kolumn Magazine: p. 29. / Library of Congress: pp. 1, 41, 87, 97, 119, 165, 177, 193, 195, 209. / Los Angeles Times: p. 123. / Metro-Goldwyn-Mayer: p. 95. / Metropolitan Museum of Art: p. 227. / Montana State Capitol: p. 187. / Montikamoss (Wikicommons): p. 99. / NASA: pp. 111, 175. / National Archives at College Park: p. 117. / National Institutes of Health: p. 89. / National Photo Company Collection, Library of Congress: p. 207. / National Portrait Gallery: pp. 73, 151, 211. / New York World-Telegram: pp. 59, 69, 75, 107. / Schlesinger Library, RIAS, Harvard University: p. 161. / David Shankbone: pp. 105, 129. / Shutterstock: pp. 3, 33, 43, 53, 67, 77, 93, 115, 125, 149, 153, 155, 163, 173, 197, 205, 219, 231, 243. / John Mathew Smith & www.celebrity-photos.com: p. 127. / Smithsonian Istitution: pp. 47, 143, 145, 185, 239. / Sharon Styer: p. 135. / TechCrunch (Wikicommons): p. 235. / Time, Inc.: p. 141. / Kyle Tsui: p. 11. / Underwood & Underwood: pp. 63, 191. / U.S. Air Force Space Command: p. 225. / U.S. Army: pp. 19, 61. / U.S. Congress: pp. 121, 179. / U.S. Department of Commerce: p. 131. / U.S. Department of ▮▮▮▮: p. 79. / U.S. Department of Health and Human Services: p. 171. / ▮▮▮ Department of ▮▮▮▮ p. 169. / U.S. Fish and Wildlife Service: p. 35. / U.S. National Library ▮▮ Medicine: p. 24▮ ▮▮▮ Navy: p. 101. / Romana Vysatova: p. 113. / Keith Weller: p. 85. / World Economic Forum: p. 109. / Public domain: pp. 5, 13, 15, 17, 51, 81, 133, 137, 139, 147, 189, 201, 217, 223, 229, 233, 245.

INTRODUCTION

Famed women's rights activist and suffragist Susan B. Anthony once advised women to "Forget what the world will say; think your best thoughts, speak your best words, work your best works, looking to your own consciences for approval." Here are the inspiring stories of extraordinary American women from colonial times to the present whose impressive achievements illustrate Susan B. Anthony's wise words.

Many of the women in this book are so famous it's no surprise to find them here; many others you'll discover for the first time. Their lives and accomplishments are unique and diverse, but they all share one thing in common: they challenged American society's traditional, frequently male-dominated notions of gender roles: what women could and should achieve and how they should behave once they succeeded in their chosen fields. Many faced such obstacles as poverty, racism, sexism, and illness while growing up and in their struggle to succeed, but they never wavered in their determination to reach their goals. They transformed their lives, and in turn they influenced the lives of countless others and had a major impact on the history of our nation.

Women have always fought for change, and sometimes the cost of that fight was high. Elizabeth Cady Stanton's insistence that the campaign for women's rights needed to include demands for a woman's right to vote was met with jeers and anger. Labor leader Mary Harris Jones was jailed for protesting business owners' treatment of their workers; birth control activist Margaret Sanger suffered the same fate when she opened an illegal birth control clinic in 1916. Social worker Jane Addams, once the most admired woman in America, was despised and berated for advocating the cause of peace during World War I; southern civil rights leader Fannie Lou Hamer was the target of violence during the movement to end segregation in America.

The accomplishments of American women in every field of endeavor have been remarkable. Writers such as Toni Morrison and Amy Tan changed the way we look at women and the world. Activists Dolores Huerta and Wilma Mankiller worked to better conditions for Latinx and Native Americans in society and in the workplace. Education for African American girls became a reality, thanks to the efforts of educator Mary McLeod Bethune. Amelia Earhart, Jacqueline Cochran, and Sally Ride influenced young women to seek careers in aviation and space flight. The work of scientists Gertrude Elion, Rachel Carson, Grace Hopper, and Katherine Johnson transformed our understanding of disease, the environment, computers, and physics. Billie Jean King, Althea Gibson, and Wilma Rudolph defied racism and sexism to become world-class athletes.

These are just some of the many amazing women whose stories are featured in this book. They reflect the words of celebrated Supreme Court Justice Ruth Bader Ginsburg, who once said: "Real change, enduring change, happens one step at a time." The women in this book did just that: They took one step, then another. and another, continuing to persist until their outstanding achievements changed our history and blazed a path for other women to follow.

Jane Addams (1860–1935)
Social Reformer

C alled the "beloved lady" of American reform, Jane Addams was a pioneering social worker, reformer, and pacifist, most widely known as the founder and director of Chicago's Hull House settlement house. For her efforts to promote world peace, she was awarded the Nobel Peace Prize in 1931, the first American woman to receive the award.

Born in the small farming town of Cedarville, Illinois, Addams was the eighth of the nine children of John and Sarah Addams. Growing up, she was greatly influenced by her father, a prominent businessman and state senator. Highly regarded in his community, he passed on to his daughter his strong sense of civic responsibility. Addams graduated at the top of her class from Rockford Female Seminary in 1881 and planned to study medicine. However, on a trip abroad in 1888, she became impressed with Toynbee Hall, the settlement house created by British reformer Arnold Toynbee to alleviate the extreme poverty of London's East End. Returning home, Addams began to make plans to establish a similar settlement house in the United States. With her longtime friend Ellen Gates Starr, Addams moved to Chicago and began seeking financial support from philanthropists.

In 1899, they acquired and fully renovated a rundown, two-story mansion, originally built by real estate developer Charles Hull in 1856 and located in a slum neighborhood of Chicago populated by European immigrants. The goal was for educated women to share all kinds of knowledge, from basic skills to arts and literature, with the poor in the neighborhood, and with the women living in the community center among the people they served. Within a year of opening Hull House, Addams and her staff of volunteers, many of whom would become leading progressive reformers, including Florence Kelly, Alice Hamilton, and Grace and Edith Abbott, attended to the needs of the struggling immigrant community with a daycare center; kindergarten; music school; vocational, recreational, and cultural programs; and classes in sewing, cooking, dressmaking, and millinery. Hull House would grow to thirteen buildings, including a summer camp.

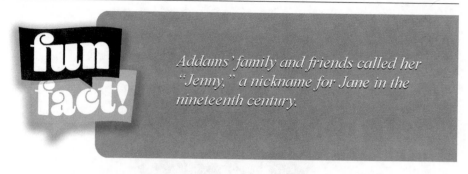

fun fact!

Addams' family and friends called her "Jenny," a nickname for Jane in the nineteenth century.

Addams wrote articles and gave speeches nationally about Hull House but also expanded her interests in social reform, successfully lobbying for the establishment of a juvenile court system, better urban sanitation and factory laws, and protective labor legislation for women. In 1907, she was a founding member of the National Child Labor Committee, which played an important role in the passage of a Federal Child Labor Law in 1916. She also served as president of the National Conference of Charities and Corrections from 1909 to 1915, the first woman to hold that title, and became active in the women's suffrage movement as an officer of the National American Women's Suffrage Association. She was also among the founders of the National Association for the Advancement of Colored People.

An outspoken pacifist, Addams was elected chair of the Women's Peace Party, and in 1919, she became the first president of the Women's International League for Peace and Freedom. Her opposition to America's entry into World War I brought her severe criticism, but she never wavered in her pacifist beliefs. She spent much of the 1920s in Europe and Asia, working for world peace, and by 1930, with the arrival of the Great Depression and the threat of a new war in Europe, Addams's pacifism and tireless social activism gained increasing credibility and respect and was recognized in 1931 when she was awarded the Nobel Peace Prize.

After her death, Addams's body lay in state in Hull House for two days while thousands of mourners filed past to pay their respects to one of the most remarkable women of her age.

Madeleine Albright (1937–)
Diplomat, Secretary of State

When President Bill Clinton appointed Madeleine Albright as secretary of state in 1997, she became the first woman to hold that position and the highest-ranking woman ever to serve in the U.S. government.

Albright was born Maria Jan Korbel in Prague, Czechoslovakia. Her father was a Czech diplomat who fled to England with his wife and infant daughter when the Nazis invaded Czechoslovakia in 1938. The family briefly returned to Prague after World War II, but they fled again in 1948 when the communists assumed power. This time, they immigrated to the United States, where Albright's father became a professor of international studies at the University of Denver.

It was not until after her confirmation as secretary of state that Albright learned that her family members were Czech Jews and not Catholics as she had believed and that three of her grandparents perished in concentration camps during the war. Albright responded to the discovery of her ancestry by saying, "I have been proud of my heritage that I have known about, and I will be equally proud of the heritage that I have just been given."

Albright was interested in foreign affairs from an early age. "By the time I was eleven," she recalled, "I had lived in five countries and knew four languages. In my parents' homes, we talked about international relations all the time, the way some families talk about sports or other things around the dinner table." In 1959, Albright graduated from Wellesley College and married journalist Joseph Albright. After giving birth to twin girls and another daughter, Albright moved with her family to Washington, D.C., commuting from there to Columbia University in New York City to complete her Ph.D. in international relations. Albright later became a professor of international affairs at Georgetown University in Washington and a director of the Women in Foreign Service program at the university's School of Foreign Service.

A respected foreign policy expert on Eastern European and Russian affairs, Albright served as an adviser to Democratic presidential candidates Walter Mondale in 1984 and

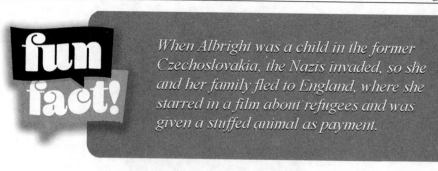

When Albright was a child in the former Czechoslovakia, the Nazis invaded, so she and her family fled to England, where she starred in a film about refugees and was given a stuffed animal as payment.

Michael Dukakis in 1988. In 1992, Bill Clinton named Albright as the U.S. ambassador to the United Nations, making her only the second woman ever to serve in that post.

The Clinton Administration was divided about selecting Albright as secretary of state with one faction arguing, "anybody but Albright," but she was appointed in 1997. Not being a natural-born citizen of the United States, she was not eligible as a U.S. presidential successor and was excluded from nuclear contingency plans. However, during her tenure, Albright influenced American foreign policy, particularly in Bosnia and the Middle East. In 2000, she became one of the highest-level Western diplomats ever to meet Kim Jong-il, leader of North Korea. She won the respect of the international community for her straightforward, no-nonsense style; her in-depth knowledge of foreign affairs; and her diplomatic skills. She proved herself to be a forceful and principled architect of U.S. foreign policy who helped to promote democracy around the world.

Following Albright's term as secretary, it was rumored that she might pursue a career in Czech politics with President Vaclav Havel discussing the possibility of her succeeding him. Albright was reportedly flattered but denied ever seriously considering the possibility. Instead, Albright remained active on various programs and initiatives of interest to her, including genocide prevention, and founded the Albright Group (later the Albright Stonebridge Group), an international strategy consulting firm based in Washington, D.C. Her many books include *Madam Secretary* (2003), *The Mighty and the Almighty* (2006), *Prague Winter* (2012), and *Fascism: A Warning* (2018).

Louisa May Alcott (1832–1888)
Novelist

A novelist and poet, Louisa May Alcott is the author of one of the most beloved novels of all time, *Little Women* (1868), based on the author's childhood experiences in Concord, Massachusetts, with her three sisters. Regarded as a children's literature classic, *Little Women* and its several sequels are written with a sophistication that defies a restriction to young readers. It can be appreciated as a women's novel, one with a strong feminist subtext. Alcott's protagonists, the March sisters, and their wise, principled mother represent five versions of nineteenth-century womanhood, as the novel dramatizes the completeness and self-sufficiency of their nearly all-female universe.

Many telling similarities exist between the March family of *Little Women* and Alcott's own family. Like the spirited, literary-inclined Jo March, Louisa May Alcott was the second oldest of four sisters. Alcott's father, Bronson Alcott, was one of the foremost intellectuals of his day and was variously a schoolmaster, educational innovator, school superintendent, transcendentalist, and lecturer. Because he was frequently absent from home, leaving his family in genteel poverty, the family turned to one another for support with Louisa turning to writing to bring in a family income after trying her hand at work as a seamstress, domestic servant, governess, and teacher.

In 1851, she published a poem in a magazine. Additional poems and serialized stories followed. A first book, *Flower Fables*, a collection of fairy tales, appeared in 1854. She achieved her first notoriety as a writer for *Hospital Sketches* (1863), which drew on her experiences as an army nurse in Washington, D.C. Her first novel, *Moods* (1864), a psychological study of a failed marriage, failed with critics. Henry James, who praised the book's "every-day virtues," felt she lacked the ability to "handle the great dramatic passions" and suggested that she should be "satisfied to describe only that which she has seen."

Alcott would respond with *Little Women*, which showcased her close observation of domestic life in a development story of the four March sisters and their mother as

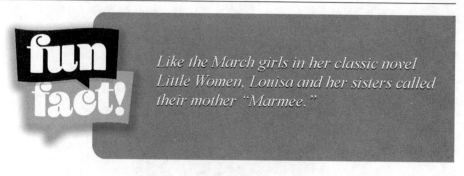

*Like the March girls in her classic novel
Little Women, Louisa and her sisters called
their mother "Marmee."*

their father is serving in the Civil War. Their stories, extended in the sequels *Good Wives* (1869), *Little Men* (1871), and *Jo's Boys* (1886), became international best-sellers, selling millions of copies and spawning three movies and two miniseries.

Alcott's novel may idealize the comforting coziness of nineteenth-century domestic life with, as one of Alcott's biographers puts it, "the vividness of a Currier & Ives print," but in Meg, Jo, Beth, and Amy, Alcott created characters whose strengths and failings, struggles and triumphs are as easily recognized to contemporary readers as they were instructive for young women marching toward a new concept called "feminism" more than one hundred years ago.

Hattie Elizabeth Alexander (1901–1968)
Physician

A pediatrician and microbiologist, Hattie Elizabeth Alexander won international acclaim for developing a serum to combat influenza meningitis, a common childhood disease that was previously nearly always fatal and, with the serum, reduced the fatality rate to 20 percent. She pioneered the study of bacterial mutation and resistance to antibiotics and became one of the first women to head a national medical association as the president of the American Pediatric Society.

Alexander was born in Baltimore, Maryland, and was more interested in athletics than academics early in her education. She attended Goucher College, graduating in 1923 with courses in bacteriology and physiology, which led to jobs as a public health bacteriologist for the U.S. Public Health Service and the Maryland Public Health Service. After three years, she enrolled at Johns Hopkins University, where she received her MD in 1930.

She continued her training in pediatrics at Johns Hopkins Hospital, Columbia-Presbyterian Medical Center in New York, and Columbia University College of Physicians and Surgeons. She was appointed adjunct assistant pediatrician at Babies Hospital and the Vanderbilt Clinic in 1933, and she remained associated with Columbia for the rest of her career. She became assistant attending pediatrician in 1938, attending pediatrician in 1951, and finally full professor in 1958.

Alexander first began researching influenza meningitis in the early 1930s. Attempts to create an anti-influenzal serum derived from horses had failed, but she noted the success of researchers using a rabbit serum to treat pneumonia. Experimenting with rabbit serums, by 1939, Alexander had developed an effective cure for influenzal meningitis and continued to refine the treatment through the early 1940s, and, within a short period, infant mortality from the disease was virtually eliminated.

Becoming one of the first medical researchers to note the development of resistance of influenza bacilli cultures to antibiotic drugs, she studied antibiotics to understand the genetic mutation of bacteria to develop resistance. Her inquiry led her into the new

While on the faculty at Columbia University, Alexander had a reputation for defending struggling students so that their professors would not kick them out of the university, and they could continue their studies.

area of microbiological genetics. Collaborating with fellow microbiologist Grace Leidy, Alexander developed techniques that produced hereditary changes in the DNA of *Hemophilus influenzae* in 1950.

Alexander authored over 150 research papers, and her achievements were recognized by receiving the E. Mead Johnson Award for Research in Pediatrics in 1942, the Stevens Triennial Prize in 1954, and the Oscar B. Hunter Memorial Award of the American Therapeutic Society in 1961. In 1964, she was chosen as the first female president of the American Pediatric Society. After retiring in 1966, Alexander remained active as a teacher and consultant. She died of cancer in New York City at the age of sixty-seven.

Marian Anderson (1897–1993)
Singer

Marian Anderson, who electrified and inspired audiences with her vocal power and range, is celebrated as one of the greatest singers of the twentieth century. The first African American to become a permanent member of New York City's Metropolitan Opera Company, Anderson achieved both artistic greatness and triumphed over racial discrimination with an undaunted spirit.

Anderson was born in Philadelphia, the oldest of three daughters in a poor but loving family. At the age of six, she joined the junior choir at the Union Baptist Church, where she impressed the director by learning all the vocal parts of the hymns. As a teenager, she performed at churches and local organizations, often accompanying herself on the piano. She was prevented from enrolling in a Philadelphia music school because of her race, but members of the city's black community began the "Fund for Marian's Future" to allow her to study with leading vocalists. Anderson enjoyed acting and wanted to try opera, but the exclusion, up until then, of African Americans from the field discouraged her.

In 1925, Anderson won first prize in a New York Philharmonic voice competition; however, despite her critically acclaimed performance as a soloist with the New York Philharmonic and at Carnegie Hall, she had difficulty gaining bookings for performances in the United States because of her race. Anderson received a scholarship from the Rosenwald Foundation that allowed her to study in England and Germany in the late 1920s. She then toured Europe from 1930 to 1935. When she returned to the United States for a concert, the music critic for *The New York Times* proclaimed, "Marian Anderson has returned to her native land one of the greatest singers of our time."

In 1939, in an incident that garnered national headlines, the Daughters of the American Revolution barred Anderson from performing at Constitution Hall, their national headquarters, because of her race. First Lady Eleanor Roosevelt resigned from the D.A.R. in protest, and other prominent women followed suit. Anderson subsequently

Despite being a famous singer, Marian Anderson was often refused service at hotels that were for whites only. When she was traveling in his neck of the woods, Anderson was a welcome guest in the home of Albert Einstein, who despised discrimination in all its forms.

performed in a concert at the Lincoln Memorial before a live audience of seventy-five thousand and millions more who listened to the radio broadcast.

Anderson went on to shatter the racial barrier that had kept black singers from pursuing careers in opera by joining the Metropolitan Opera in 1955. She sang at the inaugurals of President Eisenhower and President Kennedy, and she performed again at the Lincoln Memorial during the memorable 1963 civil rights March on Washington when Martin Luther King Jr. gave his famous "I Have a Dream" speech.

For her service on behalf of racial justice and her contributions to music, Anderson received the U.S. Presidential Medal of Freedom in 1991.

Maya Angelou (1928–2014)
Essayist, Memoirist, Poet

One of America's most popular and acclaimed American poets, storytellers, and essayists, Maya Angelou was also a memoirist whose most famous work, *I Know Why the Caged Bird Sings* (1969), became a pioneering work on gender and race and one of the first autobiographies by an African American woman. Selected by Bill Clinton to read her poem "On the Pulse of Morning" at his 1993 inauguration, Angelou was proclaimed "the black woman's poet laureate."

Born Marguerite Anni Johnson in St. Louis, Missouri, Angelou and her brother were sent to live with her grandmother in Arkansas when her parents' marriage collapsed. Angelou recorded in *I Know Why the Caged Bird Sings* how she was raped by her mother's boyfriend when she was seven. When the man was murdered by her uncles for his crime, Angelou felt responsible and stopped talking, remaining mute for the next five years. During these silent years, Angelou developed her love for books and reading and her ability to listen and observe the world around her. Angelou credits a teacher, Mrs. Bertha Flowers, with helping her to speak again. At the age of fourteen, she and her brother moved with their mother to Oakland, California, where Angelou attended the California Labor School and, at the age of sixteen, became the first black, female cable car conductor in San Francisco. She married a white ex-sailor in 1950, and, after they separated, Angelou sang at the Purple Onion cabaret in San Francisco before becoming a cast member of a touring production of *Porgy and Bess*.

In the 1950s, inspired by Dr. Martin Luther King, Angelou became the northern coordinator of Dr. King's Southern Christian Leadership Conference. In the 1960s, she moved to Cairo with her son and to Ghana. Returning to the United States in the mid-1960s, Angelou was encouraged by author James Baldwin and an editor at Random House to write an autobiography. *I Know Why the Caged Bird Sings,* which chronicles Angelou's childhood, became an immediate popular and critical success and the first of six autobiographical volumes, concluding with the final volume, *A Song Flung up to Heaven*,

Angelou won a Grammy Award in 1994 for her recorded poem "On the Pulse of Morning," which she read at President Bill Clinton's inauguration. She won twice more for Best Spoken Word Album in 1996 for "Phenomenal Woman" and 2003 for "A Song Flung Up in Heaven."

in 2002. Her memoirs helped to define the evolving genre of creative nonfiction that employs fiction-writing techniques such as dialogue and nonchronological narrative.

Angelou also became a popular poet in such collections as *Just Give Me a Cool Drink of Water 'fore I Diiie* (1971), which was nominated for a Pulitzer Prize, *Oh Pray My Wings Are Goona Fit Me Well* (1975), *And Still I Rise* (1978), and *Shaker, Why Don't You Sing?* (1983). Her *Complete Collected Poems* appeared in 1994. She also pursued a career in film and television, becoming the first black woman to have a screenplay (*Georgia, Georgia*) produced in 1972, and received an Emmy nomination for her performance in *Roots* in 1977. She became the first African American woman to direct a major film, *Down in the Delta*, in 1998.

Over a remarkably productive and diverse career, Maya Angelou was an unapologetic voice for racial and gender empowerment. Angelou deserves the credit for writing, in the words of critic Hilton Als, "about blackness from the inside, without apology or defense."

Susan B. Anthony (1820–1906)
Suffragist

Susan B. Anthony is renowned as one of the most prominent leaders of the suffragist movement in the battle to gain the vote for American women. Her efforts of more than fifty years finally led to the passage in 1920 of the Nineteenth Amendment, also known as the Susan B. Anthony Amendment.

Born in Adams, Massachusetts, Susan Brownell Anthony was the second of the six children of Quaker abolitionist parents. Educated at a Quaker school in Philadelphia, she began her career as a teacher in rural New York state, where she campaigned for equal pay for women teachers, coeducation, and college training for girls.

In 1848, Anthony's parents and younger sister attended the first women's rights convention in Seneca Falls, New York. From them, Anthony learned of Elizabeth Cady Stanton, whose groundbreaking Declaration of Rights and Sentiments had become a rallying cry for women's rights and the suffrage movement. Anthony first met Stanton in 1851, and the two joined forces to lead the crusade for women's suffrage. In 1869, they formed the National Woman Suffrage Association to lobby for a constitutional amendment for their cause. Anthony would devote thirty years of her life to traveling around the country to gather support for women's suffrage.

Anthony and Stanton believed that women were entitled to vote under the postwar constitutional amendments that enfranchised former slaves and guaranteed equal rights to all citizens. In 1872, Anthony attempted to vote in the presidential election and was arrested, tried, found guilty, and fined $100, which she refused to pay. No action was taken to enforce the court action, however, which meant that Anthony was unable to challenge the law, as she had hoped, before the U.S. Supreme Court.

Each year beginning in 1876, advocates for women's suffrage presented Congress with a constitutional amendment extending voting rights to women, and each year, Congress ignored or rejected it. However, largely through Anthony's efforts, four states did grant women the right to vote in state and local elections. In 1890, the National

The USS Susan B. Anthony (AP-72) was named after the women's rights activist. Built in 1930 by the Grace Steamship Company, it was turned over to the U.S. Navy in 1942 and used for troop transport in the South Pacific.

Woman Suffrage Association merged with the American Woman Suffrage Association to form the National American Woman Suffrage Association (NAWSA), for which Anthony served as president from 1892 to 1900.

In 1906, the year she died, Anthony attended her last women's suffrage convention. There, she delivered the message that "failure is impossible." It would take another fourteen years and a new generation of suffragists led by Carrie Chapman Catt and Alice Paul for Anthony's conviction to make the passage of the Nineteenth Amendment a reality.

Today, Susan B. Anthony is revered as one of the most influential figures in American history for her dedication to the cause of women's rights and her leadership in the women's suffrage movement.

Dorothy Arzner (1897–1979)
Film Director

Dorothy Arzner was the first female film director in the Hollywood studio system. From 1927 until her retirement from feature directing in 1943, she was also the only female director working in Hollywood. She made a total of twenty films and launched the careers of a number of Hollywood stars, including Katharine Hepburn, Rosalind Russell, and Lucille Ball. She was also the first woman to join the Directors Guild of America and the first woman to direct a sound film.

She was born in San Francisco but grew up in Los Angeles, where her father owned a restaurant. It was frequented by many silent film stars, including Mary Pickford, Mack Sennett, and Douglas Fairbanks and was the first place that Arzner came into contact with the movie business. After finishing high school, she enrolled at the University of Southern California, studying medicine in the hopes of becoming a doctor. During World War I, she joined a local ambulance unit, but working in the office of a surgeon convinced her that a career in medicine was not for her. Instead, she tried the film industry, which was in need of workers after the war. She was given the opportunity to choose a job she preferred, and, after spending a week observing, she decided, "If one was going to be in this movie business, one should be a director because he was the one who told everyone else what to do."

She started in the script department and edited fifty-two films. Asked to edit Rudolph Valentino's film *Blood and Sand* (1922), she shot some of the bullfighting scenes for the film and intercut them with stock footage, saving the studio thousands of dollars. She caught the attention of director James Cruze and became his trusted "right arm." She used a threat to leave Paramount for Columbia to land her first directing job, *Fashions for Women* (1927).

Its success led to her directing three more silent films, and she was given the assignment to direct Clara Bow in her first talkie, *The Wild Party* (1929). Since early talkies were much harder to make, established male directors were content to stay with

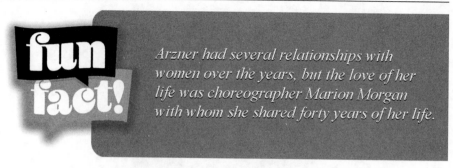

fun fact!

Arzner had several relationships with women over the years, but the love of her life was choreographer Marion Morgan with whom she shared forty years of her life.

silent films, allowing Arzner to deal with the challenges of sound. To ease Bow's discomfort from acting beside a stationary microphone, Arzner had a technician rig a microphone on the end of a fishing rod so a technician could maneuver the mic, following Bow as she moved. Arzner had invented the "boom microphone."

In 1932, Arzner left Paramount to freelance for other studios. When MGM released *The Bride Wore Red* (1937), it advertised it as "A Woman's Love Story Directed by Hollywood's Only Woman Director." During World War II, Arzner made training films for the Women's Army Corps. After the war, she focused on making commercials. Arzner was rediscovered in the 1970s by feminists reviewing older films to screen at film festivals. She was honored by the Director's Guild in 1975, and Katharine Hepburn sent her a congratulatory telegram reading: "Isn't it wonderful that you had such a great career, when you had no right to have a career at all?"

Lucille Ball (1911–1989)
Actress, Comedian, Studio Owner

C omic actor Lucille Ball is the most popular and influential woman in the history of early television. The star and cocreator of *I Love Lucy*, Ball continues to entertain millions of people around the world through the syndication of the show in reruns more than fifty years after its debut.

Born near Jamestown, New York, Lucille Ball left home at the age of fifteen to pursue an acting career in New York City. In acting school, she was repeatedly told that she had no talent and should return home. Determined to succeed in show business, she worked as a waitress and a model before getting her first national attention in 1933 as the Chesterfield Cigarette Girl. Ball was invited to Hollywood to try her luck in the movies, and in the late 1930s and early 1940s, she had some modest success as a featured actress in a variety of comedies and dramas.

In 1940, she married Cuban bandleader Desi Arnaz, whom she had met while the two were making a film. In 1950, the couple formed Desilu Productions to enable them to work together in movies and television. Ball and Arnaz tried to sell a husband-and-wife comedy series starring themselves to a TV network, but executives were convinced that the public would not accept the Cuban-born Arnaz as Ball's on-screen husband. To prove the networks wrong, Ball and Arnaz embarked on a nationwide tour performing their husband-and-wife sketches to live audiences. Finally, they found a sponsor for their concept, and *I Love Lucy* debuted on CBS on October 15, 1951. From 1951 to 1957, each week, nearly forty million viewers watched the zany antics of "America's Favorite Redhead." Since Ball and Arnaz controlled the production of the show, they held the residual rights to reruns, and when the show went to syndication, it made them enormously wealthy. One of the most-watched episodes concerned the birth of Lucy and Ricky Ricardo's (Ball and Arnaz's characters) baby. Making television history as the first real pregnancy to be openly depicted in a broadcast, the event was the culmination of a season in which Ball carried her daughter, Lucie. Ball and Arnaz would have a second child, Desi Arnaz Jr., in 1953.

On her hit TV sitcom I Love Lucy, Lucy's best friend, Ethel Mertz, was portrayed by actress Vivian Vance. In real life, Vance and Ball were not very close at all, but they convinced audiences that they were inseparable pals.

Ball and Arnaz's collaboration ended with their divorce in 1960. In 1962, Ball bought Arnaz's share in Desilu and became sole head of the company. This made her the first woman to head a major Hollywood studio. While busy as an executive, Ball continued to perform on television as well as onstage in the musical *Wildcat* (1960) and on-screen in such films as *Critic's Choice* (1963), *Yours, Mine, and Ours* (1968), and *Mame* (1974). In the 1960s, she starred in two additional television series, *The Lucy Show* and *Here's Lucy*. In 1985, Ball played a spunky bag lady in the television movie *Stone Pillow* and in 1986 attempted a comeback, playing a grandmother in the short-lived situation comedy *Life with Lucy*.

Although all three of her 1950s and 1960s series are television rerun staples, her first series remains her funniest. With *I Love Lucy*, Ball became the first and only female actor to raise slapstick comedy to a fine art while at the same time helping to firmly establish the situation comedy as a major television entertainment form for future generations of viewers.

Clara Barton (1821–1912)
Army Nurse

Called the "Angel of the Battlefield" for nursing soldiers during Civil War battles, Clara Barton went on to establish the American Red Cross, one of the most notable humanitarian organizations in the United States.

Born in North Oxford, Massachusetts, Barton was the youngest of the five children of a farmer and sawmill owner. She was educated by her older brothers and sisters and at local schools. Barton became skilled at nursing when, beginning at the age of eleven, she nursed one of her brothers through a persistent illness for two years. When she was eighteen, she began to work as a teacher in neighboring schools. In 1852, she founded one of the first free public schools in New Jersey and later moved to Washington, D.C., where she worked as a clerk in the U.S. Patent Office.

When the Civil War began, Barton witnessed the first significant battle of the war at Bull Run. Shocked to find a severe lack of first-aid facilities and provisions for the wounded, she quit her job and arranged her small residence as a storeroom, bypassing government and military red tape and inefficiency to accumulate bandages, medicine, and food for the troops. With the help of a few friends, she distributed these supplies to the Union soldiers on the battlefields. Often under fire, Barton ministered to the wounded on both the Union and the Confederate sides at every major battle in Maryland, Virginia, and South Carolina. She was officially named head nurse for one of General Benjamin Butler's units in 1864, even though she had no formal medical training.

After the war, Barton ran the Missing Soldiers Office. While there, she helped find or identify soldiers killed or missing in action and marked thousands of graves. Barton and her assistants would eventually locate more than twenty-two thousand missing men. She spent the summer of 1865 helping to find, identify, and properly bury thirteen thousand individuals who died in the Andersonville prison camp in Georgia. From 1865 to 1868, Barton received widespread recognition for a series of lectures she delivered throughout the United States on her wartime experiences. During this time, she

While nursing a wounded soldier on a Civil War battlefield, Barton nearly lost her life when a bullet ripped through the sleeve of her dress. The same bullet fatally wounded her patient. She never mended her sleeve as a reminder of his wartime sacrifice.

met Susan B. Anthony and Frederick Douglass and became active in both the women's suffrage and postwar civil rights movements.

Mentally and physically exhausted after her countrywide tours, Barton traveled to Europe in 1869 to regain her health. While in Switzerland, she learned of the International Committee of the Red Cross, which had been created in 1863 to relieve the suffering of soldiers on the battlefield. Barton managed to convince eleven European governments to respect the neutrality of ambulance and health care workers on the battlefield, who were identified by the sign of a red cross on a white background. This arrangement became part of the rules of the Geneva Convention and its international treaty regarding wartime behavior.

Back in the United States, Barton began a campaign to create an American Red Cross chapter and to push the American government into ratifying the Geneva Treaty. To help gain support, she supported Red Cross involvement in disasters such as floods, fire, railway accidents, and epidemics. In 1881, Barton organized the American Association of the Red Cross, and the following year, the U.S. Senate ratified the Geneva Treaty.

Barton would lead the American Red Cross for the next twenty-three years, providing relief in twenty-one disasters. Rejecting government subsidies, Barton appealed directly to the public for contributions, using her personal savings when funds were low.

Barton retired as president of the Red Cross in 1904 and spent her last years at her home near Washington. Both the Glen Echo, Maryland, house in which she spent the last fifteen years of her life and the Missing Soldiers Office in Washington, D.C., are now museums.

𝓕𝓵𝓸𝓻𝓮𝓷𝓬𝓮 𝓑𝓪𝓼𝓬𝓸𝓶 (1862–1945)
Geologist

Pioneering American female geologist Florence Bascom is considered the "first woman geologist" in America, who founded a leading academic center of geology and would train and open the door for following generations of notable female geologists. Bascom would become the second woman to earn a Ph.D. in geology (after Mary Emilie Holmes in 1888), the first woman to earn a Ph.D. from Johns Hopkins University (1893), the first woman to work for the U.S. Geological Survey (1889), the first female geologist to present a paper before the Geological Survey in Washington (1901), and the first woman to be elected to the Council of the Geological Society of America (1924).

Bascom was born in Williamstown, Massachusetts. Her father was a professor at Williams College and later the president of the University of Wisconsin, who would provide his daughter with her first exposure to the field of geology. Her mother was a women's rights activist involved in the suffrage movement. Both parents encouraged their daughter to pursue a college education. Bascom earned her bachelor's degree in arts and letters at the University of Wisconsin in 1882. She would earn a B.S. degree from there in 1884 as well as a master's degree in 1887. She pursued doctoral work in geology at Johns Hopkins University at a time when it was a discipline for men only. She was required to sit behind a screen in class in order not to distract the male students, who were the priority. Her doctorate explored the origins and formation of the Appalachian Mountains, and she became the first woman to receive a Ph.D. from Johns Hopkins in 1893.

Bascom went to work as an assistant geologist for the U.S. Geological Survey, serving as an associate editor of the magazine *American Geologist* from 1896 to 1908. In 1906, the first edition of *American Men of Science* rated her among the top one hundred geologists in the country. After teaching at Ohio State University (1893–1895), Bascom moved to Bryn Mawr College, where, for the next thirty-three years, she created its Department of Geology and developed its library, collections, and laboratories. Her students became her colleagues: four would go on to earn doctoral degrees, and three worked for the Geological Survey. In addition to teaching, Bascom was active in field research,

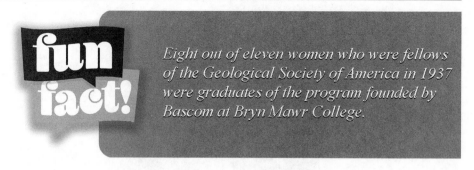

and her work on the geology of the Piedmont remains important today. She published more than forty scholarly articles.

Bascom would retire from teaching in 1928 but continued to work at the Geological Survey until 1936. She died of a stroke at the age of eighty-two, having laid the foundation for American female geologists. In a kind of testimony to both her career and its focus, Bascom observed in 1928, "The fascination of any search after truth lies not in the attainment … but in the pursuit, where all the powers of the mind are absorbed in the task. One feels oneself in contact with something that is infinite, and one finds a joy that is beyond expression in 'sounding the abyss of science' and the secrets of the infinite mind."

Mary McLeod Bethune (1875–1955)
Educator, School Founder

One of the most influential and important African American women in American history, Mary McLeod Bethune was a stalwart advocate for the African American community as an educator and political leader.

Bethune was born in Mayesville, South Carolina, one of the seventeen children of former slaves Sam and Patsy McLeod. On a scholarship, she was able to attend the Scotia Seminary in North Carolina, a school for black girls that emphasized religious and industrial education. She later studied at the Bible Institute for Home and Foreign Missions (later the Moody Bible Institute) in Chicago, where she was the only black student. After graduating in 1895 and failing to find work as a missionary, she began teaching at the Haines Institute in Georgia and the Kendall Institute in North Carolina, where she met and married teacher and salesman Albertus Bethune.

In 1904, Bethune founded a school in Daytona Beach, Florida, for the daughters of African American laborers, raising money for the school by baking pies, selling ice cream, and going door to door seeking donations. In 1923, it merged with the Cookman Institute, a men's school, to become a coeducational college, renamed Bethune–Cookman College, in 1929. Bethune served as its president until 1942, taking a break to concentrate on fundraising, then resuming the presidency until her retirement in 1947.

Bethune's efforts as an educator and advocate for improved race relations brought her to national attention. She cofounded the National Council of Negro Women in 1935 and served as its president until 1949. Bethune became the first African American, female presidential adviser when Franklin Roosevelt named her director of Negro Affairs of the National Youth Administration. During World War II, Bethune was an adviser on minority affairs to Roosevelt and assisted the secretary of war in selecting officer candidates for the U.S. Women's Air Corps.

In 1930, journalist Ida Tarbell named Bethune in the top ten of her list of America's greatest women. Multiple honors followed, including becoming the first woman to receive

Bethune was the only woman of color to attend the first conference of the United Nations in 1945. She was selected to go by President Harry S. Truman. A businesswoman, too, she cofounded the Central Life Insurance Company in Tampa and was part owner of a resort in Daytona.

the National Honor of Merit, Haiti's highest award. Inducted into the National Women's Hall of Fame in 1973, Bethune became the first African American woman to have a monument in her honor erected in Washington, D.C. On the pedestal is engraved a passage from her Last Will and Testament: "I leave you love. I leave you hope. I leave you the challenge of developing confidence in one another. I leave you a thirst for education."

Margaret Bourke-White (1904–1971)
Photographer

Margaret Bourke-White took her camera where no woman had previously dared. A pioneer in her field, she worked as an industrial photographer and a photojournalist at a time when both jobs were considered exclusively the province of men and then rose to the top of both professions.

Born in New York and raised in New Jersey, Bourke-White attributed her determination to excel to her parents' emphasis on effort and achievement, which she described as "perhaps the most valuable inheritance a child could receive." After attending Columbia University, the University of Michigan, and Cornell University, Bourke-White began a career as a photographic specialist in architectural and industrial subjects, taking photos of bridges, smokestacks, and factories, which she sold to various magazines.

In 1929, she became the first photographer for the new magazine *Fortune*, where she began to gain a reputation for taking physical risks and going anywhere to follow a story and get the best shots. While working for *Fortune*, Bourke-White made several trips to the Soviet Union, becoming the first Western photographer to be allowed into the country for many years. In the 1930s, as one of the four staff photographers for *Life* magazine, Bourke-White began to shift her focus from industrial to human subjects, taking poignant photographs of drought victims of the Dust Bowl. In 1936, she spent months traveling throughout the South with writer Erskine Caldwell, documenting the lives of poor southern sharecroppers during the Great Depression. Their work together resulted in the acclaimed 1937 book *You Have Seen Their Faces*. Bourke-White married Caldwell, and they collaborated on two more books: *North of the Danube* (1939), a depiction of life in Czechoslovakia before the Nazi occupation, and *Say, Is This the U.S.A.* (1941), a chronicle of life in America on the eve of the U.S. entry into World War II.

During World War II, Bourke-White became the first U.S. Army Air Force female photographer to see action in North Africa and Italy. She flew on bombing missions and was torpedoed on a boat off North Africa. In 1945, while attached to the U.S.

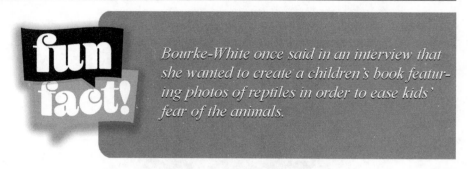

Bourke-White once said in an interview that she wanted to create a children's book featuring photos of reptiles in order to ease kids' fear of the animals.

Army as it raced into Germany, Bourke-White was one of the first photographers to enter the Nazi concentration camps, and her chilling photographs of the conditions and the survivors shocked the world.

By the mid-1970s, Bourke-White was suffering from Parkinson's disease, and it curtailed her career. She completed her last photo essay in 1957; during her tenure at *Life*, she had produced some the most significant photographs of the twentieth century. In 1963, she published her autobiography, *Portrait of Myself*. She died in Connecticut at the age of sixty-seven.

Ruby Bridges (1954–)
Civil Rights Activist

In 1960, at the age of six, Ruby Bridges became the first African American student to integrate an all-white elementary school in the South. She would become an iconic symbol of the civil rights movement and its youngest activist.

The oldest of five siblings, Bridges was born into a farming family in Tylertown, Mississippi. When she was two years old, her parents moved to New Orleans, Louisiana. Her birth coincided with the U.S. Supreme Court's landmark ruling in *Brown v. Board of Education*, which ended racial segregation in public schools. Southern states, however, continued to resist integration, and in 1959, Bridges attended a segregated New Orleans kindergarten. In 1960, a federal court ordered New Orleans to desegregate, and the school district created an entrance examination for African American students to see whether they could compete academically at the all-white school. Bridges and five other students passed the exam.

Her parents were conflicted about whether to let her attend the all-white William Frantz Elementary School a few blocks from their home. Her father feared for his daughter's safety, while her mother wanted her to have the educational opportunities that her parents had been denied. Four federal marshals escorted Bridges and her mother to the school every day; mother and child walked past crowds screaming vicious slurs at them. She would later say that she was only frightened when she saw a woman holding a black baby doll in a coffin. The ardent segregationists pulled their children from the school, and only one of the white teachers, Boston native Barbara Henry, was willing to teach her. For the entire year, Bridges was in a class of one. She ate lunch alone and sometimes played with her teacher at recess, but she never missed a day of school that year. At Bridges's home, her father lost his job, and the grocery stores refused to sell to the family; her sharecropping grandparents were evicted. Eventually, though, others in the community, both black and white, began to show support; families gradually started to send their children back to the school, and the protests began to subside. A neighbor provided Bridges's father with a job, and others volunteered

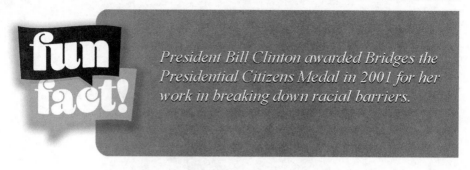

President Bill Clinton awarded Bridges the Presidential Citizens Medal in 2001 for her work in breaking down racial barriers.

to watch the house as protectors. In Bridges's second year, Barbara Henry's contract was not renewed, the federal marshals were gone, and Bridges walked to school every day by herself. However, she had other African American students in her second-grade class, and the school began to see full enrollment again.

In 1964, artist Norman Rockwell celebrated Bridges's courage in a famous painting entitled *The Problem We All Live With*. Bridges graduated from a desegregated high school, became a travel agent, married, and had four sons. She reunited with her first teacher in the 1990s, and the pair did speaking engagements together. In 1993, Bridges began working as a parent liaison at her old elementary school, which had by that time become an all-black school. A lifelong activist for racial equality, in 1999, Bridges established The Ruby Bridges Foundation to promote tolerance and create change through education. She also published her memoir, *Through My Eyes* (1999). In 2011, Rockwell's painting, now part of the permanent collection of the Norman Rockwell Museum, was on display, at the request of President Barack Obama, in the West Wing of the White House for four months.

Gwendolyn Brooks (1917–2000)
Poet

One of the most revered and distinguished poets of the twentieth century, Gwendolyn Brooks was the first African American to win a Pulitzer Prize for Poetry and, in 1976, became the first black woman to be inducted into the National Institute of Arts and Letters. Able to move effortlessly between formal conventions and eloquent language and street talk and the rhythm of black urban life, which became her distinctive subject, Brooks produced a treasury of important and influential works that were all informed by her original and humanistic vision.

Although born in Topeka, Kansas, Brooks grew up on the South Side of Chicago, her mother a teacher and her father a janitor who studied to become a doctor. Her parents taught her the value of literature and learning, and Brooks began to write at the age of seven, composing her first poem, a two-line verse. She filled notebooks with her poetry from the age of eleven. At thirteen, her poem "Eventide" was published in *American Childhood* magazine. Despite her writing success, Brooks's school years were largely unhappy. She was ridiculed for her dark skin by blacks who regarded light skin as the standard of beauty and shunned by whites for being black. Brooks would use her school experiences as the basis for her 1953 novel, *Maud Martha*, one of the first novels to explore theme of a black girl's coming of age. After graduating from high school, Brooks attended a junior college and produced a newspaper focusing on racial and cultural issues. In 1939, she married writer Henry Lowington Blakely, whom she had met through her involvement with the NAACP. The first of the couple's two children was born in 1940.

Brooks's first poetry collection, *A Street in Bronzeville*, was published in 1945, the same year she was selected as one of ten women to receive the *Mademoiselle* magazine Merit Award for Distinguished Achievement. Her second collection, *Annie Allen* (1949), received the Pulitzer Prize for Poetry. In the 1950s, she published a novel, *Maud Martha,* about a woman who stands up to a racist store clerk. She continued through the 1950s and 1960s to publish volumes of children's poetry and adult collections, including *The*

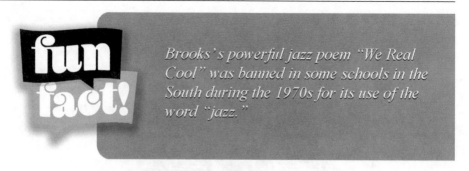

Brooks's powerful jazz poem "We Real Cool" was banned in some schools in the South during the 1970s for its use of the word "jazz."

Bean Eaters (1960), *Selected Poems* (1963), and *Riot* (1969). Her subject matter dealt with the experiences of the African American community with a style that rivaled such modernist writers as Ezra Pound and T. S. Eliot.

In 1967, Brooks attended the Second Black Writers' Conference at Fisk University and was influenced by the energy and perspective of the black writers she met there. The experience would lead to the exploration of the implications of her own black identity. Before 1967, she recalled, "I wasn't writing consciously with the idea that blacks *must* address blacks, *must* write about blacks.... I'm trying to create new forms, trying to do something that would be presented in a tavern atmosphere." She set out "to clarify my language," creating poems in new forms that would be "direct without sacrificing the kinds of music, the picture making I've always been interested in." Her first collection in her new style was *In the Mecca* (1968), subtle portraits of black urban life. From the 1970s to the 1990s, Brooks continued to publish important volumes: *Aloneness* (1971), *Beckonings* (1975), *Primer for Blacks* (1980), *Blacks* (1987), *Winnie* (1988), and *Children Come Home* (1991). In all her works, an original and unique poetic voice is heard capturing the intimate experiences of daily life. As Brooks once described her method, she "scrapes life with a fine-tooth comb."

$\mathscr{Pearl\ S.\ Buck}$ *(1892–1973)*
Novelist

In 1938, writer and novelist Pearl Sydenstricker Buck became the third American and the first of two American women to receive the Nobel Prize in Literature for "her rich and truly epic descriptions of peasant life in China and for her biographical masterpieces." Buck was a tireless advocate of women's rights and of Chinese and Asian cultures.

Born in West Virginia to Presbyterian missionaries, Buck moved to China when she was five months old, remaining there until 1911 (she learned Chinese before she learned English). When she returned to the United States for college at Randolph-Macon Woman's College in Lynchburg, Virginia. She described her childhood as living in "several worlds": the "small, white, clean Presbyterian world of my parents" and the "big, loving merry not-too-clean Chinese world." After graduation, she returned to China, and from 1914 to 1932, she served as a missionary, marrying fellow missionary John Lossing Buck in 1917. Together, they moved to Suzhou, Anhui Province, the region she would memorialize in *The Good Earth.* From 1920 to 1933, the couple lived in Nanjing, where they taught at the University of Nanking. They were swept up in the violence known as the Nanking Incident of 1927 that pitted Chiang Kai-shek's nationalist and communist forces and local warlords against each other. They sought refuge in Japan, where Buck lived for a year before returning to China and devoting herself full time as a professional writer, publishing essays and stories in various magazines in the 1920s.

Buck published a first novel, *East Wind: West Wind,* in 1930 and, working each morning in the attic room of their bungalow in Nanking, completed her masterpiece, *The Good Earth,* published in 1931, the first book of a trilogy that includes *Sons* (1932) and *A House Divided* (1935). The trilogy, collectively called *The House of Earth,* provides an intimate saga of a family and village life in China in the early years of the twentieth century. Buck's realistic and sympathetic depiction of Chinese life and culture was groundbreaking. According to scholar Kang Liao, Buck played a "pioneering role in de-mythologizing China and the Chinese people in the American mind." By her death in 1973, Buck would publish over seventy books, including novels, a collection of short

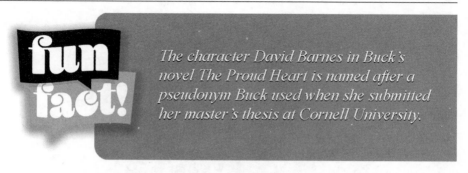

The character David Barnes in Buck's novel The Proud Heart *is named after a pseudonym Buck used when she submitted her master's thesis at Cornell University.*

stories, biographies, an autobiography, poetry, drama, children's books, and translations from the Chinese.

After returning to live in the United States in 1934, living in a farmhouse in Bucks County, Pennsylvania, Buck became active in the American civil rights and women's rights movements. In 1942, she and her second husband, Richard Walsh, founded the East and West Association, which was dedicated to cultural exchange and understanding between Asia and the West. In 1949, she established Welcome House, the first international, interracial adoption agency, and in 1964, she established the Pearl S. Buck Foundation, providing scholarships for thousands of Asian children. In 1973, Buck was inducted into the National Women's Hall of Fame and in 1983 was honored with a postage stamp, part of the Great Americans series. In 2004, *The Good Earth* returned to the best-seller list when it was selected by Oprah Winfrey for her book club.

Tarana Burke (1973–)
Civil Rights Activist

In 2006, Tarana Burke began using the phrase "me too" to raise awareness about the pervasiveness of sexual abuse and assault in society, and in 2017, use of the #MeToo hashtag on social media created a broader movement and a cultural phenomenon. Burke was named by *Time* magazine, among a group of other prominent activists, as one of "the silence breakers," making them the *Time* Persons of the Year for 2017.

She was born in the Bronx, New York, and grew up in a low-income, working-class family in a housing project. She experienced rape and sexual assault as a child and teenager. She has stated that the violence she experienced has inspired her to work to improve the lives of other victims of sexual abuse. She attended Alabama State University before transferring to and graduating from Auburn University.

After college, she began working in Selma, Alabama, with the 21st Century Youth Leadership Movement, the National Voting Rights Museum & Institute, and the Black Belt Arts and Cultural Center. In 2003, she cofounded Jendayi Aza, which became Just Be, Inc., a nonprofit, all-girls program for young, black teenagers. She coined the phrase "me too" while working at Just Be, Inc., in 2006 after hearing stories by victims of sexual abuse and was searching for the right words to express empathy with the young women and girls who disclosed their experiences to her. "Me too" was meant to express, "You are not alone. This happened to me, too." As Burke has described the expression, "On one side, it's a bold declarative statement that 'I'm not ashamed' and 'I'm not alone.' On the other side, it's a statement from survivor to survivor that says 'I see you, I hear you, I understand you and I'm here for you and I get it.'" Burke used the term to raise awareness of the pervasiveness of sexual abuse and assault.

The Me Too movement was transformed into #MeToo in 2017 when actress Alyssa Milano used the social media platform Twitter to invite those who have experienced sexual harassment, abuse, or assault to share their stories in order that "we might give people a sense of the magnitude of the problem." In the first 24 hours, the hashtag was

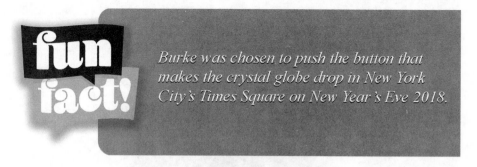

fun fact!

Burke was chosen to push the button that makes the crystal globe drop in New York City's Times Square on New Year's Eve 2018.

shared in more than twelve million posts and reactions, and the #MeToo movement, connecting abuse survivors around the globe, had become a cultural phenomenon.

In 2018, Burke received the Prize for Courage from the Ridenhour Prizes, awarded to individuals who demonstrate courageous defense of the public interest and passionate commitment to social justice. Burke works as the senior director at Girls for Gender Equity and organizes workshops to help improve gender policies at schools and in the workplace. She continues to focus on helping victims of sexual violence as one of the core public faces of the #MeToo movement.

Rachel Carson (1907–1964)
Biologist

Marine biologist and nature writer Rachel Carson, perhaps more than anyone else, catalyzed the global environmental movement with her 1962 book, *Silent Spring*, a controversial and groundbreaking study of the dangers of chemical pesticides. The book led to a nationwide ban on DDT and other pesticides and sparked the movement that eventually led to the creation of the U.S. Environmental Protection Agency.

Rachel Louise Carson was born on a farm in Springdale, Pennsylvania. She described herself as a "rather solitary child" who "spent a great deal of time in woods and beside streams, learning the birds and the insects and flowers. Carson became a published writer by the age of ten, writing for children's magazines. While attending the Pennsylvania College for Women (later Chatham College), she studied literature with the goal of becoming a writer. However, a required biology course ignited her passion for science, and she changed from an English major to a biology major, graduating magna cum laude in 1929. She next studied at the oceanographic institution in Woods Hole, Massachusetts, and at Johns Hopkins University, where she received a master's degree in zoology.

Carson was forced to forego the pursuit of a doctorate to support her mother and two orphaned nieces. She became only the second woman hired by the U.S. Bureau of Fisheries, where she worked for the next fifteen years as an aquatic biologist, writing brochures and educational materials for the public. She eventually would be promoted to editor-in-chief of all publications for the U.S. Fish and Wildlife Service.

An article she wrote for the bureau on marine life was accepted by *Atlantic Monthly*, and it grew into her first book, *Under the Sea World* (1941). In 1951, a second book, *The Sea Around Us* (1951), became a worldwide best-seller; it was translated into thirty-two languages and won the National Book Award for Nonfiction. A companion volume, *The Edge of the Sea*, was published in 1955. Both books are vivid accounts of the ocean and shorelands that combine keen scientific observation with rich, poetic descriptions.

Because of her book sales, Carson was able to move to Southport, Maine, to concentrate on her writing. She would then move to Silver Spring, Maryland, to care for

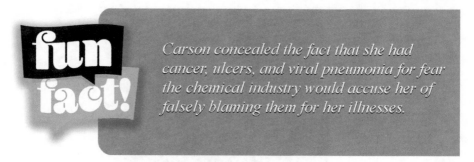

fun fact!

Carson concealed the fact that she had cancer, ulcers, and viral pneumonia for fear the chemical industry would accuse her of falsely blaming them for her illnesses.

her aging mother, and in 1958, she received a letter from a friend describing the devastating effects on her private bird sanctuary in Duxbury, Massachusetts, after it was sprayed with the pesticide DDT under the state's mosquito control program. Carson investigated and began to document the impact of DDT and other chemicals on plants, animals, and people. She published her findings in *Silent Spring* in 1962, detailing pesticides' effects on ecosystems and the health risk for humans. She also accused the chemical industry of spreading misinformation and ridiculed public officials' inaction.

Chemical companies sought to discredit her as a communist or hysterical woman, and when a CBS special, *The Silent Spring of Rachel Carson*, aired in 1963, chemical companies pulled their ads. Fifteen million people viewed the program, and President John F. Kennedy's Science Advisory Committee validated Carson's research, launching a national debate on the use of pesticides that eventually led to the banning of DDT and increased sensitivity to environmental dangers that ignited the modern environmental movement. In addition to having won a crucial battle on behalf of the environment, Carson also touched off a much-wider debate that challenged the assumptions that industrial progress must come at the expense of the environment. *Silent Spring* had fundamentally altered the way many people saw the world and the responsibility of humans to protect it.

Carson would be honored for her work, receiving medals from the National Audubon Society and the American Geographical Society and induction into the American Academy of Arts. At the pinnacle of her notoriety and acclaim, Carson, seriously ill with breast cancer, died two years after her book's publication. In 1980, she was posthumously awarded the Presidential Medal of Freedom. According to environmental engineer and Carson scholar H. Patricia Hynes, "*Silent Spring* altered the balance of power in the world. No one since would be able to sell pollution as the necessary underside of progress so easily or uncritically." In certain fundamental ways, Carson created a new science: environmental studies.

Mary Cassatt (1845–1926)
Painter

The only woman in the Impressionist group of artists who helped to redirect modern art, Mary Cassatt is universally regarded as the greatest female artist of the nineteenth century. She has also been called "the most significant American artist, male or female, of her generation." As friend and influential art editor and critic Forbes Watson said, rejecting her title as America's best female painter, "Much more interesting and revealing would be a list of men who painted better than Mary. It would be a very short list."

Born in Pittsburgh, Pennsylvania, Cassatt was the daughter of a successful stockbroker and real estate speculator. She was inspired to become a painter when at the age of seven she accompanied her family on an extended four-year European trip to France and Germany, where she was exposed to great European works of art for the first time. While there, she developed an enduring love for Paris and French culture and was determined to return to study painting.

In 1861, she began to study at the Pennsylvania Academy of Fine Arts. When she declared to her father her intention to become a professional painter, he said, "I would almost rather see you dead." However, he supported her decision to return to Europe to study, and, in 1866, she moved to Paris and began her training by copying paintings in museums. After additional time in Italy and Spain, she began exhibiting regularly in the 1870s at the Paris Salon, but she stopped when its jury disapproved of the avant-garde direction of her work. In 1877, Edgar Degas invited her to exhibit with the Independents (called Impressionists by hostile critics). As Degas told Cassatt, "Most women paint as though they are trimming hats.... Not you." Cassatt and the other Impressionists began the greatest redefinition of art since the Renaissance. Committed to truthful depiction of ordinary life, the Impressionists sought to recreate an artist or viewer's impressions of a scene and explored the effect of light on a subject. Cassatt's works are characterized by their unusual angles of vision and natural and unposed portraits. Cassatt is most famous for her many depictions of mothers and their children.

After seeing an exhibition in Paris in 1890 featuring works of Japanese painters, Cassatt became inspired by the Ukiyo-e genre, admiring its emphasis on simple lines and use of color blocking.

In 1893, Cassatt bought a chateau in Oise, where she lived and worked until her death. In 1904, she was made a chevalier of the French Legion of Honor. Her artistic greatness was finally recognized in the United States when the Pennsylvania Academy and the Chicago Institute awarded her several prizes (all of which Cassatt rejected). Cassatt lost her eyesight in her later years and was forced to stop painting. She died at her chateau at the age of eighty-two, having achieved during her long life the double distinction of pioneering a new art and a new role for female artists.

Julia Child (1912–2004)
Chef, Television Personality

A chef and cookbook author who brought the art of French cooking to kitchens across the United States, Julia Child also brought her techniques to millions with her award-winning television cooking show *The French Chef*.

Child was born Julia Carolyn McWilliams on August 15, 1912, in Pasadena, California. She was tall and athletic and grew up playing tennis, golf, and basketball. She attended a private boarding school and in 1934 graduated from Smith College, where she majored in history. After graduation, she worked as a copywriter in New York City.

During World War II, she served in the Office of Strategic Services (OSS), first as a top-secret researcher in Washington and later on assignment for the OSS in Ceylon and China. In China, she met a fellow OSS employee, Paul Child; they married after the war in 1946. In 1948, they moved to Paris, where Paul was assigned as an officer with the U.S. Information Agency (USIA). In Paris, she attended the Cordon Bleu school and through a women's cooking club met her future coauthors Simone Beck and Louisette Bertholle. Their landmark book, *Mastering the Art of French Cooking*, published in 1961, became an immediate best-seller and is still in print today.

Child's NET (later PBS) television show, *The French Chef*, premiered in 1963 and introduced her friendly and entertaining, yet expert, style to the American public. The show won a Peabody Award in 1965 and an Emmy Award in 1966 and ran nationally for ten years. She went on to publish more books, including *The French Chef Cookbook* and *Mastering the Art of French Cooking, Volume 2*. For the next thirty-five years, she continued her television and publishing career while living in Cambridge, Massachusetts. Paul Child died in 1994, and Julia moved to Montecito, California, in 2001. In her later years, she received many national and international awards, including the U.S. Presidential Medal of Freedom and France's Legion of Honor. In 1995, she established the Julia Child Foundation to support the culinary arts. The National Museum of American History at the Smithsonian Institution in Washington, D.C., includes an exhibit titled Bon Appetit! Julia Child's Kitchen.

While serving in the OSS during World War II, Child worked with a team of scientists to successfully develop a shark repellant for the Navy.

Shirley Chisholm (1924–2005)
Congresswoman

The first African American woman in Congress and the first woman and African American to seek the nomination for president of the United States from one of the two major political parties, Shirley Chisholm was an inspirational trailblazer, noted for her outspoken advocacy for women and minorities.

Born Shirley Anita St. Hill in Brooklyn, New York, Chisholm was the daughter of immigrants from the West Indies island of Barbados. After graduating from Brooklyn College in 1946, Chisholm worked as a teacher in a childcare center before serving in New York City's Bureau of Child Welfare, helping to set up daycare centers for working women. In 1949, she married Conrad Chisholm. They divorced in 1977, and she subsequently married Arthur Hardwick Jr. The marriage lasted until his death in 1986. In the 1950s and early 1960s, Chisholm began to work for better minority and female participation in local politics. At that time, white males represented most neighborhoods and districts in New York, even those areas, like the one where Chisholm resided, that were made up largely by African Americans. In 1964, Chisholm ran for and won a seat in the New York Assembly, becoming one of only six African Americans in that body and the only black, female member. In 1968, Chisholm was elected as a Democrat to the U.S. House of Representatives, becoming Brooklyn's first black representative and the nation's first African American, female member of Congress. At the time, only eight other African Americans were members of the House, which had only ten female members. New representatives were expected to wait their turn patiently before speaking up or offering initiatives. Chisholm did neither. She became an outspoken opponent of U.S. policy in Vietnam, a highly visible supporter of the Equal Rights Amendment, and a tireless campaigner for jobs, education, and enforcement of antidiscrimination laws. Referred to as "Fighting Shirley," she introduced more than fifty pieces of legislation and championed racial and gender equality and the plight of the poor. She was cofounder of the National Women's Political Caucus in 1971 and in 1977 became the first black woman and second woman ever to serve on the powerful House Rules Committee.

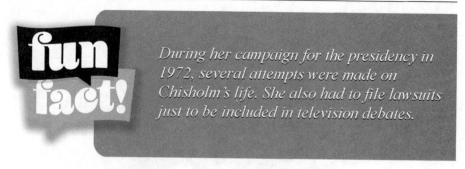

fun fact!

During her campaign for the presidency in 1972, several attempts were made on Chisholm's life. She also had to file lawsuits just to be included in television debates.

In 1972, she became the first woman to make a serious bid for the presidential nomination of a major political party. Discrimination followed her quest for the Democratic Party presidential nomination. She was blocked from participating in the televised primary debate. Still, students, women, and minorities followed her on the "Chisholm Trail," and she entered twelve primaries and garnered 152 delegates' votes (10 percent of the total). Her effort paved the way for other African American candidates, including Jesse Jackson and Barack Obama, as well as the candidacy of Hillary Clinton.

Chisholm retired from Congress in 1983 to return to teaching at Mount Holyoke College, where she remained for four years. In 1985, she helped found the National Political Congress for Black Women and served as its first president. In 1993, President Clinton named her ambassador to Jamaica, but she declined the nomination due to ill health. Chisholm authored several books, including *Unbought and Unbossed* (1970) and *The Good Fight* (1973). Chisholm died in Florida at the age of eighty-one after suffering several strokes. Of her legacy, Chisholm said, "I want to be remembered as a woman … who dared to be a catalyst of change."

Hillary Clinton (1947–)
First Lady, Secretary of State

In summarizing her resume—First Lady of Arkansas, First Lady of the United States, first First Lady to win political office, first female senator from the State of New York, first woman to win a nominating primary of a major party, first woman nominated for president by a major party, first female presidential candidate—it is hard to argue that Hillary Clinton is one of the most accomplished political figure in American history. Despite her loss to Donald J. Trump in 2016, she still managed to become the fourth-largest popular-vote winner in American history (behind Barack Obama's two presidential elections, and Joe Biden's win in 2020). She is also one of the most polarizing political figures—both admired and vilified—and a projection (both good and ill) of the status of women in politics at the highest level.

Born Hillary Rodham in Chicago, she was the oldest of five children in a conservative Republican family. While attending Wellesley College in the 1960s, she shifted her political views to the left and became a committed social progressive and political activist. Attending Yale Law School, she began dating fellow law student Bill Clinton, and the couple campaigned together in Texas in 1972 for the unsuccessful Democratic presidential candidate George McGovern. She received her law degree in 1973, having stayed on an extra year to be with Clinton. She declined his first proposal following graduation, but they eventually married in 1975.

Following her graduation from law school, she served as staff attorney for the Children's Defense Fund and was a member of the impeachment inquiry staff in Washington, D.C., to advise the House Committee on the Judiciary during the Watergate scandal. After failing the District of Columbia Bar and passing the Arkansas Bar, she made the decision to follow Clinton to Arkansas: "I chose to follow my heart instead of my head." Clinton was teaching law and running for a seat in the U.S. House of Representatives in his home state. She also began teaching criminal law courses at the University of Arkansas and became the first director of a new legal aid clinic on campus. After losing the Arkansas congressional race in 1974, Clinton was elected Arkansas at-

Clinton won a Grammy award in 1997 for the audiobook version of her best-selling book It Takes a Village.

torney general in 1976, and she joined the Rose Law Firm, specializing in patent infringement and intellectual property law while also working *pro bono* in child advocacy.

In 1978, she became Arkansas's first lady when Bill Clinton was elected governor, a position she would hold from 1979 to 1981 and then again from 1983 to 1992. In 1980, she gave birth to their only child, their daughter Chelsea. Clinton drew national attention for the first time when her husband became a candidate for the 1992 Democratic presidential campaign in her defense of her husband against charges of extramarital affairs and her advocacy of careers for women instead of pursuing the traditional role as homemaker. When Bill Clinton was elected president in 1992, he named Hillary to lead a commission to draft a proposal for national health care reform. It was the most important political role ever assigned to a first lady. Although the health care initiative ultimately failed, she earned respect for her expertise and ability, though also fire from those who were uncomfortable with her prominent role in the administration as well as with allegations over supposed impropriety in real estate deals in which the Clintons had been involved in Arkansas.

During Clinton's second term, Hillary again supported her husband despite the evidence of sexual infidelity with White House intern Monica Lewinsky that led to his impeachment. Some admired her strength and poise in private matters that were made public and sympathized with her as a victim of her husband's behavior; others criticized her as an enabler to her husband's indiscretions or accused her of cynically staying in a failed marriage to further her own political aspirations.

Before the end of the Clinton Administration, Clinton was elected to the Senate from New York in 2000, making her the only woman to serve in an elected office while and after serving as first lady. In 2007, she announced her candidacy for the Democratic nomination for the U.S. presidency. No woman had ever been nominated by a major party for the presidency, and no first lady had ever run for president. Although she lost the nomination to Barack Obama, she had received seventeen million votes during the nomination and had won 1,640 pledged delegates to Obama's 1,763. She was the first woman to run in the primary or caucus of every state, and she substantially eclipsed the totals for Shirley Chisholm's 1972 nomination run in votes and delegates won.

After a hard-fought and contentious primary, Barack Obama made the surprising decision after he was elected president of naming Clinton as U.S. secretary of state. Clinton proved to be a key team player within the administration and earned high praise for her diplomatic skills. She advocated what became known as the "Hillary

Doctrine," which asserted that women's rights were critical for U.S. security interests. She visited 112 countries during her tenure as secretary of state, which ended in 2013, making her the most widely traveled secretary of state ever. *Time* magazine wrote that "Clinton's endurance is legendary."

After announcing her candidacy for the presidency in the 2016 election, Clinton endured a nomination battle with Vermont Senator Bernie Sanders. She was formally nominated at the 2016 Democratic National Convention, becoming the first woman to be nominated by a major U.S. political party. Leading her opponent Donald J. Trump in all the national polls up to the election, she lost the Electoral College total needed. She had won the popular vote by almost three million and became the fifth presidential candidate in U.S. history to win the popular vote but lose the election. She won the most votes of any candidate who did not win the election. Clinton confessed that her loss was painful but called on her supporters to accept Trump as president, saying, "We owe him an open mind and a chance to lead." After losing the Democratic primary in 2008, Clinton famously said, "Although we weren't able to shatter that highest glass ceiling, thanks to you, it's got about 18 million cracks in it."

Jacqueline Cochran (1906–1980)
Army Air Force Pilot

An important contributor to the formation of the Women's Auxiliary Army Corps (WAAC) and director of the Women's Airforce Service Pilots (WASP) during World War II, Jacqueline Cochran became the first woman to pilot a bomber across the North Atlantic. Cochran was also the first woman to break the sound barrier and, at the time of her death, held more speed, altitude, and distance-flying records than any other pilot, male or female.

Born Bessie Lee Pittman in Pensacola, Florida, Cochran was the daughter of a mill-wright who set up and reworked sawmills in various towns. Bessie married Robert Cochran in 1920 and had a son who died at the age of five. After the marriage ended, Cochran kept the name Cochran and began using Jacqueline as her given name. Her second husband was industrialist Floyd Odlum, whom she married in 1936. The couple remained married until Odlum's death in 1976.

Cochran, who was known to her friends as Jackie, worked as a hairdresser during the late 1920s and early 1930s first in Pensacola and then in New York City. After a friend offered Cochran a ride in her airplane, Cochran began taking flying lessons at Roosevelt Field on Long Island, learned to fly an aircraft in three weeks, soloed, and within two years had obtained her commercial pilot's license. She started a cosmetics line called Wings to Beauty and flew her own airplane around the country promoting her products. In the 1930s, she was one of a handful of barnstorming female pilots competing in air races, and by 1938, she was considered the best female pilot in the United States after setting a new transcontinental speed record as well as an altitude record.

Before the United States entered World War II, Cochran was part of Wings for Britain, an organization that ferried aircraft to Britain, becoming the first woman to fly a bomber across the Atlantic. She volunteered for the Royal Air Force and worked for the British Air Transport Auxiliary (ATA), recruiting female pilots in the United States and taking them to England to join the ATA. In 1939, Cochran wrote to Eleanor Roosevelt proposing a women's flying division in the Army Air Force. In 1943, Cochran

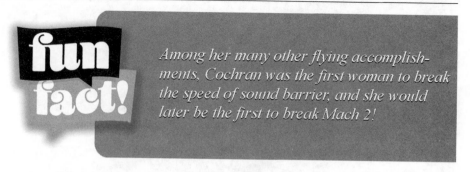

Among her many other flying accomplishments, Cochran was the first woman to break the speed of sound barrier, and she would later be the first to break Mach 2!

was named director of the Women's Airforce Service Pilots (WASP), which supplied more than a thousand auxiliary pilots for the armed forces. She was awarded three Distinguished Service Crosses and commissioned a lieutenant colonel in the Air Force Reserve. She was promoted to colonel in 1969 and retired in 1970.

In 1953, Cochran became the first woman to break the sound barrier and the first woman to pilot a jet aircraft across the Atlantic Ocean. Considered the first female pilot in the U.S. Air Force, Cochran was also the first woman to land and take off from an aircraft carrier, the first pilot to make a blind (instrument) landing, and the first pilot to fly above twenty thousand feet with an oxygen mask.

Jacqueline Cochran's biographer Maryann Bucknum Brinley called Cochran "an irresistible force…. Generous, egotistical, compassionate, sensitive, aggressive—indeed an explosive study in contradictions—Jackie was consistent only in the overflowing energy with which she attacked the challenge of being alive."

Joan Ganz Cooney (1929–)
Television Producer

A s the creator of *Sesame Street*, perhaps the most influential educational TV program in history, Joan Ganz Cooney helped transform children's television in the United States. *Sesame Street* was created to educate preschoolers, particularly those from disadvantaged homes, in basic number, language, and reasoning skills while at the same time entertaining them with humor, music, snappy visuals, and a comical cast of Muppets. The show, which premiered in 1969, would eventually reach an estimated 235 million viewers each week in more than 140 countries.

Joan Ganz Cooney was born and raised in Phoenix, Arizona. After graduating in 1951 with a degree in education from the University of Arizona, she worked as a newspaper reporter before moving to New York City in 1954 to work in television publicity. In 1962, she began producing public affairs documentaries for the New York educational television station, winning an Emmy Award for her documentary *Poverty, Anti-Poverty, and the Poor*.

In 1966, Cooney was asked to prepare a report on how television could be better used to educate the very young. She saw in the assignment a great opportunity. "I could do a thousand documentaries on poverty and poor people that would be watched by a handful of the convinced," she recalled, "but I was never really going to have an influence on my times. I wanted to make a difference." Her report, "The Potential Uses of Television in Preschool Education," demonstrated the educational value of television for preschoolers and became the genesis of *Sesame Street*.

In 1968, with the help of funding from several foundations and the federal government, Cooney cofounded the Children's Television Workshop (CTW), gathering together teams of researchers, writers, teachers, animated cartoonists, and television producers. The group designed a program that would make learning the alphabet and numbers easy and fun by using the same techniques that made cartoons and commercials so successful—animation, songs, puppets, and humorous skits.

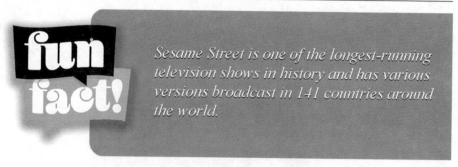

fun fact!

Sesame Street is one of the longest-running television shows in history and has various versions broadcast in 141 countries around the world.

The success of *Sesame Street* led Cooney to produce other highly regarded educational programs that focused on the building of specific skills, such as reading (*The Electric Company*), science (*3-2-1 Contact*), mathematics (*Square One*), and geography (*Where in the World Is Carmen Sandiego?*). Some critics have argued that the CTW technique of teaching children by entertaining them can lead them to expect the same kind of entertainment when they attend school. However, studies have shown that *Sesame Street* has had a positive impact on the learning skills of preschoolers. After fifty years, the program that Joan Ganz Cooney pioneered is still enormously popular and entertaining the young children of many parents who grew up watching the show.

Cooney remained the chairman and chief executive of CTW until 1990 and continued on its executive board. In 1990, she became the first female nonperformer to be inducted into the Academy of Television Arts & Sciences Hall of Fame and was awarded the U.S. Presidential Medal of Freedom in 1995.

Anna Julia Cooper (1858–1964)
Educator

One of the most historically significant African American teachers and scholars, Anna Julia Cooper's life spanned the Civil War through the civil rights movement, which she reflected in important contributions to sociology, history, and African American studies. As a teacher and administrator, she insisted on the importance of education, particularly for African American women. Her lessons and examples of racial and gender empowerment earned her the description "mother of black feminism."

Born a slave in Raleigh, North Carolina, Cooper's father is believed to have been her mother's white master. In 1868, when Cooper was nine, she received a scholarship to enroll in the newly opened Saint Augustine's Normal School and Collegiate Institute in Raleigh, founded by the local Episcopal diocese to train teachers to educate former slaves and their families. She excelled as a student, but her feminism started early when she discovered that her male classmates were encouraged to study a more rigorous curriculum than were the female students. The experience would motivate her for the rest of her life to advocate for the education of black women.

Cooper enrolled in Oberlin College, graduating in 1884 with a B.S. degree in mathematics and a master's degree in 1888. In 1887, she joined the faculty at the M Street High School in Washington, D.C., established in 1870 as the Preparatory High School for Negro Youth. There, she taught mathematics, science, and Latin. While teaching, she completed her first book, *A Voice from the South: By a Black Woman of the South* (1892), which is considered the first book about black feminism. In 1902, Cooper was named principal of the school, and, under her leadership, its academic reputation increased, with several graduates being admitted to Ivy League schools. Cooper's emphasis on college preparatory courses put her at odds with critics like Booker T. Washington, who favored vocational education for blacks. Her contract was not renewed in 1905, and Cooper next taught at Lincoln University, a historically black college in Jefferson City, Missouri, and in 1910, she was rehired at M Street (renamed Dunbar High School in 1916), where she remained until 1930.

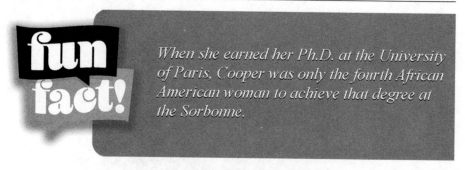

When she earned her Ph.D. at the University of Paris, Cooper was only the fourth African American woman to achieve that degree at the Sorbonne.

In 1911, Cooper began studying part time for a doctoral degree and received her doctorate from the Sorbonne in 1925, at the age of sixty-seven, with her dissertation, written in French but published in English, *Slavery and the French Revolutionists, 1788–1805.*

Cooper's later years were devoted to Frelinghuysen University, an extension program for working African Americans, as its president. She died in Washington, D.C., at the age of 105. Cooper has the distinction of being the only woman who is quoted in current U.S. passports: "The cause of freedom is not the cause of a race or a sect, a party or a class—it is the cause of humankind, the very birthright of humanity."

Barbara Corcoran (1949–)
Entrepreneur

One of the ways in which women have found great success in business is in the real estate industry as brokers and as entrepreneurs, especially in New York. By 2014, women such as Bonnie Stone Sellers (Christie's International Real Estate), Dolly Lenz (Dolly Lenz Real Estate), and Diane Ramirez (Halstead Property) dominated the New York real estate market and were among the nation's most powerful business leaders. The woman who paved the way for them is Barbara Corcoran, founder of The Corcoran Group, a real estate and brokerage company. In 1973, Corcoran borrowed $1,000, quit her job as a waitress, and started a small real estate company in New York City. Over the next twenty-five years, she grew her company into a $5 billion real estate empire.

Born and raised in Edgewater, New Jersey, Corcoran attended a local Catholic elementary school and Sr. Cecilia High School in Englewood. She graduated from St. Thomas Aquinas College in New York in 1971 with a degree in education. She has admitted to having held as many as twenty jobs before she was twenty-three, including renting out apartments in New York City, although she was not yet interested in real estate as a profession. Nevertheless, in 1975, she cofounded a real estate business called The Corcoran-Simonè with her boyfriend, who contributed a $1,000 loan. When the couple split up, Corcoran formed her own firm, The Corcoran Group, and began publishing *The Corcoran Report*, covering real estate trends in New York City. Having grown her company into one of the largest in the city, Corcoran sold her business for $66 million in 2001. The current president and CEO of The Corcoran Group is Pamela Liebman.

The decision to sell was prompted by her giving birth to her son, Tommy, when she was forty-five after seven years of trying to conceive a child with her husband, Bill Higgins, whom she married in 1988. However, Corcoran realized that the life of a stay-at-home mother was not enough for her. "I thought I had made a terrible mistake," she says. "I had no identity. My ego took a hit." She wrote an autobiography, *If You Don't Have Big Breasts, Put Ribbons on Your Pigtails: and Other Lessons I Learned from My Mom* (2003), and pitched herself to TV networks as a real estate expert. She landed a job on

Corcoran has helped about 150 people become successful in business by investing in their ideas and becoming partners in their businesses. She also created an online test to see whether people have what it takes to be an entrepreneur.

Good Morning America, then on the *Today* show, as a regular contributor and offered business advice on CNBC's *The Big Idea with Donny Deutsch*. In 2018, producer Mark Burnett (*Survivor*) approached Corcoran to participate in a not-yet-named reality TV show that would become *Shark Tank*. Corcoran has served on all nine seasons of *Shark Tank* as one of the investment experts who determine whether or not to financially back contestants who pitch their products and inventions on the show. Corcoran has pledged more than $5.4 million in investments in the many deals she has made. She is also the author of the best-selling book *Shark Tales: How I Turned $1,000 into a Billion Dollar Business!* (2011).

Angela Davis (1944–)
Civil Rights Activist, Educator

A radical African American advocate on behalf of civil rights and other social issues, Angela Davis was perhaps the most notorious counterculture activist of the 1960s. She was a member of the Black Panther Party and the Communist Party of America, was twice a vice presidential candidate on the Communist Party ticket, and at one time was the third woman listed on the FBI's Ten Most Wanted Fugitive List.

Born in Birmingham, Alabama, the daughter of a service station-owner father and a schoolteacher mother, Davis lived in the "Dynamite Hill" neighborhood, so called because of all the bombings of houses intended to drive out middle-class blacks who lived there. She attended segregated local public schools. Her mother, Sallye Bell Davis, was a national leader and organizer of the Southern Negro Youth Congress, which was aimed at building alliances among African Americans in the South. Davis finished high school in New York's Greenwich Village and was awarded a scholarship to Brandeis University, one of only three black students in her class. She was influenced by philosopher Herbert Marcuse whom, Davis would say, "taught me that it was possible to be an academic, an activist, a scholar, and revolutionary." As a graduate student at the University of California–San Diego in the late 1960s, she joined several radical groups, including the Black Panthers and the Che-Lumumba Club, the all-black branch of the Communist Party.

In 1969, Davis joined the philosophy department at the University of California–Los Angeles; however, she was fired from her position because of her membership in the Communist Party. She went to court to get her job back but still left when her contract expired in 1970. Davis became a strong supporter of three prison inmates of Soledad Prison known as the Soledad Brothers, who were accused of killing a prison guard after several African American inmates had been killed in a fight with another guard. Suspected of complicity in an abortive escape and kidnapping at the Marin County courthouse involving George Jackson, one of the Soledad Brothers, Davis was a fugitive and finally was arrested in New York City in 1970 and returned to California

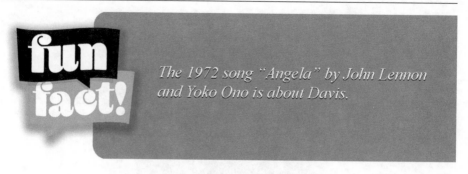

fun fact! *The 1972 song "Angela" by John Lennon and Yoko Ono is about Davis.*

to face charges of kidnapping, murder, and conspiracy. She was acquitted of all charges in 1972.

After a time traveling and lecturing, Davis returned to teaching as a professor of ethnic studies at San Francisco State University from 1980 to 1984 and as a professor of the history of consciousness and feminist studies at the University of California–Santa Cruz and Rutgers University from 1991 to 2008. She is the cofounder of Critical Resistance, an organization dedicated to the abolishing of the prison-industrial complex, and is the author of several books, including *Angela Davis: An Autobiography* (1974), *Women, Race, and Class* (1980), *Women, Culture and Politics* (1989), *Are Prisons Obsolete?* (2003), *Abolition Democracy* (2005), and *The Meaning of Freedom* (2012).

Agnes de Mille (1905–1993)
Choreographer, Dancer

A choreographer, dancer, teacher, and author, Agnes de Mille was one of the most influential figures in American dance. She combined classical and modern dance with the spirited rhythms of American folk dances and helped to transform the American musical theater by bringing the beauty of ballet to a wider audience.

De Mille was a member of a distinguished American theatrical family, which included her father, playwright and director William de Mille, and her uncle, film producer–director Cecil B. de Mille. Born in New York City, she grew up in Hollywood, and, at the age of ten, after seeing the great dancer Anna Pavlova perform, was determined to become a dancer herself. Her parents discouraged her from considering a stage career and initially refused her dancing lessons; eventually they relented, and she began to study ballet. To please her parents, she deferred her dream of becoming a dancer to attend the University of California. Following graduation, de Mille went to New York City to establish a career as a dancer and choreographer. She met with little success because Broadway producers were not interested in her attempt to incorporate classical and American folk elements in her dances in place of the conventional chorus-line dancing popular at the time.

Frustrated, in the early 1930s, de Mille went to Europe, where she studied, worked, and performed for a number of years, meeting with greater success. In 1939, she returned to the United States and was asked to join the newly formed New York Ballet Theatre, which would later become the American Ballet Theatre. With this group, de Mille choreographed *Black Ritual*, the first ballet performed entirely by black dancers in a classic American ballet company. Her ballet *Rodeo*, a celebration of the American West with music by Aaron Copeland, would become a landmark in dance and theater history featuring an innovative mixture of folk dancing, modern dance, and classical ballet.

De Mille also made history with her dances for the Rodgers and Hammerstein musical *Oklahoma!* The show featured an integration of story, song, and dance for the first

Before she became a choreographer whose dances changed Broadway musicals forever, her uncle, famed Hollywood director Cecil B. De Mille, hired her to stage and perform a dance on the back of a live bull for one of his films. She walked off the set when "Uncle C" complained that her dance was terrible.

time in a musical comedy and ushered in a new era of sophistication and artistry in the musical theater. De Mille would also go on to choreograph such classic musicals as *Carousel* and *Brigadoon*. In the 1960s, de Mille became cofounder and president of the Society of Stage Directors and Choreographers. In 1973, she founded the Heritage Dance Theatre, which was devoted to traditional American dance. De Mille's achievement in transforming American dance was acknowledged with a Kennedy Center Award in 1980 and a National Medal for the Arts in 1986.

Katherine Dunham (1909–2006)
Choreographer, Dancer

African American dancer, choreographer, anthropologist, educator, and social activist Katherine Dunham has been called the "matriarch and queen mother of black dance." She had one of the most successful dance careers of the twentieth century, directing her own dance company for many years. She introduced authentic African dance movements and exploded the possibilities of modern dance expression.

She was born Kaye Dunn in Chicago but grew up in Glen Ellyn, Illinois, about twenty-five miles west. Her father was a descendant of slaves, and her mother was of mixed French Canadian and Native American heritage. After her mother died when Dunham was three, her father remarried and moved the family to Joliet, Illinois, where Dunham graduated from high school in 1928. In high school, she studied and performed dance and opened a private dance school for young, black children. After completing Joliet Junior College, she studied anthropology and dances of the African diaspora at the University of Chicago. In 1935, on a travel fellowship, she did ethnographic study of dance in the Caribbean with fellow anthropology student Zora Neale Hurston. She would receive her bachelor's degree in social anthropology in 1936 but abandoned graduate work to relaunch her performance career.

In 1938, she joined the Federal Theatre Project in Chicago and composed a ballet, *L'Ag'Ya*, based on Caribbean dance. Two years later, she formed an all-black dance company that toured extensively, featuring works such as *Tropics* (1937) and *Le Jazz Hot* (1938), based on her research. The Dunham Company toured for two decades around the globe in fifty-seven countries, introducing to Europe for the first time to black dance as an art form. Dunham also choreographed for Broadway stage productions and opera as well as in such films as *Carnival of Rhythm* (1942), *Stormy Weather* (1943), and *Casbah* (1947).

Dunham was a social activist who fought racial discrimination and segregation, creating *Southland*, a ballet that depicted a lynching in 1951, and in 1992, at the age of eighty-

In high school, Dunham joined the Terpsi-
chorean Club, where she was inspired by the
modern styles of Austro-Hungarian Rudolf
von Laban and Swiss music composer Émile
Jaques-Dalcroze, developer of Dalcroze
eurythmics, which teaches music through the
study of movement.

three, staged a forty-seven-day hunger strike to highlight the plight of Haitian refugees.
She is the author of an autobiography, *A Touch of Innocence* (1959). She received a Kennedy
Center Honor in 1983 and a National Medal of Arts in 1989. She died of natural causes a
month before her ninety-seventh birthday. Dance critic Wendy Perron celebrated her
legacy by saying that Dunham "was the first American dancer to present indigenous forms
on a concert stage, the first to sustain a black dance company.... She created and performed
in works for stage, clubs, and Hollywood films; she started a school and a technique that
continue to flourish; she fought unstintingly for racial justice."

Ann E. Dunwoody (1953–)
Army Officer

The first woman to serve as a four-star general in both the Army and the U.S. Armed Forces, Ann E. Dunwoody completed a thirty-eight-year military career in 2012. Her other notable firsts include being the first woman to command a battalion in the 82nd Airborne Division, Fort Bragg's first female general officer, and the first woman to command the Combined Arms Support Command.

Dunwoody was born at Fort Velvoir, Virginia. Her father was a career Army officer, and the family lived in Germany and Belgium while she was growing up. She graduated from Supreme Headquarters Allied Powers Europe American High School in 1971 and attended the State University of New York College–Cortland to pursue a career in physical education. During her junior year, Dunwoody attended a four-week introductory Army program followed by an eleven-week women's officer orientation course, the result of which would be a two-year commitment in the military. After graduating from Cortland in 1975, she received a commission as a second lieutenant in the Quartermaster Corps. She would later earn two master's degrees—in logistics management from the Florida Institute of Technology (1988) and in national resource strategy from the Industrial College of the Armed Forces (1995).

After her initial two-year commitment in the Army, Dunwoody decided to become a career soldier. Her major staff assignments included service as the parachute officer in the 82nd Airborne Division; strategic planner for the chief of staff of the Army; executive officer to the director, Defense Logistics Agency; and deputy chief of staff for Logistics G-4. She was deployed to Saudi Arabia for Operation Desert Shield/Operation Desert Storm in 2001 and for Operation Enduring Freedom and to Uzbekistan in support of Combined Joint Task Force-180. As commander of surface deployment and distribution command, Dunwoody supported the largest deployment and redeployment of U.S. forces since World II, and as commander of the Army Materiel Command, she was in charge of the largest commands in the Army, employing more than sixty-nine thousand personnel across all fifty states in 145 countries.

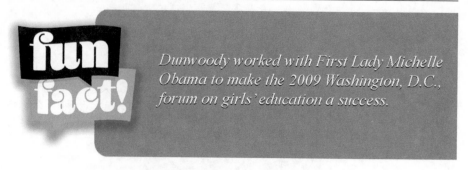

fun fact!

Dunwoody worked with First Lady Michelle Obama to make the 2009 Washington, D.C., forum on girls' education a success.

In 2008, Dunwoody was promoted to general, the first woman in the U.S. military to be promoted to that rank. Chief of Staff of the Army General Ray Odierno stated that while the promotion was significant for women, Dunwoody did not get it because of her gender: "It wasn't because you were a woman. It was because you were a brilliant, dedicated officer, and you are quite simply the best logistician the Army has ever had." Dunwoody subsequently pushed for a decrease in sexual assault in the Army as well as greater opportunities for female soldiers.

Dunwoody retired in 2012. In 2015, she published *A Higher Standard: Leadership Strategies from America's First Female Four-Star General*. It is worth noting that when Dunwoody first became a soldier, women served in the Women's Army Corps. "Over the past 38 years," Dunwoody remarked at her retirement celebration, "I have had the opportunity to witness women Soldiers jump out of airplanes, hike 10 miles, lead men and women, even under the toughest circumstance. And over the last 11 years I've had the honor to serve with many of the 250,000 women who have deployed to Iraq and Afghanistan on battlefields where there are no clear lines, battlefields where every man and woman had to be a rifleman first. And today, women are in combat, that is just a reality. Thousands of women have been decorated for valor and 146 have given their lives. Today, what was once a band of brothers has truly become a band of brothers and sisters."

Amelia Earhart (1897–1937)
Aviator

The most famous female aviator of the twentieth century, Amelia Earhart opened up the field of aviation for women as pilots and engineers. She followed her own particular path of adventure by purposely challenging and rejecting the gender roles of her time.

Born and raised in Atchison, Kansas, Earhart was a tall and lanky girl who enjoyed playing boys' sports. She graduated from Chicago's Hyde Park High School in 1916. She attended Columbia University for a year, pursuing medical studies before working as a nurse in a Toronto military hospital during World War I. She became captivated by flying when she took her first airplane ride. After taking lessons from pioneer female pilot Netta Snook, Earhart soloed for the first time in 1921. A year later, she bought her first plane in which she set a women's altitude record of fourteen thousand feet.

In 1928, Earhart became the first woman to fly across the Atlantic Ocean as one of three crewmembers on a flight of 20 hours and 40 minutes from Newfoundland to Wales. In 1929, she became a founding member and president of the Ninety-Nines, the first U.S. organization of licensed female pilots. In 1931, she married publisher George Putnam, who became her manager and the publisher of the several books she wrote about her experiences. The following year, she became the first woman—and only the second person (after Charles Lindbergh)—to make a transatlantic solo flight. On her trip across the Atlantic, she set a new speed record and earned the first Distinguished Flying Cross given to a woman.

Earhart's many flying achievements in the 1920s and 1930s made her an inspiration to women and a closely followed celebrity. She lectured extensively, encouraging women to pursue their ambitions in careers that had previously been restricted to men.

Between 1930 and 1935, Earhart set seven women's speed and distance records in a variety of aircrafts. In 1935, Earhart became the first aviator to fly solo from Honolulu, Hawaii, to Oakland, California. The same year, she flew solo from Los Angeles to Mexico City and then nonstop from Mexico City to New York. In June 1937, Earhart

Amelia Earhart organized an all-women group of pilots called the Ninety-Nines. She even designed the pilots' uniforms, which were advertised in Vogue magazine.

embarked on a daring, twenty-seven-thousand-mile trip around the equator—the longest flight in aviation history. The most dangerous part of the journey would be across the Pacific from New Guinea to the tiny island of Howland 2,500 miles away. With only primitive navigational equipment, finding such a small landmark in the middle of the Pacific was a daunting prospect.

On July 2, 21 hours after the expected 18-hour flight had begun, the Coast Guard received a final message from Earhart that she and her navigator, Fred Noonan, had approximately 30 minutes of fuel remaining but still had not sighted land. The plane's subsequent disappearance prompted the largest naval search in history but no trace of her, Noonan, or the aircraft was ever found. The fact that Earhart vanished without a trace at the height of her popularity has fueled many rumors and theories, and the mystery of her final flight contributed to the legendary status that she has gained as a great American adventurer.

Earhart has emerged as a feminist icon: independent, cool under pressure, courageous, defiant, and goal oriented. Her accomplishments in aviation inspired a generation of female aviators, including the more than one thousand female pilots of the Women Airforce Service Pilots (WASP), who ferried military aircraft and served as transport pilots in World War II.

Gertrude Elion (1918–1999)
Biochemist, Pharmacologist

Biochemist and pharmacologist Gertrude Elion received the Nobel Prize in Physiology or Medicine in 1988. Among the many drugs she developed were the first chemotherapy for childhood leukemia; the immunosuppressant that made organ transplants possible; the first antiviral medication; and treatment for lupus, hepatitis, arthritis, gout, and the first drug for effectively treating patients with AIDS. She became the fifth female Nobel laureate in Physiology or Medicine and the ninth in science—all without earning a Ph.D.

Elion was born in New York City to immigrant parents from Lithuania and Poland. An excellent student, Elion graduated from Walton High School at the age of fifteen. "I had no specific bent toward science," she recalled, "until my grandfather died of stomach cancer. I decided that nobody should suffer that much." She attended Hunter College, majoring in chemistry, and graduated in 1937. She went on to earn a master's degree from New York University in 1941. Unable to find a job in a research laboratory because she was a woman, she found work at a laboratory for A&P supermarkets performing tedious tasks such as measuring the acidity of pickle juice. "I hadn't been aware," Elion recalled, "that any doors were closed to me until I started knocking on them." She did brief stints teaching before accepting a research assistant position for George H. Hitchings (1905–1998) at Burroughs Wellcome & Company, the pharmaceutical company where she would spend the rest of her career. While working with Hitchings, she started a Ph.D. program taking evening classes at Brooklyn Polytechnic Institute, but after several years of long commutes, she realized that she would be unable to complete her degree without becoming a full-time student. She decided instead to forego the Ph.D. and focus on her research (she would eventually receive honorary doctorates from George Washington University, the University of Michigan, and Brown University).

Working with Hitchings, Elion would revolutionize drug making using a method known as "rational drug design," replacing the conventional method of trial and error with a close study of how organic compounds operated and what could be done to in-

Elion was the first woman inducted into the National Inventors Hall of Fame (in 1991), the same year she was inducted into the National Women's Hall of Fame. The next year, she joined Engineering and Science Hall of Fame, and in 1995 she was named a Foreign Member of the Royal Society.

terfere with harmful effects. Examining the differences between the biochemistry of normal human cells and those of cancer cells, they formulated drugs that could kill or inhibit the production of particular pathogens, leaving the normal cells undamaged. Elion would publish 225 papers on her findings, and by 1950, Hitchings and Elion successfully synthesized the compounds that for the first time interfered with the formation of leukemia cells, putting leukemia patients in remission. Elion would next discover how to make the compounds less toxic to patients, with fewer side effects as a result. This led to one of the first effective chemotherapy treatments.

Elion's innovative research method would lead to the development of multiple new drugs, including Purinethol, the first to treat leukemia; Azathioprine, the first immune-suppressive agent; Allopurinol for treating gout; Pyrimethamine for malaria; Trimethoprim for meningitis, septicemia, and bacterial infections; Acyclovir for viral herpes; and Nelarabine for cancer treatment. Elion's research has affected countless individuals.

Elion officially retired in 1983, but she continued her research, overseeing the development of azidothymidine (AZT), the first drug used in the treatment of AIDS. In 1991, she was awarded a National Medal of Science, and she was presented with the Lemelson-MIT Lifetime Achievement Award in 1997. She died at the age of eighty-one. In what can serve as a fitting testimonial and encouragement for those who will follow her, Elion observed, "Don't be afraid of hard work. Nothing worthwhile comes easily. Don't let others discourage you or tell you that you can't do it. In my day I was told women didn't go into chemistry. I saw no reason why we couldn't."

Peggy Fleming (1948–)
Figure Skater

Born in San Jose, California, figure skater Peggy Fleming began to compete on the junior circuit, winning her first gold medal in the Pacific Coast Juvenile Championship in 1960. She continued a string of successes and in 1964 won her first U.S. Championship as a senior-level skater, which qualified her to represent the United States at the 1964 Winter Olympic Games in Innsbruk. She did not receive a medal at the Olympics but later that year won a bronze medal at her first World Championship.

A stunning series of gold-medal wins followed: in the U.S. Championships in 1965 through 1968; World Championships in 1966 through 1968; and women's singles gold at the 1968 Winter Olympic Games in Grenoble. Although Fleming's performance at the Olympics was deemed not her best, her characteristic grace and skill dominated the competition. She was the only U.S. gold winner at the 1968 Olympics, which added to the attention and acclaim she received in the United States. She turned professional at the end of the 1968 season.

Fleming appeared in her first TV special in 1968 and went on to star in five NBC specials of her own. She regularly skated with the Ice Capades, the Ice Follies, and the Holiday on Ice programs. In 1980, Fleming began her career as a skating analyst on the ABC network. A breast cancer survivor, she became a spokesperson for women's health issues and devotes time to other philanthropic causes.

The Peggy Fleming Trophy is an ice-skating competition founded in 1998 and hosted at the Broadmoor World Arena in Colorado Springs, Colorado. Because of the COVID-19 pandemic, in 2020 it was organized as a virtual skating competition.

Betty Friedan (1921–2006)
Author, Women's Rights Activist

If Catherine East was, in Betty Friedan's words, the "midwife of the contemporary women's movement" of the 1960s and 1970s, then Friedan can be considered the movement's first parent. Her groundbreaking 1963 book, *The Feminine Mystique*, was absorbed into the hearts and minds of American women and is widely regarded as the spark that would ignite the women's movement. Friedan would go on to become one of the most influential leaders of the movement she helped set in motion.

Born Bettye Naomi Goldstein, Friedan was born in Peoria, Illinois, the oldest child in a family of two daughters and a son. Her father, Harry, was a jeweler; her mother, Miriam Horowitz Friedan, had been a journalist who gave up her career when her daughter was born. While growing up, Friedan often felt lonely and isolated as a Jewish child in the largely Christian community of Peoria and later ascribed her commitment to social justice as stemming from her awareness of the injustice of anti-Semitism. Friedan's sense of exclusion did not prevent her from excelling in school. A voracious reader in childhood, she was an academically gifted student who was involved in her high school newspaper. When her application to write a column for the paper was turned down, she founded a literary magazine called *Tide*, won a dramatic award (for a time she aspired to become an actor), and graduated as valedictorian of her class.

In 1938, Friedan entered Smith College, where she studied psychology. After graduating cum laude in 1943, she won a fellowship to study at the University of California–Berkeley. There, she dropped the "e" from her first name. Unwilling to commit to a doctorate and a career as a psychologist, Friedan left after a year at Berkeley to move to New York City. Due to the shortage of men in civilian jobs because of World War II, Friedan was able to find work as a journalist first for the Federated Press, a news agency for labor unions with left-wing newspapers, and later for the *UE News*, the official publication of the United Electric, Radio, and Machine Workers of America. One of her assignments was to report on the House Un-American Activities Committee (HUAC), which began investigating supposed communists in the United States not

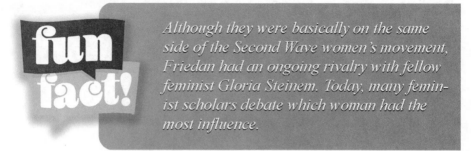

Although they were basically on the same side of the Second Wave women's movement, Friedan had an ongoing rivalry with fellow feminist Gloria Steinem. Today, many feminist scholars debate which woman had the most influence.

long after the war. She also authored union pamphlets arguing for workplace rights for women. In 1947, she married Carl Friedan, a theater producer, and the following year, she gave birth to the couple's first of three children. After twelve stormy years together, the Friedans divorced.

In the 1950s, Friedan was fired from her job with the *UE News* because she was pregnant with her second child and had requested her second maternity leave. She then became a freelance writer for various women's magazines. Concurrent with Friedan's growing dissatisfaction with her primary role as wife and mother was the notion, popular in American society and promoted in the magazines for which Friedan wrote, that the highest achievements to which a woman should aspire were marriage, motherhood, and homemaking. Friedan began to wonder if other women shared her discontent, and in 1957, she sent a questionnaire to two hundred of her Smith College classmates. The answers she received convinced her that her ailment, a psychic distress she came to call "the problem that has no name," was widespread. She began several years of research into the origins of, as she later wrote, "the discrepancy between the reality of our lives as women and the image to which we were trying to conform." Friedan analyzed that image and found it to be a fantasy of post–World War II, happy, suburban, female domesticity created and supported by educators, sociologists, psychologists, and the media. She called the image and the book that resulted from her research *The Feminine Mystique*. An immediate success, the book spoke to the legions of women who had sacrificed their identities and sense of self-worth by succumbing to the gilded cage of the suburban home. Although it continues to be read as a classic work in the history of twentieth-century American women, *The Feminine Mystique* has also drawn criticism over the years for its focus on the lives of white, middle- and upper-middle-class women to the exclusion of working-class women and women of color.

The Feminine Mystique was seen as a new, unifying force in second-wave feminism, and its now famous author emerged as a leading figure in the women's movement that followed. In 1966, she cofounded the National Organization for Women (NOW) and served as NOW's president until 1970. In the 1960s and 1970s, she helped found the National Association for the Repeal of Abortion Laws (1969), renamed several times and now known as NARAL Pro-Choice America, organized the Women's Strike for Equality on the fiftieth anniversary of the ratification of the Nineteenth Amendment to raise awareness of gender discrimination, and was a cofounder of the National Women's Political Caucus (1971). Through her activism within these organizations, Freidan was influential in helping to change unfair hiring practices, gender inequality, and pregnancy discrimination in the workplace.

Friedan's sometimes abrasive and imperious personality led to clashes with others in the women's movement, and as more diverse voices emerged, she was criticized for her focus on issues facing middle-class, educated, heterosexual women. Friedan's emphasis on retaining the movement's mainstream ties alienated her from younger, more radical feminists who were increasingly becoming an influential force within the women's movement. Nevertheless, Friedan remained a visible and passionate activist on behalf of women's rights, who has been described as the "mother of the modern women's movement."

In addition to her activism, Friedan taught at New York University and the University of Southern California and frequently lectured at women's conferences around the world. In 1976, she published *It Changed My Life: Writings on the Women's Movement*, in which she assessed the progress of the movement and her relationship with it. Concerned with the splintering of the movement into smaller groups with a variety of agendas, she called for an end to polarization and a new emphasis on "human liberation." Friedan's other works include *The Second Stage* (1981), *The Fountain of Age* (1993), *Beyond Gender* (1997), and a memoir titled *Life So Far* (2000). The recipient of many awards throughout her career, Friedan's papers are held at the Schlesinger Library at Harvard University's Radcliffe Institute.

Margaret Fuller (1810–1850)
Author, Editor, Journalist

The first female full-time book reviewer, author, editor, and journalist, Margaret Fuller also produced what is considered to be the first major feminist work in the United States, *Woman in the Nineteenth Century* (1845). Susan B. Anthony would write that Fuller "possessed more influence on the thought of American women than any woman previous to her time."

Born in Cambridge, Massachusetts, the first child of Congressman Timothy Fuller, her father provided her with an education as rigorous as any boy's, forbidding her the standard feminine fare of the time such as etiquette books and sentimental novels. Educated at schools in Boston and Groton, Fuller would earn, by the time she was thirty, the reputation of being the best-read person—male or female—in New England and became the first woman to be allowed to use the library at Harvard. Fuller's reputation as an intellectual drew prominent women, including the wives of Ralph Waldo Emerson and Hawthorne, Lydia Maria Child, and Mrs. Theodore Parker, to a series of classes called "Conversations" that Fuller hosted from 1839 to 1844, giving women a rare forum to discuss academia and issues of the day.

With Emerson, Fuller founded *The Dial* in 1940. It was a literary and philosophical journal that Fuller edited and to which she contributed articles and reviews, including in 1843 her groundbreaking feminist manifesto "The Great Lawsuit," which called for women's equality. When *The Dial* ceased publication in 1844, Fuller moved to New York to join Horace Greeley's *New York Tribune* as a literary critic and reviewer. In 1845, she expanded her *Dial* essay "The Great Lawsuit" into *Woman in the Nineteenth Century*, a classic of the women's movement. In 1846, she became the first female foreign correspondent for the *Tribune*. In Italy, she fell in love with Giovanni Ossoli, a lieutenant of Giuseppe Mazzini in the cause of Italian Unification, with whom she had a son. On the front lines in the revolution for the establishment of a Roman Republic that failed, Fuller, Ossoli, and her son sailed back to America, where, within one hundred yards of Fire Island, their ship went aground and sank, and no trace of Fuller, Ossoli, or her son were ever found.

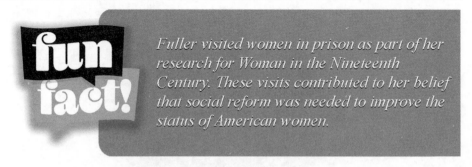

Fuller visited women in prison as part of her research for *Woman in the Nineteenth Century*. These visits contributed to her belief that social reform was needed to improve the status of American women.

Edgar Allan Poe, who both admired Fuller's integrity as a writer and decried some of her ideas, famously declared that "humanity is divided into men, women, and Margaret Fuller," a testimony to a singular figure in American women's history.

Fuller was inducted into the National Women's Hall of Fame in 1995.

Althea Gibson (1927–2003)
Tennis Player

A pioneering African American tennis player, Althea Neale Gibson was born in Silver, South Carolina. In 1930, her parents moved to Harlem, where they lived on a block that was barricaded during the day so that neighborhood children could play organized sports. Gibson learned paddle tennis there, and by 1939, at the age of twelve, she was the New York City women's paddle tennis champion. Members of the Cosmopolitan Tennis Club noticed her athletic prowess and paid for a junior membership as well as lessons.

Many of the national tennis tournaments were closed to African Americans, so Gibson began to compete in tournaments sponsored by the American Tennis Association (ATA), an organization founded in 1916 to promote tennis for African Americans. Gibson's first tournament win was the 1941 ATA New York State Championship when she was fourteen. She was the national junior champion in 1944 and 1945 and national singles champion for ten straight years (1947–1956). During this time, Gibson attended Florida A&M University and graduated in 1953.

Despite Gibson's outstanding level of play, she was barred from entering the U.S. National Championships (now the U.S. Open). Although U.S. Tennis Association rules prohibited racial or ethnic discrimination, players gained points at official tournaments, most of which were held at white-only clubs. In 1950, in response to lobbying by ATA officials and prominent tennis stars, Gibson became the first black player to receive an invitation to the U.S. Nationals, where she played in her first tournament on her twenty-third birthday. Although she did not win a title, she gained attention for her talent and skill as well as for her barrier-breaking participation. She went on to win other tournaments and in 1952 was ranked seventh nationally by the USTA.

As an amateur, she made no money from competitions, and, after graduation, she began teaching physical education at Lincoln University in Jefferson City, Missouri. Her tennis career was reinvigorated when the U.S. State Department invited her on a

fun fact!

In addition to her attempt at a singing career and playing golf, Gibson also played the saxophone quite well.

six-week "goodwill tour" of Asia, where an integrated group of tennis stars played exhibition matches. She remained abroad after the tour, winning sixteen of the eighteen tournaments in Europe and Asia. In 1956, she became the first African American to win a Grand Slam tournament, the French Championships singles event.

Throughout 1957 and 1958, Gibson dominated women's tennis. In 1957, she won the Wimbledon and U.S. National singles titles, the Wimbledon and Australian doubles titles, and the U.S. mixed doubles title. In 1958, she successfully defended her Wimbledon and U.S. National singles titles and won her third straight Wimbledon doubles championship. She was the number-one-ranked woman in the world and in the United States in both 1957 and 1958 and was named Female Athlete of the Year by the Associated Press in both years as well. She became the first black woman to appear on the covers of *Sports Illustrated* and *Time*. Gibson ended her amateur career in 1958 with five Grand Slam singles titles, five Grand Slam doubles titles, and one mixed doubles title.

After relinquishing her amateur status, Gibson faced the need to make a living. No professional tours existed for women, which meant that her opportunities were limited to promotional events such as playing before Harlem Globetrotters games. She attempted a singing career and recorded an album but was not particularly successful. She appeared in the 1959 film *The Horse Soldiers* and worked as a sports commentator and advertising spokesperson. In 1960, she published her first memoir, *I Always Wanted to Be Somebody* (written with Ed Fitzgerald). Racial barriers, however, prevented her from obtaining the financial endorsements of other tennis stars.

In 1964, at the age of thirty-seven, Gibson broke another barrier as the first African American woman to join the Ladies Professional Golf Association (LPGA) tour. Although she achieved some success, the financial rewards were low, and she retired from the golf circuit in 1978.

In 1968, Gibson published her second memoir, *So Much to Live For* (with Richard Curtis). In the early 1970s, she began working in sports administration for both local and state governments in New Jersey. She also devoted time to clinics and coaching, particularly for the underprivileged. Her later years were marked by health problems, including a stroke and serious heart problems.

Ruth Bader Ginsburg (1933–2020)
Attorney, U.S. Supreme Court Justice

The second female justice on the U.S. Supreme Court (following Sandra Day O'Connor), Ruth Bader Ginsburg is a widely admired jurist for the probity of her decisions and for her indefatigable commitment to service.

Born Ruth Joan Bader in Brooklyn, New York, she grew up in a working-class neighborhood. Her father was a merchant. Her older sister died of meningitis at the age of six when Ginsburg was fourteen months old. Outside the family, Ginsburg began to go by the name "Ruth" to help teachers distinguish her from other students named Joan. The Baders were an observant Jewish family, and she attended synagogue regularly. When she started James Madison High School, her mother was diagnosed with cancer and died just days before her daughter's graduation, which Ginsburg did not attend. As Ginsburg recalled, "My mother told me two things constantly. One was to be a lady, and the other was to be independent."

She attended Cornell University on a full scholarship, graduating with a B.A. degree in government in 1954. The same year, she married law student Martin D. Ginsburg. He began army service, and they had their first child in 1955. In 1956, Ginsburg enrolled in Harvard Law School, one of only nine women in a class of about five hundred men. She was asked by the law school dean, "Why are you at Harvard Law School, taking the place of a man?" When her husband took a job in New York City, Ginsburg transferred to Columbia Law School, becoming the first woman to be on two major law reviews at both Harvard and Columbia. She earned her law degree in 1959, tying for first in her class.

Despite her outstanding academic record, Ginsburg experienced gender discrimination while seeking employment after graduation. After clerking for a U.S. District Court judge (1959–1961), Ginsburg taught at Rutgers University Law School (1963–1972) and at Columbia (1972–1980), where she became the school's first female tenured law professor. In the 1970s, she also served as the director of the Woman's

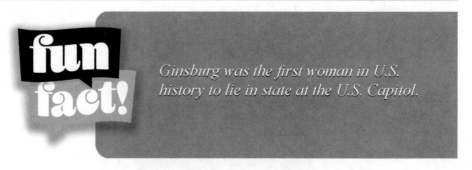

Ginsburg was the first woman in U.S. history to lie in state at the U.S. Capitol.

Rights Project of the American Civil Liberties Union, arguing six landmark cases on gender equality before the U.S. Supreme Court.

In 1980, President Jimmy Carter appointed her to the U.S. Court of Appeals for the District of Columbia, where she served until she was appointed to the U.S. Supreme Court by President Bill Clinton in 1993. As a justice, Ginsburg was on the Supreme Court's moderate-liberal bloc, whose opinions are generally marked by moderation and restraint but are also a strong voice in favor of gender equality. In 1996, she wrote the court's landmark decision in *United States v. Virginia* that determined that the state-supported Virginia Military Institute could not refuse to admit women. She strongly dissented in the case of *Bush v. Gore,* which effectively decided the 2000 presidential election.

In 2010, her husband, Martin, died of cancer, ending their marriage of fifty-six years. Ginsburg would call him her biggest booster and "the only young man I dated who cared that I had a brain." The day after her husband's death, Ginsburg was back at work on the court. It is this devotion to her job and her apparently steadfast focus and energy that has turned Ginsburg into a cultural icon and the subject of two feature films, the documentary *RBG* (2018) and the biopic *On the Basis of Sex* (2018), which is about the first case she argued before the Supreme Court on gender equality. She also became a recurring character played by Kate McKinnon on *Saturday Night Live.* In 1999, Ginsburg was diagnosed with colon cancer. She underwent surgery, chemotherapy, and radiation treatments and never missed a day on the bench. In 2018, she was hospitalized after fracturing three ribs in a fall. A day later, she returned to her regular judicial work schedule. The scan of her ribs showed cancerous nodules in her lungs, and she underwent a left lung lobectomy. On January 7, 2019, for the first time since joining the court more than twenty-five years earlier, Ginsburg missed an oral argument while she recuperated. She returned to work on February 15, 2019.

After a long struggle with metastatic cancer of the pancreas, Ginsburg died at her home in Washington, D.C. Her casket was on display outside the Supreme Court building for two days before being moved to Congress, where memorials were attending by numerous dignitaries. She had served as a Supreme Court justice for twenty-seven years.

When asked when enough women would be on the Supreme Court, Justice Ginsburg notoriously replied, "When there are nine."

Maria Goeppert-Mayer (1906–1972)
Physicist

Theoretical physicist Maria Goeppert-Mayer became the second woman to be awarded a Nobel Prize in Physics (after Marie Curie) and the first American woman. She is best known for proposing the nuclear shell model of the atomic nucleus: inside the nucleus, protons and neutrons are arranged in a series of layers, like the layers of an onion, with neutrons and protons rotating around each other at every level. Her discovery was foundational in the development of nuclear physics.

Goeppert-Mayer was born in Kattowitz, Germany (now Poland), the only child of a professor of pediatrics at the University of Göttingen and a former music teacher. Goeppert-Mayer was educated at a girls' grammar school operated by suffragettes. When it went bankrupt after her junior year, she passed the collegiate examination to enter the University of Göttingen without a high school diploma. She earned her Ph.D. there in 1930, the same year she married American chemical physicist Joseph Edward Mayer, and the couple moved to the United States, where he was offered a faculty position at Johns Hopkins University. Policies at the university prevented them from hiring both spouses in faculty positions, so for the next nine years, Goeppert-Mayer worked at Johns Hopkins as a volunteer associate. After becoming an American citizen in 1933, Mayer and her husband both received appointments at Columbia University, although Goeppert-Mayer's was without a salary. She gained her first paid faculty position teaching science part-time at Sarah Lawrence College.

In 1942, Goeppert-Mayer joined the Manhattan Project and worked on the separation of the uranium isotopes for the atomic bomb. Through her friend Edward Teller, Goeppert-Mayer was given a position at Columbia with the Opacity Project, a program to develop thermonuclear weapons. After the war, her husband became a professor in the Chemistry Department at the new Institute of Nuclear Studies at the University of Chicago, and Mayer became a voluntary associate professor of physics at the school. When the nearby Argonne National Laboratory was founded, Goeppert-Mayer was offered a part-time job there as a senior physicist in the Department of Theoretical

It wasn't until the invention of the laser in 1961 that experimental physicists were able to verify Goeppert-Mayer's 1930 doctoral thesis about the possibility of two-photon absorption (TPA) in atoms. TPA would have applications in such areas as 3D optical data storage and imaging.

Physics, although, Goeppert-Mayer admitted, "I don't know anything about nuclear physics." It was at Chicago and Argonne that Goeppert-Mayer developed the mathematical model of nuclear shells. Three other German scientists were also working on the same problem, and, although Goeppert-Mayer's discovery preceded theirs, they were able to publish first and received much of the credit. Goeppert-Mayer would collaborate with one of the scientists, Hans D. Jensen, on the book *Elementary Theory of Nuclear Shell Structure* (1950) and would share the Nobel Prize in Physics in 1963 for their work.

In 1960, Goeppert-Mayer became a full professor of physics at the University of California–San Diego. Suffering a stroke shortly after her appointment, she continued to teach and conduct research for a number of years until her death in 1972. After her death, the Maria Goeppert Mayer Award was created by the American Physical Society to honor young, female physicists at the beginning of their careers.

Martha Graham (1894–1991)
Choreographer, Dancer

Known as the "mother of modern dance," Martha Graham revolutionized the way dancers communicate with their audiences. Born in Allegheny, Pennsylvania, Graham was the oldest of the three daughters of George Graham, a psychiatrist. Her family moved to Pittsburgh and then to Santa Barbara, California, when Graham was fourteen. She was inspired to become a dancer after attending a recital given by the popular dancer Ruth St. Denis in 1911. In 1916, Graham went to Los Angeles to enroll in the Denishawn School of Dancing run by St. Denis and her husband, dancer and choreographer Ted Shawn. Graham made her debut with the Denishawn Company in 1920, dancing the lead in an Aztec-inspired ballet, *Xochitl*, which had been created for her. She left the company in 1923 to work as a solo dancer in the Greenwich Village Follies; two years later, she accepted a teaching position at the Eastman School of Music in Rochester, New York. There, Graham worked on training her body to move in new ways to form a unique and daring style of modern dance that focused on body movement, breathing, and gravity.

Graham performed her new dance style at her first independent dance concert in 1926. Many critics disliked her choreography, but most audiences loved it. She continued to experiment, using dance to explore mood, emotion, and physical expression in ways that were completely different from classical ballet and contemporary modern dance. In 1930, Graham created one of her most famous works, *Lamentations*, a solo piece in which she wore a long tube of material that she stretched out and pulled back to show the reactions of the body to grief.

In the 1930s, Graham founded the Martha Graham School of Contemporary Dance and the Martha Graham Dance Company, both of which would become internationally renowned. In 1934, she began teaching summer workshops at Bennington College in Vermont. There, she created one of her most important works, *Letter to the World*, an interpretation of Emily Dickinson's poetry and life. Graham also created works based on other great women from literature, history, and Greek mythology such as Charlotte and

In addition to being an innovative choreographer, Graham also created her own costumes for her performances, and she directed the makeup design of her dancers.

Emily Brontë (*Death and Entrances*), Joan of Arc (*Seraphic Dialogue*), and Medea (*Cave of the Heart*). Her interest in American themes would result in her best-known ballet, *Appalachian Spring*, which premiered in 1944, with music by composer Aaron Copeland.

Graham was a major influence on two generations of dancers; many of her performers went on to become choreographers and directors of their own companies. She continued to dance until she was in her seventies and to create ballets and teach classes well into her nineties.

𝒯emple 𝒢randin (1947–)
Autism Advocate, Scientist

Temple Grandin is one of the first individuals on the autism spectrum to share her personal experience with autism. She first gained national attention when she was profiled in Oliver Sacks's 1995 book, *An Anthropologist on Mars* (the title refers to Grandin's description of how she feels in social settings). Grandin first spoke publicly about autism in the 1980s at the request of one of the founders of the Autism Society of America. She has since become an influential and eloquent advocate for the autistic community and on behalf of the humane treatment of animals.

Born in Boston into a wealthy family, Grandin was the oldest of the four children of her father, a real estate agent and heir to the largest corporate wheat farm business in America at that time, Grandin Farms, and an actress-singer mother. Grandin was never formally diagnosed with autism but with "brain damage" at the age of two. Grandin did not begin to speak until the age of four. When she was in her teens, her mother saw a checklist on autism created by Dr. Bernard Rimland, founder of the Autism Research Institute, and thought that Grandin's symptoms indicated autism. A formal diagnosis consistent with being on the autism spectrum was only carried out when Grandin was in her forties.

To treat her condition of "brain damage," Grandin worked with a speech therapist, and a nanny was hired to play educational games with her. She was able to attend a supportive kindergarten and elementary school; she was expelled from her private high school for throwing a book at a schoolmate who taunted her. After her expulsion, Grandin's parents divorced, and she spent a summer on an Arizona ranch that would prove formative in her subsequent career interest of animal science. She was sent to a private boarding school for children with behavioral problems, where she met science teacher William Carlock, who would become an important mentor figure. Carlock gave Grandin the idea to build herself a "hug box," a device to calm herself, which Grandin later shared with others on the autism spectrum. Encouraged by Carlock in her academic potential, Grandin went on to earn a bachelor's degree in psychology

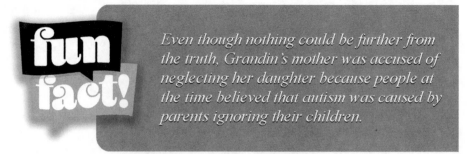

fun fact!

Even though nothing could be further from the truth, Grandin's mother was accused of neglecting her daughter because people at the time believed that autism was caused by parents ignoring their children.

from Franklin Pierce College in 1970, a master's degree in animal science from Arizona in 1975, and a doctoral degree in animal science from the University of Illinois–Urbana-Champaign in 1989. She then worked as a consultant to livestock companies, advising them on ways to improve the quality of life of their cattle. Grandin is the author of numerous scientific papers on animal behavior and has lectured widely on animal welfare. "I think using animals for food is an ethical thing to do," she has said, "but we've got to do it right. We've got to give those animals a decent life, and we've got to give them a painless death. We owe the animals respect."

As a high-functioning autistic person, Grandin has articulated her experiences to increase understanding both for those dealing with autism and the general public. She advocates early intervention, including teacher training, to address autistic children's specific fixations. She is also a champion of "neurodiversity" and opposes the notion of a comprehensive cure for autism, arguing that her contributions to the field of animal welfare would not have been possible without the insights and sensitivities that are a consequence of her autism.

In 2010, she was selected for the Time 100, an annual list of the one hundred most influential people in the world. She was the subject of the Emmy- and Golden Globe-winning biographical film *Temple Grandin,* starring Claire Danes in the title role.

Carol W. Greider (1961–)
Molecular Biologist

Molecular biologist Carol W. Greider was awarded (with Elizabeth H. Blackburn and Jack W. Szostak) the 2009 Nobel Prize in Physiology or Medicine for her research into telomeres (segments of DNA occurring at the ends of chromosomes) and for her discovery of the enzyme telomerase that revolutionized our understanding of the aging process and degenerative diseases and opened the door to new treatments for both.

Carol Greider was born in San Diego, the daughter of scientists: a physicist father and biologist mother. Her mother, suffering from depression, committed suicide when Greider was six, and she grew up in Davis, California, with her father and older brother. Afflicted with dyslexia, Greider managed through memorization to excel in chemistry and biology. She graduated with a bachelor's degree in biology from the University of California–Santa Barbara in 1983. Greider had difficulty getting into graduate school based on low test scores due to her dyslexia but was accepted at the University of California–Berkeley, where she began to work in Elizabeth Blackburn's laboratory on telomeres.

Blackburn and Greider searched for the telomere's mysterious regulating enzyme that protected the cell. Greider, in what the Lasker Award Committee would later describe as "a *tour de force* of biochemistry," painstakingly tried one method after another to purify and observe the proteins found in the telomeres to identify the enzyme they were searching for. After nearly eight months of failure, Greider and Blackburn altered their experiment using oligonucleotides of DNA produced in a chemical synthesizer rather than bacteria. This led to evidence of the enzymatic action they had been looking for. They named the enzyme telomerase, and the revelation of their finding caused a sensation, leading to new avenues for treatments of degenerative diseases and cancer.

In 1987, Greider received her Ph.D. from the University of California–Berkeley in molecular biology and was awarded a research fellowship at the Cold Spring Harbor Laboratory in New York, where she continued her research into telomerase. In 1990, she was named an assistant investigator at the Cold Spring Harbor Laboratory, an asso-

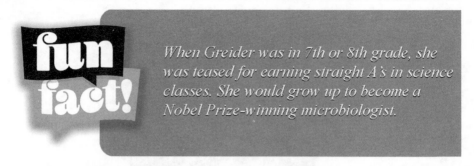

fun fact! When Greider was in 7th or 8th grade, she was teased for earning straight A's in science classes. She would grow up to become a Nobel Prize-winning microbiologist.

ciate in 1992, and a full investigator in 1994. Throughout the 1990s, Greider's work with telomeres focused on cancer and the discovery that inhibiting telomerase activity in cancer cells can slow tumor growth. This research has led to telomerase as a promising subject for the development of anticancer drugs. In 1997, Greider accepted a professorship at Johns Hopkins University School of Medicine, where she serves as the director of its Department of Molecular Biology and Genetics.

In addition to the 2009 Nobel Prize, Greider has been the recipient of the Lewis S. Rosenstiel Award for Work in Basic Medical Science (1999), the Albert Lasker Basic Medical Research Award (2006), and the Wiley Prize in Biomedical Sciences (2006).

Greider has stated, "One of the lessons I have learned in the different stages of my career is that science is not done alone. It is through talking with others and sharing that progress is made.... The ideas generated are not always the result of one person's thoughts but of the interactions between people; new ideas quickly become part of collective consciousness. This is how science moves forward and we generate new knowledge."

Fannie Lou Hamer (1917–1977)
Civil Rights Activist

A grassroots activist for civil rights and voting rights, Fannie Lou Hamer worked to desegregate the Democratic Party in Mississippi by cofounding the Mississippi Freedom Democratic Party (MFDP). She also organized Mississippi's Freedom Summer and was a cofounder of the National Women's Political Caucus.

Born Fannie Lou Townsend in Montgomery County, Mississippi, she was the last of the twenty children of her sharecropper parents. She grew up in poverty and, at the age of six, joined her family picking cotton. From 1924 through 1930, she attended a one-room school for sharecroppers' children, open between picking seasons. At the age of twelve, she left school to support her aging parents. By the age of thirteen, she could pick between two hundred and three hundred pounds of cotton daily, despite having a leg disfigured by polio.

In 1944, she married a tractor driver, Perry Hamer, and the couple labored on a Mississippi plantation until 1962. Because Hamer was the only worker who could read and write, she also served as the plantation timekeeper. In 1961, Hamer received a hysterectomy by a white doctor without her consent while undergoing surgery to remove a uterine tumor. Such forced sterilization of black women was so widespread at the time, it was called a "Mississippi appendectomy." Unable to have children of her own, the Hamers adopted two daughters.

In 1962, Hamer became a Student Nonviolent Coordinating Committee (SNCC) organizer and led a group to register to vote at the Indianola Mississippi Courthouse. Denied due to an unfair literacy test, the group was harassed on their way home, stopped by police, and fined $100 because the bus they were in was "too yellow." In addition, Hamer was fired by the plantation owner she worked for, and much of the Hamers' property was confiscated. In 1963, after successfully registering to vote, Hamer and several other black women were arrested for sitting in a "whites-only" bus station restaurant in Charleston, South Carolina. At the jailhouse, she was brutally beaten, leaving her with lifelong injuries from a blood clot in her eye and kidney and leg damage.

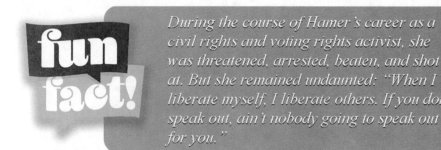

During the course of Hamer's career as a civil rights and voting rights activist, she was threatened, arrested, beaten, and shot at. But she remained undaunted: "When I liberate myself, I liberate others. If you don't speak out, ain't nobody going to speak out for you."

In 1964, Hamer cofounded the Mississippi Freedom Democratic Party to challenge the local Democratic Party's ban on black participation. Hamer and other MFDP members went to the Democratic National Convention, where Hamer called for mandatory integrated state delegation. By 1968, racial parity in delegations became a reality, and Hamer was a member of Mississippi's first integrated delegation. Also, in 1964, Hamer helped organize Freedom Summer, which brought hundreds of college students to help with African American voter registration. She also announced her candidacy for the Mississippi House of Representatives but was barred from the ballot. A year later, Hamer, Victoria Gray, and Annie Devine became the first black women to stand in the U.S. Congress when they protested the Mississippi House election of 1964.

In the late 1960s, Hamer turned her attention from politics to economics in pursuit of greater racial equality. In 1968, she began a "pig bank" to provide free pigs to black farmers to breed, raise, and slaughter. In 1969, she launched the Freedom Farm Cooperative, which bought land that blacks could own and farm collectively. She supervised the building of two hundred units of low-income housing. In 1971, Hamer cofounded the National Women's Political Caucus to empower women to exercise their political power as a voting majority.

Extensive travel and past health issues took a toll. In 1972, Hamer was hospitalized for nervous exhaustion, and in 1974, she suffered a nervous breakdown. She died in 1977 of complications of hypertension and breast cancer at the age of fifty-nine. Her tombstone is engraved with one of her most famous statements: "I am sick and tired of being sick and tired."

Alice Hamilton (1869–1970)
Physician, Researcher

A pioneer in the field of public health and industrial medicine, Dr. Alice Hamilton helped show the need for ridding U.S. factories, mines, and mills of the industrial poisons that were the cause of many illnesses and deaths of American workers. Through her research and public advocacy of better health conditions in the workplace, Hamilton saved and extended the lives of countless workers.

Hamilton grew up in Indiana and attended boarding school in Connecticut. She decided to become a doctor based on her desire for an independent and adventurous life. "I wanted to do something that would not interfere with my freedom," she recalled. "I realized that if I were a doctor, I could go anywhere I wanted—to foreign lands, to city slums—and while carrying on my profession, still be of some use." After graduating from the University of Michigan and doing research in bacteriology and pathology in Germany, in 1897, Hamilton became a professor of pathology at the Women's Medical College of Northwestern University in Chicago and went to live at Jane Addams's Hull House. There, she founded one of the first child welfare and outpatient clinics in the United States.

Hamilton's experience working in the Chicago slums prompted her scientific interest in the environmental factors that contributed to human illnesses, and in 1911, she produced the first American study of industrial diseases. Hamilton identified the impact of lead poisoning and labeled tuberculosis as "a disease of the working classes" aggravated by poor nutrition, inadequate housing, and fatigue caused by long work shifts prevalent among mill workers.

In 1919, Hamilton became the first female professor at Harvard University. As a professor of industrial medicine at Harvard Medical School and at Harvard's School of Public Health, Hamilton lobbied for increased government programs to protect citizens against sickness, disability, unemployment, and old age. These reforms were partially realized during the New Deal of the 1930s, while other reforms she advocated, such as health programs for the elderly and indigent, were enacted as Medicare and Medicaid in the 1960s. In 1925, Hamilton published *Industrial Poisons in the United States,* the first

This physician and pioneer in workplace health and safety descended into mines and bluffed her way into factories to uncover industrial toxins that threatened the lives of American workers.

such text on the subject, making her one of the few worldwide authorities in the field. From 1924 to 1930, she served on the Health Committee of the League of Nations.

In 1935, Hamilton retired from Harvard to serve as a special adviser on industrial medicine for the U.S. Labor Department's Bureau of Labor Standards. There, she pressed for the complete elimination of child labor, and the passage of the Fair Labor Standards Act of 1938 accomplished that goal.

Hamilton published her autobiography, *Exploring the Dangerous Trades*, in 1943, and she continued to remain active in the fields of public health and industrial medicine that she pioneered into her eighties.

Mia Hamm (1972–)
Soccer Player

Soccer star Mia Hamm was born Mariel Margaret Hamm in Selma, Alabama. She first played soccer in Florence, Italy, where her father was stationed with the U.S. Air Force, and she joined her first soccer team at five in Wichita Falls, Texas. A natural athlete, she excelled on the boys' football team in junior high school and starred on her high school soccer team. From 1989 to 1994, Hamm attended the University of North Carolina–Chapel Hill and led the women's team to four NCAA Division I Women's Soccer Championships. She was named the Atlantic Coast Conference (ACC) Player of the Year for three consecutive years.

Hamm's college stardom brought her to the U.S. women's national team in 1987. The youngest player ever to play on the team, Hamm continued to play with them until 2004. She and the team competed in the first four FIFA Women's World Cup tournaments in 1991, 1995, 1999, and 2003. Hamm led the U.S. team in the first three Olympic Games to include women's soccer: 1996 in Atlanta (gold), 2000 in Sydney (silver), and 2004 in Athens (gold).

In 2001, Hamm was a founding player in the first professional women's soccer league in the United States, the Women's United Soccer Association (WUSA), and played for the Washington Freedom from 2001 to 2003. She and the Freedom won the Founders Cup in 2003. Hamm retired from competitive soccer in 2004 after the 2004 Summer Olympic Games. At the time, she had a record 158 international goals, which she held until 2013, when her record was broken by fellow American star Abby Wambach. Hamm's outstanding accomplishments at a time when women's soccer first reached the highest international level made her the sport's first superstar.

Since retirement, Hamm has been involved in both charitable and business ventures. In 1999, she founded the Mia Hamm Foundation following the death of her adopted brother, Garrett, in 1997 from complications of aplastic anemia, a rare blood disease. The foundation is dedicated to promoting awareness of and raising funds for families in

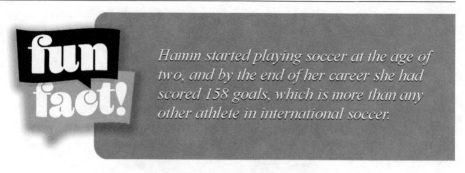

fun fact!

Hamm started playing soccer at the age of two, and by the end of her career she had scored 158 goals, which is more than any other athlete in international soccer.

need of a bone marrow or cord blood transplant. It also focuses on creating opportunities to empower women through sport. She described the importance of soccer in her life in her book *Go for the Goal: A Champion's Guide to Winning in Soccer and Life*. She has also been involved in many product endorsements, commercials, and television productions and is a co-owner of the Los Angeles Football Club of Major League Soccer.

Kamala Harris (1964–)
Vice President of the United States of America

In 2016 Kamala Devi Harris became the first South Asian American to be elected to the U.S. Senate and the second African American woman to enter that chamber. Four years later, she was elected vice president of the United States as Joe Biden's running mate, making her the first woman and first Asian American to hold the office.

Born October 20, 1964, in Oakland, California, Harris is the daughter of Shyamala Gopalan Harris, a breast cancer researcher who immigrated from India, and Donald Harris, a Stanford University economics professor originally from Jamaica. When she was 12, her parents divorced, and she moved to Quebec, Canada, with her mother. Here, she learned French, cofounded a dance troupe, and participated in protests.

Harris returned to the United States to attend Howard University in Washington, D.C., where she earned a B.A. in political science and economics. This was followed by a J.D. in 1989 from Hastings College of Law at the University of California. After passing the California State Bar exam the next year, she worked as the deputy district attorney for Alameda County. This was followed in 1998 by work with the Career Criminal Unit at the San Francisco District Attorney's Office and, two years later, chief of the Community and Neighborhood Division there. While in this position, Harris founded the Bureau of Children's Justice.

Continuing to move up the ladder, in 2003 Harris was elected San Francisco's district attorney. During her campaign, she promised that, if elected, she would not seek the death penalty for a gang member convicted of killing a police officer in 2004. When she made good on that promise, she was criticized by many San Franciscans. In this post, she meanwhile worked to reduce crime by creating job training and educational programs for low-risk criminal offenders.

In 2010, Harris was elected California's first woman and first African American state attorney general. As the AG, she played hardball with financial institutions for their improper mortgage practices, successfully suing them for $20 million. She also

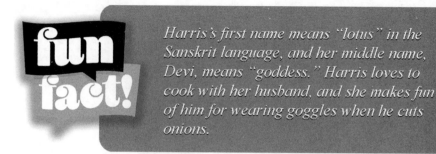

Harris's first name means "lotus" in the Sanskrit language, and her middle name, Devi, means "goddess." Harris loves to cook with her husband, and she makes fun of him for wearing goggles when he cuts onions.

was against Proposition 8, which was against same-sex marriages. When the law was reversed and the marriages were again allowed, Harris officiated the first same-sex marriage in California in 2013.

Continuing her political rise, Harris won a U.S. Senate seat in 2016, defeating incumbant Loretta Sanchez. She has served on several important committees, including the Homeland Security and Governmental Affairs Committee, Select Committee on Intelligence, Committee on the Judiciary, and Committee on the Budget. As a member of the Judiciary Committee, Harris entered the spotlight for assailing U.S. Supreme Court nominee Brett Kavanaugh with questions about alleged sexual assaults, and she was a key player in the impeachment hearings of President Donald Trump. As a senator, some of her positions included efforts to keep down rising housing costs and supporting a single-payer healthcare system.

After calling off her own campaign for U.S. president in 2019, Harris was selected by Democratic nominee Joe Biden to be his running mate, making her the first black woman and person of South Asian descent to be nominated by a major U.S. political party. When Biden won the election, she became the first woman to serve as a U.S. vice president.

Harris, who married attorney Douglas Emhoff and is the mother of two children, is the author of the books *Smart on Crime: A Career Prosecutor's Plan to Make Us Safer* (2009) and the autobiographical *The Truths We Hold: An American Journey* (2019). She also penned a children's book called *Superheroes Are Everywhere*.

Katharine Hepburn (1907–2003)
Actress

K atharine Hepburn is recognized as one of the most distinguished and unique movie actresses in the history of motion pictures. In a career that spanned more than fifty years, Hepburn dazzled audiences with her portrayal of strong, spirited, independent women and won four Academy Awards, the most achieved by any actor.

Born in Hartford, Connecticut, Hepburn was the daughter of a well-to-do surgeon and a mother who scandalized conservative Hartford by working for such controversial causes as birth control and women's suffrage. The Hepburn children were encouraged to be independent, self-reliant, and inquisitive. She was educated by private tutors and at the age of sixteen entered Bryn Mawr College, where she studied drama and appeared in school productions. After graduating in 1928, Hepburn moved to New York to pursue a theatrical career. Her early stage appearances, however, were dismal failures. Her acting was artificial; her voice was high and tinny, and she suffered from stage fright. Her breakthrough came in 1932 when she was cast as the queen of the Amazons in *The Warrior's Husband*, and her beauty, athletic grace, and performance as an emancipated, spirited woman captivated audiences.

Hepburn's stage success led to movie work in Hollywood, where she received good reviews for her first film, *A Bill of Divorcement* (1932). She went on to attain stardom in a long series of memorable roles, portraying such characters as feisty Jo March in *Little Women* (1933), icy socialite Tracy Lord in *The Philadelphia Story* (1940), a world-famous political commentator in *Woman of the Year* (1942), a straitlaced missionary in *The African Queen* (1951), and Eleanor of Aquitaine in *The Lion in Winter* (1968), for which she won her third Oscar. Hepburn's other Oscar-winning performances were in the films *Morning Glory* (1933), *Guess Who's Coming to Dinner* (1967), and *On Golden Pond* (1981).

After an early brief marriage to Philadelphia socialite Ludlow Ogden Smith and her subsequent divorce, Hepburn never remarried. However, beginning in the early

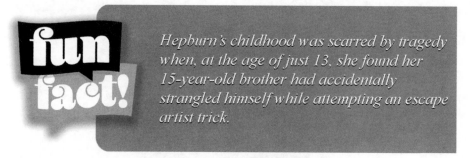

Hepburn's childhood was scarred by tragedy when, at the age of just 13, she found her 15-year-old brother had accidentally strangled himself while attempting an escape artist trick.

1940s, she became romantically involved with her *Woman of the Year* costar Spencer Tracy. They made nine films together, and, although many inside Hollywood knew of their longtime affair, it was a well-kept secret from the public because Tracy's Roman Catholicism was an impediment to his getting a divorce. Even after his death in 1967, Hepburn would never comment publicly on their twenty-five-year relationship.

Through her long career, Hepburn led a life as far removed as possible from Hollywood stardom. Strong-minded, dignified, and outspoken, she demanded and won the respect of nearly everyone she ever worked with. A true original—on and off the screen—she has influenced generations of young women who followed her to Hollywood to make acting their career.

Billie Holiday (1915–1959)
Singer

Regarded by most jazz critics as the greatest jazz singer ever recorded, Billie Holiday revolutionized vocal performing, taking it from the accompaniment position of the big band "girl singer" to center stage and the main attraction. Her highly emotional renditions and skill in improvisation are the hallmarks of great jazz soloists. Vocal artists as far ranging in style as Sarah Vaughn, Lena Horne, Carmen McCrae, and Frank Sinatra have been influenced by her. Others continue to be judged by her standard.

Born Eleanora Fagan, she grew up in Baltimore, raised by her mother and relatives. Before she was ten, she began to work for the proprietress of a local brothel performing menial chores and running errands. It was here that she first heard the recordings of Bessie Smith and Louis Armstrong, who would become major influences on her singing career. "I always wanted Bessie's sound and Pop's feeling," she recalled. In 1927, after completing fifth grade, she joined her mother in New York City, working as a maid and possibly a prostitute. She also sought work as a dancer in Harlem nightclubs; in one she was encouraged to sing, and she began to perform at various New York clubs.

Her style was unique from the start. Instead of the high-volume dramatics of Smith and Armstrong, she offered subtlety and nuance. In 1933, she was discovered by jazz enthusiast and record producer John Hammond, who arranged her first recordings within 24 hours after producing Bessie Smith's final album. Hammond recalled that Holiday "was not a blues singer, but she sang popular songs in a manner that made them completely her own. She had an uncanny ear, an excellent memory for lyrics, and she sang with an exquisite sense of phrasing." She began to tour with the Count Basie and Artie Shaw bands, becoming one of the first black performers in Shaw's otherwise all-white band.

From 1937 to 1941, Holiday performed regularly at Café Society in Greenwich Village, a club opened for the purpose of providing entertainment to integrated audiences. There, Holiday adopted as her closing number "Strange Fruit," a song about lynching

Holiday was on one of the first reality shows broadcast on TV when she appeared in the show The Comeback Story in 1953. The program was focused on true stories of people who overcame adversity to achieve celebrity.

and the "bitter crop" of southern racial politics. Columbia Records refused to let her record the song, but it was released on an independent label. On the Decca label, she recorded her most famous songs, "Lover Man" and her own compositions "God Bless the Child" and "Don't Explain." In 1947, Holiday entered a clinic to try to kick a drug addiction that had escalated after the collapse of her marriage to nightclub manager Jimmy Monroe. After her discharge, she was arrested for narcotics possession and served nine and a half months in a federal reformatory for women in West Virginia. Upon her release, her cabaret license was revoked, and Holiday could no longer perform in local clubs. Instead, she toured outside New York and in Europe. She continued to record and perform in the 1950s despite health issues exacerbated by drugs and alcohol. She died of liver failure at the age of forty-four. Holiday's life was a sad litany of neglect, divorce, arrests, and addiction interspersed by remarkable vocal and musical achievement. As jazz performer Anita Day observed, Billie Holiday remains "the one true genius among jazz singers.... Only somebody who'd gone through the things she did and survived, could sing from the soul the way she did."

bell hooks (Pseudonym of Gloria Jean Watkins, 1952–)
Author, Educator

Born Gloria Jean Watkins but better known by her pen name, hooks is an author, scholar, feminist, and social activist whose work has focused on intersectionality and race, capitalism, and gender in the context of oppression and class domination and has examined the varied perceptions of African American women and the development of feminist identities. She is credited with coining the terms "imperialist white-supremacist capitalist patriarchy" and "oppositional gaze," which describes the reflexive ways in which people look back at each other and which often reflects the unconscious attitudes of the "gazer."

Bell hooks was born in Hopkinsville, Kentucky, one of the six children of Veodis Watkins, a custodian, and Rosa Bell Watkins, a homemaker. Hooks began her education in racially segregated schools and has written of the difficulties she encountered when she made the transition to an integrated school with predominantly white teachers and students. After her graduation from Hopkinsville High School, she attended Stanford University, where she received her B.A. degree in English in 1973. She received an M.A. degree in English from the University of Wisconsin–Madison in 1976 and a doctorate in literature at the University of California–Santa Monica in 1983. Hooks's doctoral dissertation was on author Toni Morrison.

From 1976 to 1979, hooks was an English professor and senior lecturer in ethnic studies at the University of Southern California (UCLA), where she published her first book, a chapbook of poems titled *And There We Wept* (1978). The book was written under her pen name, which she borrowed from her outspoken maternal great-grandmother, Bell Blair Hooks, whom she greatly admired.

Hooks taught English, ethnic studies, and women's studies at a variety of colleges and universities in the 1980s and 1990s. In 2004, she became a professor-in-residence at Berea College in Berea, Kentucky. In the 1980s, hooks established a support group for African American women called the Sisters of the Yam, which she later used as the title for a 1993 book celebrating black sisterhood.

fun fact!

hooks's decision to present her pen name in lowercase letters came from her desire for readers to focus attention on her books and her message rather than on herself.

When hooks was nineteen, she began writing what would become her first full-length book, *Ain't I a Woman?: Black Women and Feminism*, published in 1981. The book examines the effects of racism and sexism on African American women in the context of the civil rights and feminist movements from the women's suffrage era to the 1970s. In 1992, *Publishers Weekly* named *Ain't I a Woman?* one of the most influential books of the last twenty years. Hooks's other works include *Feminist Theory: From Margin to Center* (1984), *All About Love: New Visions* (2000), and *We Real Cool: Black Men and Masculinity* (2004). She has also published numerous scholarly articles, appeared in documentary films, participated in public lectures, and received several honors and awards. In 2014, she established the bell hooks Institute at Berea College.

Grace Hopper (1906–1992)
Computer Scientist, Navy Rear Admiral

Grace Hopper's pioneering work in computer technology helped to bring about the computer revolution. Hopper's development of the automatic programming language called COBOL (Common Business Oriented Language) helped to simplify the technology that ultimately made the computer accessible and essential.

Hopper was born in New York City and graduated from Vassar College in 1928. She went on to receive her Ph.D. in mathematics from Yale University in 1934. After teaching mathematics at Vassar for twelve years, in 1943, determined to help in the war effort, Hopper enlisted and was accepted into the WAVES (Women Accepted for Voluntary Emergency Service) branch of the Navy, even though she was considered overage and underweight. She attended the U.S. Naval Reserve Midshipman School and graduated with the rank of lieutenant junior grade. She was then assigned to the Bureau of Ordnance Computation Project at Harvard University.

At Harvard, Hopper developed the programs for the Mark I, the first automatically sequenced digital computer, a predecessor of today's electronic computer. She continued to work on the second and third series of Mark computers for the Navy before she rejoined the private sector in 1949. Working for the Eckert–Mauchly Computer Corporation, she assisted in the development of the first commercial, large-scale electronic computer, UNIVAC. Hopper and her staff would go on to create the first computer language compiler, a program that translates programming code into a machine language that a computer can understand. Her work led to the development of COBOL.

Throughout her career, Hopper maintained close contact with the naval reserve. She retired from the Navy in 1966 but was recalled to supervise the service's computer language and programs. In 1969, Hopper became the first person to receive computer science's "Man of the Year" award from the Data Processing Management Association. In 1983, President Ronald Reagan appointed her a rear admiral, and when she finally retired from the Navy in 1986 at the age of eighty, she was the oldest officer on active duty in the armed services.

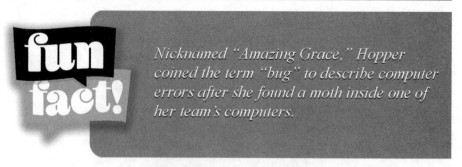

Nicknamed "Amazing Grace," Hopper coined the term "bug" to describe computer errors after she found a moth inside one of her team's computers.

Hopper later served as a senior consultant to the Digital Corporation, a position she held until her death. In 1991, Hopper became the first woman to receive, as an individual, the U.S. Medal of Technology, awarded "for her pioneering accomplishments in the development of computer programming languages."

An often combative and unorthodox computer scientist, Hopper spent her career trying to convince "the Establishment," as she called the computer science community, that computers were capable of becoming more than just highly efficient calculators. Hopper's understanding that a computer could imitate the seemingly inexhaustible process of the human intellect would set in motion one of the greatest technological revolutions in human history. Few others contributed as much to that revolution as Grace Hopper.

Dolores Huerta (1930–)
Labor Leader

For more than thirty-five years, Dolores Huerta has fought to gain justice, dignity, and a decent standard of living for one of the country's most disadvantaged and exploited groups—the migrant farm workers.

Huerta was born Dolores Fernández in the small mining town of Dawson, New Mexico. Her father was of Native American and Mexican heritage; her mother was a second-generation New Mexican. Her parents divorced when she was a toddler, and her mother moved her daughter and two sons to Stockton, California, where Huerta grew up in a mixed neighborhood of farm workers and laborers. Unlike most Hispanic women of her generation, she continued her education after graduating from high school, receiving a degree in education from Stockton College. She took a job teaching at an elementary school, but her interest soon shifted to social activism.

In 1955, Huerta began to work with the Community Service Organization, a Mexican American self-help association that sponsored voter registration drives and social reforms in the Hispanic community. Huerta was drawn to the plight of the migrant farm workers, who labored for low pay and were forced to live in cars, shacks, and tents; exposed to deadly pesticides; and deprived of health and welfare benefits. In 1962, she joined César Chávez in organizing the Farm Workers Association, which later became the United Farm Workers, to fight for workers' rights, paid holidays, improved housing, unemployment insurance, and pension benefits. Huerta recruited union members and in 1965 helped to organize a nationwide grape boycott when California's grape pickers went on strike for better working conditions. Huerta was tireless in rallying support during the bitter, five-year strike. As a result of efforts of Huerta and other union leaders, the growers finally gave in and negotiated a historic contract with the union that set an hourly wage, established low-cost housing for workers, health benefits, and a total ban on toxic pesticides used in California vineyards.

During her early years in the labor movement, Huerta met her second husband, Ventura Huerta, who was also an activist. The marriage did not last, partly as a result of

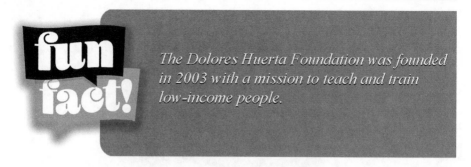

The Dolores Huerta Foundation was founded in 2003 with a mission to teach and train low-income people.

her devotion to her work. Although she has admitted to placing her labor activities above concerns for her family, Huerta raised eleven children from her two marriages.

In 1988, during a peaceful demonstration in San Francisco, Huerta suffered broken ribs and a ruptured spleen when police officers swung their batons at protesters. The incident made headlines and caused the San Francisco police to change their crowd-control policies. Huerta recovered from her injuries and returned to work for the UFW as a negotiator and vice president. She retired from active union service in 1999.

Arianna Huffington (1950–)
Company Executive, Entrepreneur

Greek American businesswoman Arianna Huffington is the founder of *The Huffington Post* and the founder and CEO of the health and wellness start-up Thrive Global. She has also been a board member of Uber since 2016.

Born Arianna Stassinopoulos, Huffington is the daughter of a Greek newspaper owner. She moved to England as a teenager and pursued an economics degree from Cambridge University, earning a master's in 1972. While at Cambridge, she served as president of its debating society, the Cambridge Union, the first foreign-born student to do so. After graduation, she lived in London for a time before relocating to the United States, settling in California with Republican politician Michael Huffington, whom she married in 1986 and divorced in 1997.

Huffington began her political and journalistic career as a Republican. She contributed to the conservative *National Review*, and, in 1994, she worked on her husband's unsuccessful campaign for U.S. Senate. In the late 1990s, however, Huffington shifted to the left politically and became active in progressive causes, particularly efforts to combat global warming. After an unsuccessful run in the 2003 California governor's race, Huffington launched *The Huffington Post* website in 2005, serving as its cofounder and editor-in-chief. It was set up as a group blog, publishing hundreds of guest contributors while providing news updates and links to other news sources and columnists. In 2011, AOL acquired *The Huffington Post* for $315 million. Huffington launched a new venture as president and editor-in-chief of The Huffington Post Media Group, which she ran until 2016, when she left to start Thrive Global, which has raised over $43 million in funding.

A prolific author, some of her books include *The Female Woman* (1973), *After Reason* (1978), *Maria Callas* (1981), *Greetings from the Lincoln Bedroom* (1998), *How to Overthrow the Government* (2000), *Pigs at the Trough* (2003), *On Becoming Fearless ... In Love, Work, and Life* (2007), and *The Sleep Revolution: Transforming Your Life, One Night*

Huffington tried her hand at acting when she appeared as the recurring character Arianna the Bear, in the animated TV sitcom The Cleveland Show.

at a Time (2016). Huffington was named to *Time* magazine's list of the 100 Most Influential People and to *Forbes* magazine's Most Powerful Women list.

Zora Neale Hurston (1891–1960)
Novelist, Short Story Author

An anthropologist, novelist, short-story writer, and essayist, Zora Neale Hurston was one of America's most influential African American writers. A central figure in the Harlem Renaissance of the 1920s and 1930s, Hurston recorded and incorporated black folk tales and traditions into her work, invigorating American literature with the power and expressiveness of the African American vernacular. A brash and opinionated woman, she produced a series of novels and folklore collections that significantly gave voice to segments of American society, most notably women and African Americans who had previously been silent or unheard.

Hurston was born in Eatonville, Florida, the first incorporated black community in the United States. Her father was the mayor of Eatonville and a Baptist preacher. The town's vibrant folk tradition and its frequent "lying" sessions of tall tales had a great impact on Hurston, who absorbed many of the stories told by her elders and eventually began to make up tales of her own. When her mother died and her father remarried, Hurston was passed about from boarding school to friends and relatives. At sixteen, she worked as a wardrobe girl for a traveling light opera troupe. Quitting the show in Baltimore, she went to work as a maid for a white woman, who arranged for Hurston to attend high school. From 1918 to 1924, Hurston studied part-time at Howard University in Washington, D.C., while working as a manicurist. She eventually studied anthropology at Barnard College while writing poems, plays, articles, and stories. After graduation, she went on to Columbia University to study with eminent cultural anthropologist Franz Boas. Hurston did field research first in Eatonville, collecting data that she would include in her folklore collections and novels, and later in Haiti and Jamaica.

Hurston's two important folklore collections are *Mules and Men* (1935) and *Tell My Horse* (1938). Her novels include *Jonah's Gourd Vine* (1934), *Their Eyes Were Watching God* (1937), *Moses, Man of the Mountain* (1939), and *Seraph on the Sewanee* (1948). Her autobiography, *Dust Tracks on the Road*, was published in 1942.

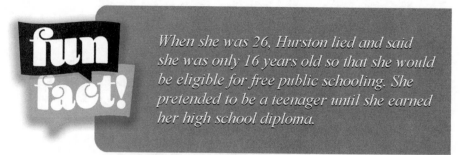

When she was 26, Hurston lied and said she was only 16 years old so that she would be eligible for free public schooling. She pretended to be a teenager until she earned her high school diploma.

Hurston's biographer, Robert Hemenway, captures her complexities and contradictions, calling her "flamboyant yet vulnerable, self-centered yet kind, a Republican conservative and an early black nationalist." African American critics complained that the folk elements in her works were demeaning and one-dimensional, and few during Hurston's lifetime credited her work as a major source of vernacular strength and lyrical power. Convinced of the vitality and promise of the African American community—no doubt influenced by her experience in Eatonville—Hurston opposed legislation that forced integration, and her stand alienated her from other African Americans, who pushed for assimilation into mainstream white culture. Her advocacy of the strength and vibrancy of black culture predated the black power and cultural movements that began in the 1960s.

During Hurston's later years, her works were neglected, and she lived in extreme poverty, working for a time as a maid, librarian, and newspaper columnist. At her death in 1960, she was buried in an unmarked grave in a cemetery in Fort Pierce, Florida, until writer Alice Walker, who was instrumental in restoring Hurston's reputation, had a headstone erected. Today, Hurston is acknowledged as one of the most important African American writers of the twentieth century. Her masterpiece *Their Eyes Were Watching God* has been described by biographer Robert Hemenway "as one of the most poetic works of fiction by a black writer in the first half of the twentieth century, and one of the most revealing treatments in modern literature of a woman's quest for a satisfying life."

Shirley Ann Jackson (1946–)
College President, Physicist

The first black woman to earn a Ph.D. from the Massachusetts Institute of Technology, which was in theoretical solid-state physics, Shirley Ann Jackson was also the first black woman to be elected president and then chairman of the board of the American Association for the Advancement of Science; the first black woman to become president of a major research university, the country's oldest, Rensselaer Polytechnic Institute in New York; the first black woman to be elected to the National Academy of Engineering; and the first African American and first woman to chair the U.S. Nuclear Regulatory Commission.

Jackson's long list of impressive accomplishments was not a surprise; she declared to her mother at four years old that she would someday be called "Shirley the Great." Born into a segregated Washington, D.C., Jackson took advantage of the Supreme Court decision *Brown v. Board of Education* of 1954, which mandated the integration of the nation's schools, to attend Roosevelt Senior High School, where she participated in the school's accelerated programs in both math and science. Graduating in 1964 as valedictorian, she entered MIT, one of fewer than twenty African American students and the only one studying theoretical physics, going on to earn her doctorate in nuclear physics in 1973 and becoming only the second African American woman in the United States to earn a Ph.D. in physics.

Jackson did postdoctoral research in subatomic particles at a number of physics laboratories in the United States and in Europe before becoming a research associate at the Fermi National Accelerator Laboratory in Illinois and joining AT&T Bell Laboratories in 1978. Jackson joined the faculty at Rutgers University from 1991 to 1995 while still consulting with Bell Labs on semiconductor theory. In 1999, Jackson became the eighteenth president of Rensselaer Polytechnic Institute. Under Jackson, Rensselaer has been transformed into a world-class technological research university due to a campaign she spearheaded that raised more than $1.25 billion and invested in state-of-the-art research facilities.

Jackson's research in theoretical, solid state, quantum, and optical physics at AT&T Bell Labs helped lead to the technology responsible for the caller ID and call waiting features on our phones.

The holder of fifty-three honorary doctoral degrees from colleges and universities worldwide, Jackson, in 2016, was awarded the National Medal of Science by President Barack Obama, the nation's highest honor for contributions in science and engineering. Few individuals who have claimed "the Great" as an honorific have earned that distinction as well as Shirley Ann Jackson.

Mae Carol Jemison (1956–)
Astronaut, Physician, Scientist

In 1992, Mae Carol Jemison became the first African American woman in space when she served as a science mission specialist during an eight-day voyage on the space shuttle *Endeavour*. Jemison put into context her achievement by stating, "There have been lots of other women who had the talent and ability before me. I think this can be seen as an affirmation that we're moving ahead. And I hope it means that I'm just the first in a long line."

Jemison was born in Decatur, Alabama, the youngest of the three children of a maintenance supervisor and an elementary school teacher. Her family moved to Chicago when she was three years old for better educational and employment opportunities. As an adolescent, she was a fan of science fiction books, movies, and television programs, particularly the TV series *Star Trek*. It was, in Jemison's words, "one of the few programs that actually had women in exploration and technology roles. It also showed people from around the world working together.... It gave a real hopeful view of the universe, of groups of people, as a species." After graduating from high school in 1973, at the age of sixteen, she attended Stanford University, where she pursued a double major in chemical engineering and African American studies. She earned her medical degree in 1981 from Cornell University after having served as a medical volunteer in Cuba, Kenya, and Thailand. She completed her internship and then worked as a general practitioner in Los Angeles. In 1985, she joined the Peace Corps as a medical officer for Sierra Leone and Liberia in West Africa.

In 1987, her application for NASA's astronaut program was accepted. Jemison remembered always being fascinated with outer space and the space program, although she remembers "being irritated that there were no women astronauts." She said applying to be a shuttle astronaut was better than "waiting around in a cornfield, waiting for E.T. to pick me up or something." She was one of fifteen individuals selected out of more than two thousand applicants. After her training program, Jemison finally took off into space with six other astronauts aboard the *Endeavour* in 1992. On board, Jemison con-

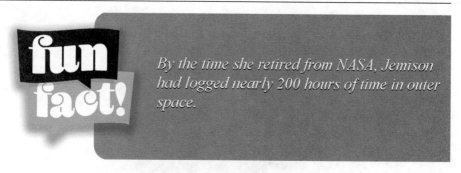

By the time she retired from NASA, Jemison had logged nearly 200 hours of time in outer space.

ducted experiments on motion sickness and the impact of weightlessness on bone density and the development of frog eggs. On the flight, Jemison took into orbit a photo of Bessie Coleman, the first African American woman ever to fly an airplane. She would say later that she was not driven to be the "first black woman to go into space. I wouldn't have cared less if 2,000 people had gone up before me.... I would still have had my hand up, 'I want to do this.'"

After her only space mission, Jemison resigned from NASA, explaining that her decision was based on her interest in exploring "how social sciences interact with technologies." She became a professor-at-large at Cornell University and a professor of environmental studies at Dartmouth College from 1995 to 2002. She has been a strong advocate in favor of science education and increasing minority student participation in science. She established the Jemison Group, a company that researches, develops, and markets space-age technology.

Gish Jen (1955–)
Novelist, Short Story Author

In 2000, when asked to name his successor in the twenty-first century, author John Updike chose Gish Jen. In 2012, writer Junot Diaz called Jen "the great American novelist we have always been hearing about." She has, in a series of cross-cultural works exploring lives both in America and China, become one of the most dominant contemporary figures in articulating a multicultural identity.

Born Lilian Jen in New York City to Chinese immigrant parents from Shanghai, Jen grew up in Yonkers and Scarsdale, New York, adopting the name Gish in high school after the actress Lillian Gish. She graduated from Harvard in 1977, majoring in English. After studying business briefly at Stanford, Jen took a position teaching English in Shandong, China, before completing an M.F.A. at the Writer's Workshop of the University of Iowa in 1983. Jen subsequently married David O'Connor, moving with him to Silicon Valley in California, where he worked. Relocating to Cambridge, Massachusetts, in 1985, Jen failed to find a secretarial job at Harvard but was awarded a fellowship at Radcliffe's Bunting Institute that allowed her to begin her first novel.

Typical American was published in 1991, describing Chinese immigrants who pursue the American Dream while struggling with assimilation. In it, and in subsequent books, Jen explores the nature of American identity from an Asian perspective. Her second novel, *Mona in the Promised Land* (1996), describes a Chinese American adolescent who converts to Judaism. Her third novel, *The Love Wife* (2004), considers a multiethnic family, including Asians, Asian Americans, and white Americans. *World and Town* (2010) explores American life post-9/11. *Who's Irish?* (1999) collects short stories that have earned Jen acclaim as a master of the story form.

Issues of culture, race, and gender that are at the center of Jen's fiction are also explored in her nonfiction books, which include *Tiger Writing: Art, Culture, and the Interdependent Self* (2013) and *The Girl at the Baggage Claim: Explaining the East–West Culture Gap* (2017). The subtitle of the *The Girl at the Baggage Claim* can stand as a fitting descriptor of Jen's

Growing up in a very traditional home of Chinese immigrants, Jen was the rebel in the family, and becoming a writer was the most rebellious occupation she could think of because it emphasized her individualism over family.

overall intention in her work: to bridge gaps in our collective identity in search of viable synthesis for our pluralistic society and increasingly globalist consciousness.

Katherine Johnson (1918–2020)
Mathematician

African American mathematician Katherine Johnson calculated the trajectory for America's first space missions in the 1960s that would be crucial for the success of the U.S. space program. Her achievement was celebrated in the 2016 film *Hidden Figures*, which dramatized the struggles of Johnson and other black women at NASA for equality. Dismissed as a "colored computer," Johnson and the other black women working in NASA's computing pool were separated from their white colleagues while she tracked the orbits of important missions such as Alan Shephard's Freedom 7 in 1961, John Glenn's Friendship 7 in 1962, and the various Apollo missions.

She was born Katherine Coleman in White Sulphur Springs, West Virginia. Her mother was a teacher, and her father was a blacksmith, farmer, and handyman. Johnson showed strong mathematical skills from an early age. "I counted everything: the steps, the dishes, the stars in the sky," Johnson recalls. With no secondary school to send her to, Johnson's parents enrolled her at the laboratory school on the campus of West Virginia State Institute, a black college one hundred miles away. She excelled at the school and entered West Virginia State as a freshman at the age of fifteen. She graduated at eighteen in 1937 with degrees in math education and French. She was selected as one of three black students to integrate the graduate program at then-all-white West Virginia University, but she left after a year to get married and start a family. She would teach mathematics, French, and music in public schools in Virginia until 1952.

When she learned that job openings were available at the National Advisory Committee for Aeronautics at the Langley Aeronautical Laboratory (now the Langley Research Center), she relocated with her husband and three daughters to Newport News, Virginia, and began to work in 1953 at Langley with engineers in the Flight Research Division on issues related to airplane gust alleviation and wake turbulence. When the National Advisory Committee was transformed into the National Aeronautics and Space Administration in 1958, the engineers of the Flight Research Division became the Space Task

The first time she applied for a job at NASA, the space agency rejected Johnson. She would go on to be a key figure in the space race and co-authored the first textbook on space travel. She also worked on the first early plans for a mission to Mars.

Force, and Johnson became a member of the inner circle working on getting the United States into space. Before computers, the calculations on trajectories were done by hand, and Johnson was given some of the most crucial tasks in designing the early space missions. She also provided trajectory work for the Lunar Orbiter Program, which mapped the Moon's surface in advance of the 1969 Moon landing, and her calculations helped to synchronize the Apollo's Lunar Module with the moon-orbiting Command Module. Johnson would play a crucial role in the calculations that made possible the safe return of Apollo 13.

Johnson retired from NASA–Langley in 1986. In 2015, President Obama awarded her the Presidential Medal of Freedom, and in 2019, NASA renamed a facility in Fairmont, West Virginia, the Katherine Johnson Independent Verification and Validation Facility. Having turned one hundred in 2018, Johnson, according to her daughter, "remains in awe and honored by" all the accolades and attention she has received, but Johnson "can't imagine why people would want to honor her for just doing a good job."

Lois Mailou Jones (1905–1998)
Painter

The longest-surviving artist of the Harlem Renaissance, Lois Mailou Jones achieved fame as an African American expatriate artist in Paris in the 1930s and 1940s. She incorporated influences from Africa and the Caribbean into her paintings and produced some of the first non-portrait paintings by an African American.

Born in Boston, she early on displayed a passion for drawing, and her parents encouraged her interest by enrolling her in the High School of Practical Arts in Boston, where she majored in art. In 1927, she graduated from the School of the Museum of Fine Arts and continued her education at the Boston Normal School of Arts and the Designers Art School in Boston. After chairing the art department at an all-black prep school in North Carolina in 1928, she accepted a faculty position at Howard University in Washington, D.C. In 1937, she took a sabbatical from Howard to study art in Paris.

Her most celebrated Parisian painting is *Les Fetiches*, a depiction of African masks in five distinct, ethnic styles reflecting her previous travels to Africa and Haiti, influences that Jones more and more incorporated into works. She painted outdoors, in the French tradition, producing landscapes and street scenes while contributing to Paris exhibitions and relishing the freedom from racial prejudice that she found in France. In 1953, she married artist Louis Vergnlaud Pierre-Noël of Haiti, and she began to incorporate into her work brighter colors and a more Expressionistic style from Haitian art. In the 1960s and 1970s, African influences reemerged in her work. In the 1980s and 1990s, Jones continued to produce important new work until she was felled by a massive heart attack on her eighty-fourth birthday. A 1990 retrospective exhibition toured the country and brought her nationwide attention and critical acclaim, which had eluded her for much of her career because her work defied typical subjects deemed suitable for African American artists. In 1994, the Corcoran Gallery of Art opened The World of Lois Mailou Jones exhibition with a public apology for its past racial discrimination. She died at the age of ninety-two at her home in Washington, D.C., after a seventy-year artistic career.

In 1941, Jones had to have her friend Céline Marie Tabary present her painting Indian Shops Gay Head at the annual Corcoran Gallery art competition in Washington, D.C., because she was black. Tabary also accepted the award on Jones's behalf when she won.

Mary Harris "Mother" Jones (1830–1930)
Labor Leader

The most influential labor organizer in the United States in the late nineteenth and early twentieth centuries, Mary Harris "Mother" Jones was a feisty and fearless agitator who devoted her adult life to helping laborers obtain better working conditions and a decent living wage.

Mary Harris was the daughter of an Irish immigrant forced to flee arrest in Ireland for his efforts to gain Irish independence from England. Raised in Toronto, she worked as a teacher and a dressmaker, and in 1860, she accepted a teaching position in Memphis, Tennessee. The following year, she married George Jones, an ironworker and organizer for the Knights of Labor, one of the earliest American labor unions.

In 1867, a yellow fever epidemic swept through Memphis, claiming the lives of George and their four children. Jones stayed on to nurse other victims and then left for Chicago, where she opened a dressmaking shop. In 1871, her shop and home were destroyed during Chicago's Great Fire. She eventually reestablished her business and began to attend Knights of Labor meetings, where she impressed union leaders with her debating skills and knowledge of labor issues. Jones recruited more workers to the union cause and, beginning in 1891, she participated in strikes in Virginia, West Virginia, Colorado, Kansas, and Pennsylvania, fighting for shorter working hours, better pay, and the right for workers to unionize. She lived wherever she found shelter, most often in workers' shanties or strikers' tent cities. Having no personal funds, she sometimes obtained income from union activities, but more often, she relied upon friends to supply her with whatever necessities she lacked.

After taking a job as a textile mill worker to investigate working conditions for children, Mother Jones saw young children who had lost fingers or hands working with dangerous machinery. In 1903, she organized the Crusade of the Mill Children, marching with them from Pennsylvania to President Theodore Roosevelt's summer home on Long Island, New York. The march of the children—many of whom were un-

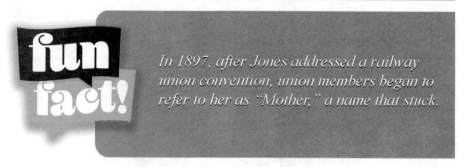

fun fact!

In 1897, after Jones addressed a railway union convention, union members began to refer to her as "Mother," a name that stuck.

dernourished and had suffered workplace accidents—brought public attention to their dangerous working conditions, and they helped to facilitate reforms. For her relentless agitation and success in organizing workers, Jones was called "the most dangerous woman in America."

Mother Jones herself was frequently jailed. In 1913, she was accused of inciting violence during a West Virginia strike and was convicted of conspiracy to commit murder. The governor commuted the sentence after a public outcry. The following year, her graphic account of the massacre of twenty people during a Ludlow, Colorado, miner's strike convinced President Woodrow Wilson to try to mediate the dispute.

A founding member of the Industrial Workers of the World (IWW), Mother Jones continued to agitate well into her nineties, rallying on behalf of garment, steel, and streetcar workers. She spent her last years in the home of a retired miner and his wife near Washington, D.C. On her one hundredth birthday, Jones received greetings from prominent Americans across the country, among them John D. Rockefeller Jr., whose father had owned some of the copper mines where she had led strikes.

Barbara Jordan (1936–1996)
Congresswoman

Congresswoman, educator, and leader of the civil rights movement, Barbara Jordan was the first African American woman to be elected to Congress from a southern state. She was also the first African American and first woman to deliver a keynote address at a Democratic National Convention, which she did in 1976. She is perhaps best known for her impassioned 1974 speech during the impeachment process against President Richard Nixon in 1974, earning her widespread praise for her oratory, morals, and wisdom.

She grew up in the largest black ghetto in Houston, Texas, the youngest of three daughters in a poor family. Her father, a Baptist preacher and warehouse laborer, taught her that race and poverty had nothing to do with her intellectual potential and her ability to achieve great things if she worked hard for them. When an African American, female lawyer visited her high school on career day, Jordan decided that a career in law would be the best way she could make a difference. Educated at Texas Southern University, where she excelled at debate, Jordan received her law degree from Boston University in 1959. She began her law practice back in Houston working at home from her parents' dining room table; after three years, she finally earned enough money to open an office.

In 1962, Jordan decided to enter politics, running unsuccessfully for the state legislature. After another failed attempt two years later, she finally won in 1966, becoming the first African American since the 1870s to serve in the Texas Senate and the first African American woman ever to be elected to the Texas legislature. During her six years as a state senator, Jordan worked for social reform, cosponsoring a minimum-wage bill and a workers' compensation plan. In 1972, she became the second African American woman to be elected to Congress, following Shirley Chisholm.

Jordan rose to national prominence in 1974 as a member of the House Judiciary Committee investigating whether President Nixon was guilty of impeachable offenses in concealing presidential involvement in the Watergate burglary. In a stirring and

Jordan, who was partnered with Nancy Earle for thirty years, is also considered an icon of the LGBTQI community, even though she kept her personal life out of the public spotlight.

memorable speech, Jordan justified her vote to recommend impeachment, declaring, "My faith is total. I am not going to sit here and be an idle spectator to the diminution, the subversion, the destruction of the Constitution."

In 1976, Jordan became the first African American to deliver the keynote at a national political convention. Her eloquence and principled stands on tough issues caused one writer to observe, "Few members in the long history of the House have so quickly impressed themselves upon the consciousness of the country." Jordan shocked her many supporters when she announced in 1977 that she would not seek reelection. Suffering from poor health due to leukemia and multiple sclerosis, which eventually caused her to rely on a wheelchair, Jordan left Washington to teach at the University of Texas. In 1994, she was awarded the Presidential Medal of Freedom. From 1994 until her death, Jordan chaired the U.S. Commission on Immigration Reform. President Bill Clinton said that he wanted to nominate Jordan for the U.S. Supreme Court, but her health problems prevented him from doing so. Jordan died at the age of fifty-nine from complications of pneumonia in Austin, Texas. Her 1974 speech on the articles of impeachment was listed number thirteen in American Rhetoric's Top 100 Speeches of the 20th Century, while her 1976 Democratic National Convention keynote address was listed as number five.

Helen Keller (and Anne Sullivan) (1880–1968)
Educator, Lecturer

The story of Helen Keller's triumph over disability is one of the best known and most inspiring in the history of women. Born in Tuscumbia, Alabama, left blind and deaf at nineteen months after an attack of scarlet fever by the age of six, she was, as she later wrote, "a phantom living in a 'no world' ... I had neither will nor intellect." She could not speak, and her parents had no way of communicating with her. She was indulged and spoiled, undisciplined, and unrestrained. Advised to confine her to a mental asylum, her parents sought the advice of a family friend, Alexander Graham Bell, who suggested they request a teacher from Boston's Perkins Institute, a training school for the blind.

In 1887, twenty-year-old Anne Sullivan arrived. The "creator of a soul," as educator Maria Montessori later called her, Sullivan had survived a sordid childhood as a half-blind orphan in a squalid Massachusetts almshouse to come to the Perkins Institute alone at fourteen, illiterate and almost as unruly as Helen was when the two met. Sullivan was provided with an education and several operations that improved her eyesight. Perhaps seeing herself in Helen, Sullivan was determined not to break the child's spirit as she took on the formidable task of trying to tame and teach her.

As Sullivan worked to discipline Helen Keller and build a trusting relationship with her, she would spell out words with her fingers into the child's hands and then give her the object she spelled to touch. It made no impression on Helen until one day, Sullivan took Keller to the water pump and let the cold water spill over one of the child's hands while spelling "water" in the other. "Suddenly I felt a misty conscious as of something forgotten," Keller later recalled, "and somehow the mystery of language was returned to me." She spelled out "water" several times and then started touching other objects while indicating a desire to know their names. In the next five months, Keller had mastered 625 words. She went on to read braille, to write using thin rulers to keep her hand in alignment, and to use a typewriter.

When their finances began to dwindle, the two began a successful tour on the Vaudeville circuit. Billed as the "Eighth Wonder of the World" and the "brightest star of happiness and optimism," Keller answered questions about her life, which her teacher-companion, Sullivan, translated for audiences.

Sullivan accompanied Keller to the Horace Mann School in New York, where Keller took lessons in speech, and was with her when she attended the Wright-Humason School for the Deaf for advanced study in speech and lip reading. When Keller entered Radcliffe College, the result of fundraising by Mark Twain, Sullivan sat beside her and spelled her lectures into her hand. In 1904, Keller graduated *cum laude*, and at her request, Sullivan mounted the platform with her and stood beside her as she received her diploma.

After Keller's graduation, she and Sullivan settled in Wrentham, Massachusetts. A year later, Sullivan married writer John Macy, who had edited Keller's first best-selling book, *The Story of My Life* (1902). Keller continued to write and, with Sullivan, embarked on a series of lecture tours, speaking on the problems of the disabled. Keller helped organize thirteen state commissions for the blind, raised funds for the American Foundation for the Blind, and lobbied for materials for the visually impaired. In 1917, Keller and Sullivan moved to Forest Hills, New York, where they lived until Sullivan's death in 1936. Keller's other books include *The World I Live In* (1908), *The Song of the Stone Wall* (1910), *Out of the Dark* (1913), *My Religion* (1927), *Mid-Stream—My Later Life* (1930), *Helen Keller's Journal* (1938), *Let Us Have Faith* (1940), *The Open Door* (1957), and a tribute to Sullivan, *Helen Keller's Teacher: Anne Sullivan Macy* (1955).

Throughout their lives, Keller and Sullivan were frequently courted and feted by presidents, royalty, and other luminaries, yet Sullivan remained true to her mission as a teacher and educator while Keller was determined not to become a celebrated oddity, albeit a heroic one. Instead, she converted her story into moving educational lessons for her many readers and audiences on the nature of disabilities and the achievements that are possible despite severe limitations. Through all her fame as one of the most influential women of all time, Keller never forgot her first and greatest teacher, her other half who made her whole. "How much of my delight in all beautiful things is innate," she wrote, "and how much is due to her influence, I can never tell. I feel that her being is inseparable from my own, and that the footsteps of my life are in hers.... There is not a talent, or an aspiration or a joy in me that has not been awakened by her loving touch."

Billie Jean King (1943–)
Tennis Player

One of the most admired and accomplished players in American tennis, Billie Jean King can be considered the single most influential figure in the successful fight for recognition and equal treatment of female athletes.

Billie Jean Moffit was born and raised in Long Beach, California. Both of her parents were athletes, and, as a child, she played football and softball. She took up tennis at the age of eleven and, six months after taking her first lesson, played in her first tournament. Even as a youngster, she was noted for her aggressive, athletic play that seemed to clash with the then-dominate image of the ladylike tennis player.

King won her first tournament at fifteen, when she captured the southern California girls fifteen-and-under championship and advanced to the quarterfinals of the national championship. In 1960, she reached the finals of the national championship but lost to seventeen-year-old Karen Hantze. A year later, she teamed up with Hantze to win the women's doubles championship at Wimbledon. They became the youngest pair ever to win the prestigious event.

In 1965, Billie Jean married Larry King, who became her agent, business manager, lawyer, and adviser. The following year, she won her first Wimbledon singles championship. Over the next ten years, King won a record twenty Wimbledon titles—six singles, ten doubles, and four mixed doubles. During that time, she also won four U.S. Open singles titles. In 1971, she joined the newly formed Virginia Slim tour and became the first female athlete to win $100,000 in a single year.

In 1973, King accepted a challenge to play a $100,000 winner-takes-all match against long-retired former champion Bobby Riggs, who had boasted that a female player could never beat a man, even with a great disparity in age. Earlier that year, the fifty-five-year-old Riggs had beaten thirty-one-year-old Margaret Smith Court in a $10,000 match. This time, in front of thirty thousand people at Houston's Astrodome and another forty million TV viewers, King crushed him in three straight sets.

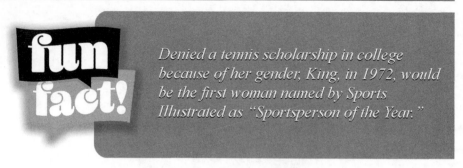

Denied a tennis scholarship in college because of her gender, King, in 1972, would be the first woman named by Sports Illustrated as "Sportsperson of the Year."

King was a founder and president of the Women's Tennis Association, a union for players, a founder of tennis and softball leagues for professional female athletes, and a publisher of *womenSports,* a magazine that reported on the progress of female athletes in a variety of sports. In 1976, she helped to create World Team Tennis, a league of male and female tennis professionals. She was also the first woman to coach male pro tennis players.

King was inducted into the Women's Sports Foundation Hall of Fame in 1980 and the International Tennis Hall of Fame in 1987.

Coretta Scott King (1927–2006)
Civil Rights Activist

Although she is best known as the wife of famed civil rights leader Martin Luther King Jr., Coretta Scott King deserves credit for her own contributions to the cause of racial justice and as an unflagging preserver of her husband's legacy for almost four decades. She took over the leadership of the civil rights movement after her husband's assassination and broadened the scope of her activism to include opposition to apartheid and LGBTQI rights.

She was born in Marion, Alabama. Her great-grandmother, a former slave, presided at her birth as a midwife. Her mother was known for her musical talent and singing voice, and her daughter shared both her mother's interest and talent in music. She attended a one-room elementary school and was bussed with the other local black teenagers to the closest black high school nine miles from home by her mother. She became the leading soprano in her school, played trumpet and piano, and sang in the chorus. She went on to receive her bachelor's degree in music at Antioch College, where she was one of only three African American, female students. In 1951, she won a scholarship to further her music studies at the New England Conservatory of Music in Boston. There, she met Boston University doctoral student Martin Luther King Jr. They began dating and were married in 1953.

After graduating from the conservatory in 1954, the couple moved to Montgomery, Alabama, where King took a position as the pastor of the Dexter Avenue Baptist Church. The church and the Kings' home would become centers for the civil rights movement as well as targets for white supremacists. Throughout the civil rights struggle, she appeared side by side with her husband as well as openly criticizing the movement's exclusion of women in leadership positions.

Following her husband's assassination in Memphis in 1968, she continued to support various causes, marching in a labor strike only days after King's funeral. She was an outspoken opponent of the Vietnam War and was placed under FBI surveillance for

Thankfully, no one was injured after an unidentified white supremacist bombed the King family home in Montgomery, Alabama, in 1956. When Coretta's father insisted that she leave Montgomery and return to Atlanta, she refused.

several years. She traveled internationally, lecturing about racism and economic issues and supporting several women's rights causes. In 1969, she published her memoirs, *My Life with Martin Luther King, Jr.* She established the King Center to advance and preserve her husband's legacy and campaigned for the federal holiday in his honor, which was signed into law in 1983.

King was the recipient of many honors and awards, among them a medal from the American Library Association named after her in 1970, which is awarded to outstanding African American writers and illustrators of children's literature; a Candace Award for Distinguished Service from the National Coalition of 100 Black Women; the prestigious Gandhi Peace Prize by the government of India in 2004; and the creation of the Coretta Scott King Forest in the Galilee region of northern Israel to perpetuate "her memory of equality and peace." Mourners at her funeral included four former U.S. presidents, one sitting president, and one future president (Barack Obama) as well as members of the Gay and Lesbian Task Force, the Human Rights Campaign, the National Black Justice Coalition, and representatives from Antioch College. The first African American to lie in honor in the Georgia State Capitol, Coretta Scott King was eulogized as the "first lady of the civil rights movement."

Maxine Hong Kingston (1940–)
Memoirist, Novelist

A memoirist and novelist, Maxine Hong Kingston is the author of *The Woman Warrior* (1976), one of the singular achievements in modern American literature. It was the first work by an Asian American writer to gain widespread popularity and critical acclaim, revolutionizing accepted literary forms, creating a new genre that has been called "the creative memoir" or creative nonfiction, and pioneering an ongoing and important exploration of the American experience from personal, ethnic, cultural, and gender perspectives. It has been followed by other works of both technical daring and vivid authenticity that have elevated Kingston into the highest rank of American writers.

The oldest of the six American-born children of Chinese immigrants, Kingston was born in Stockton, California. Her father, trained in China as a scholar and teacher, first worked in America as a laborer, saving enough to invest in a laundry in New York's Chinatown. Her mother, separated from her husband for fifteen years in China, worked as a physician before joining her husband in 1939 in California, where he managed an illegal gambling house. During World War II, they opened a laundry, where Maxine and her siblings were put to work as soon as they were old enough to help. Speaking only Chinese until she started school, Kingston eventually excelled as a student, publishing and winning five dollars for her first essay, "I Am an American," in *Girl Scouts Magazine* in 1955 while still in high school. Attending the University of California–Berkeley on a scholarship, she married fellow student Earll Kingston and worked for five years teaching English and mathematics at a California high school. Disillusioned with 1960s drug culture and the ineffectiveness of the protest movement against the Vietnam War, the couple and their young son left California in 1967, bound for Japan. Stopping off in Hawaii, they would remain there for the next seventeen years with Kingston teaching at several high schools and business and technical colleges as she began work on her first book.

The Woman Warrior was originally intended to be combined with the stories that eventually made up *China Men* (1980) to form "one big book" exploring identity formation and cultural conflict faced by Chinese Americans, based on Kingston's family

The recipient of the 1997 National Humanities Award presented by President Bill Clinton, Kingston was arrested in 2003 for participating in a protest on International Women's Day.

history and experiences. Avoiding the restrictions of standard autobiographies, which she identified as dealing with "exterior things" or "big historical events that you publicly participated in," Kingston focused instead on what she called "real stories," narratives mixing facts and the imagination, dramatizing "the rich, personal inner life." The result brought attention to one of the first Asian American experiences written from a radically new, poetic, and luminous method that would be widely imitated by future memoirists and writers of creative nonfiction. Kingston would continue to explore central issues of race, gender, and politics in such works as *Tripmaster Monkey: His Fake Book* (1989), *To Be a Poet* (2002), *The Fifth Book of Peace* (2003), *Veterans of War, Veterans of Peace* (2006), and *I Love a Broad Margin to My Life* (2011).

Juanita Morris Kreps (1921–2010)
Company Executive, Economist

An economist, businesswoman, and public official, Juanita Morris Kreps was the first woman to serve as U.S. secretary of commerce, the first woman to sit on the board of directors of the New York Stock Exchange, and the first woman to win the Director of the Year award for the National Association of Corporate Directors.

Born Juanita Morris in Lynch, Kentucky, Kreps graduated from Berea College in 1942 before earning her master's degree (1944) and Ph.D. (1948) in economics from Duke University. She married Clifton H. Kreps Jr., also an economist, and followed him to various academic positions, teaching part time at Denison and Hofstra universities and at Queens College. In 1955, she returned to Duke as a part-time instructor, and, from 1963 to 1967, she rose through the academic ranks to become a full professor and dean of the Women's College and associate provost in 1967. In 1973, she was named Duke's first female vice president. Kreps's main field of research was the changing role of women in the labor force and its effect on society. Her published works include *Sex in the Marketplace: American Women at Work* (1971) and *Sex, Age, and Work: The Changing Composition of the Labor Force* (1975).

Kreps experienced firsthand the challenges of working women while trying to coordinate teaching positions with her husband and juggling her responsibilities of raising her three children. Kreps was an early supporter of the feminist movement, publicly supporting equal opportunity employment. One of the landmarks of the feminist movement was Kreps's appointment to U.S. secretary of commerce in 1977 by President Jimmy Carter. She was the first woman to hold the office as well as the first professional economist to do so. Kreps was only the fifth woman in U.S. history to hold any Cabinet position. She focused on U.S. trade issues, development of poor regions of the United States, and labor equity issues faced by women. Named Woman of the Year by *Ladies' Home Journal* in 1978, Kreps became the first U.S. secretary of commerce to visit China to negotiate an important trade agreement. In 1979, Kreps left her cabinet post for family reasons to return to Duke and eventually retired as vice president emerita. Kreps

Kreps was the first woman to hold the influential cabinet post of Secretary of Commerce. When she was asked about the lack of qualified women for the job, Kreps replied that there were plenty of qualified women—they just had to be found.

served on numerous corporate boards, including Eastman Kodak, AT&T, J.C. Penney, United Airlines, and R.J. Reynolds. She died in Durham, North Carolina, at the age of eighty-nine. Kreps stated to the graduates in a 1977 commencement speech at Duke, "If there is one thing I could wish for you, it would be that you sense the freedom and be sensitive to the constraints that the forces of history throw in your lap. Because you face a different world, I would further hope that you feel uninhibited by the expectations of others, remembering that their notions of success or failure are not necessarily appropriate to your time and place."

Emma Lazarus (1849–1887)
Poet

A poet best known for her 1883 sonnet "The New Colossus," with its famous lines "Give me your tired, your poor, / Your huddled masses yearning to be free," which is inscribed on the pedestal of the Statue of Liberty, Lazarus is an example of a writer transformed by a cause and a consciousness driven by her awakened sense of her own Jewish identity, which made her one of the first prominent and successful writers to explore the struggles of Jews in America.

Born in New York City into a wealthy family, Lazarus was educated at home by private tutors. Her first book of verse, *Poems and Translations* (1867), was published while she was still a teenager. A second volume of poetry, *Admetus and Other Poems*, followed in 1871, along with a novel, *Alide: An Episode in Goethe's Life*, in 1874; a verse drama, *The Spagnoletto*, in 1876; and a translation of Heinrich Heine's poems in 1881. As precocious and talented as these works were, attracting attention and praise from Ralph Waldo Emerson and others, Lazarus's early verse is conventionally romantic. It was only after a reawakening of her Jewish identity that Lazarus's work assumed the focus and passion that helped establish her as more than a prodigy and dilettante and allowed her to produce works that have been admired for their passionate advocacy of the dispossessed and persecuted.

The initial stimulus in exploring her own Jewish heritage came after reading George Eliot's *Daniel Deronda* (1876) with its central theme of Jewish identity and the prejudice to which Jews were exposed. After the Russian pogroms of 1881 that followed the assassination of Tsar Alexander II, who killed or displaced thousands of Jews, many of whom immigrated to New York, Lazarus took up their cause. Lazarus helped to establish the Hebrew Technical Institute in New York to provide vocational training to assist Jewish immigrants to become self-supporting. She founded the Society for the Improvement and Colonization of East European Jews, a forerunner organization of the Zionist movement in which Lazarus promoted the creation of a Jewish state thirteen years before Theodor Herzl.

fun fact!

Fluent in English, German, Italian, and French, Lazarus found early work by translating the poems of European authors.

In 1882, she published *Songs of a Semite*, which announced her arrival as a distinctive Jewish American writer in such important poems as "The Crowning of the Red Cock"; "The Banner of the Jew"; "Dance to Death," a verse drama, which is considered her best work; and *By the Waters of Babylon*, a poetic sequence published in 1887. Her collected poems were published in 1889.

Her most famous poem, "The New Colussus," was written in 1883 to raise money to construct the pedestal for the Statue of Liberty. Her poem was praised for giving the statue, a gift from France, a spirited purpose, but it was not mentioned in the dedication ceremony in 1886 and did not appear in her *New York Times* obituary after she died a year later from cancer at the age of thirty-eight. It was only in 1903 that her words, which embodied the American vision of liberty, were cast in bronze and affixed to the statue.

Maya Lin (1959–)
Architect

In 1981, a committee of architects, artists, and designers selected the winning design for a Vietnam Veterans Memorial in Washington, D.C. They chose the work of twenty-one-year-old Maya Lin, who at the time was still an undergraduate student at Yale University. Her design of a V-shaped, black, granite wall listing the names of the nearly sixty thousand men and women killed or missing in action in Vietnam was a striking and controversial conception that radically differed from heroic monuments of the past.

Maya Ying Lin was born in Athens, Ohio, the daughter of parents who had fled China just before the Communist Revolution of 1949. Her father was a ceramic artist and dean of the Ohio University art school; her mother was a poet and professor of Asian and English literature. As a student, Lin demonstrated an aptitude for both mathematics and art. She entered Yale University, where she studied architecture and sculpture, though teachers encouraged her to choose either one discipline or the other. "I would look at my professors, smile, and go about my business," she recalled. "I consider myself both an artist and an architect. I don't combine them, but each field informs the other."

During the controversy surrounding her design for the Vietnam Memorial, Lin was subjected to racial and sexist slurs from those who felt that an Asian American woman was an inappropriate designer for a monument honoring those who lost their lives in a war fought against the Vietnamese. Through the often bitter debate, Lin held firm to her conviction that her design "does not glorify war or make an antiwar statement. It is a place for private reckoning." Dismissed by some critics as a "black gash of shame," Lin's design struck a special chord with veterans and the families and friends of the fallen who came to touch the names of loved ones and leave personal mementos behind. Lin had created, in the words of one admiring critic, "a very psychological memorial ... that brings out in people the realization of loss and a cathartic healing process." The Wall, as it has come to be called, has become the most visited monument in America, attracting more than one million people a year, a testimony to a great artist's simple but profound vision and the courage of her convictions.

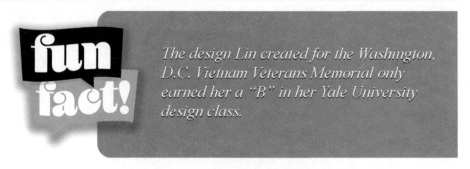

The design Lin created for the Washington, D.C. Vietnam Veterans Memorial only earned her a "B" in her Yale University design class.

In 1986, Lin earned a master's degree in architecture and went on to design the Civil Rights Memorial in Montgomery, Alabama, the Museum for African Art in New York City, and a monument commemorating women at Yale University. She has also designed numerous public and private buildings, landscape designs, and sculptures. In her many environmentally themed works, she has raised awareness of the environmental crisis. In 2000, she published the book *Boundaries,* and in 2009, Lin created the building for the Museum of Chinese in America near New York City's Chinatown. Since 2010, Lin has been working on what she calls her "final memorial": the What Is Missing? Foundation, which commemorates the biodiversity that has been lost. Using sound, media, science, and art in temporary installations and on the Internet, What Is Missing? appears in multiple sites simultaneously.

Married to New York photography dealer Daniel Wolf, Lin is the mother of two daughters. In 2005, Lin was elected to the Academy of Arts and Letters as well as the National Women's Hall of Fame. In 2009, she received the National Medal of Arts from President Barack Obama.

Eleanor Josephine MacDonald (1906–2007)
Oncologist, Epidemiologist, Researcher

The first cancer epidemiologist ever, Eleanor Josephine MacDonald was the first to precisely determine incidence rates of cancer and one of the earliest proponents that cancer was a preventable disease.

MacDonald was born in West Somerville in Boston. Her father was an engineer at AT&T, and her mother was a concert pianist. MacDonald, also a gifted musician, graduated from Radcliffe College in 1928 with B.A. degrees in music and English. For four years after graduation, she performed as a concert cellist.

Her scientific career began when a friend of the family, Dr. Robert B. Greenough, chairman of the Cancer Committee in Massachusetts, asked MacDonald for assistance in writing a research paper on cystic mastitis. This would lead to MacDonald becoming an epidemiologist, studying at Harvard University's School of Public Health. She took a job with the Massachusetts Department of Public Health, where she began a series of studies on cancer. Previously, epidemiologists had only researched communicable diseases. MacDonald was the first to study the incidence of cancer and other chronic diseases occurring in people older than forty. For a period of five years, she and her colleagues went door to door seeking information on the residents' health. When she presented her results, they were hailed as the first accurate calibration of cancer incidence in the country. MacDonald showed that with early detection, cancer could be treated successfully. MacDonald's approach to the problem of cancer made her the first epidemiologist in cancer research.

From 1940 to 1948, MacDonald worked for the Connecticut State Health Department, where she created the first population-based cancer record registry and follow-up program for the state. Over a six-year period, she and a volunteer checked all hospital records in the state for patients with cancer. They then traced each case to find out what had become of the patients. They found that 1,800 were still alive, and, as MacDonald recalled, "This was the beginning of follow-up for cancer patients." MacDonald's methods and procedures were widely copied nationwide.

An early adopter of the new computer technology that had become available to researchers, MacDonald earned honors from the American Cancer Society and the M. D. Anderson Cancer Center, and she is in the Texas Medical Center Hall of Fame.

In addition to her work in Connecticut, MacDonald worked for ten years on weekends to set up and run the statistical department at Memorial Sloane Kettering in New York as well as serving as a consultant to the National Advisory Cancer Council in Washington, D.C. In 1948, MacDonald became a full professor in epidemiology at the University of Texas MD Anderson Hospital in Houston, an association she would continue for forty-five years. Her studies included the first cancer incidence data for Hispanics and a determination that intense exposure to sunlight was linked to the rise in the occurrence of skin cancer.

MacDonald retired from her position as a professor in 1974 but continued to serve as a professor emeritus. "It has been marvelous," she recalled, "to be a pioneer. Everyone encouraged me in my work, and I did not feel they discriminated against me because I was female." She died in her home in Houston at the age of 101, having added so much to our understanding of cancer and to its treatment as a curable disease.

Dolley Madison (1768–1848)
First Lady

Dolley Madison, perhaps more than any other first lady, helped to define the role of the president's spouse, providing social occasions for members of opposing political parties so they could come together and amicably socialize, network, and negotiate. Moreover, her bravery and patriotism during a time of war later earned her a reputation as one of America's most courageous first ladies.

Born Dorothea Payne in North Carolina and raised on a plantation near Ashland, Virginia, she was the oldest daughter of nine children. Her Quaker parents doted on her and gave her the nickname "Dolley." In 1790, she married John Todd Jr., a young Quaker lawyer, who died three years later while caring for victims of a Philadelphia yellow fever epidemic. Dolley and her sons, a two-year-old and a newborn, also became ill. She and her older son survived, but the infant died.

In 1794, after a fourteen-month courtship, she married Virginia congressman James Madison. The Quakers disowned her because she married outside her faith. This meant that she was free from their restrictions and could attend social occasions that Quakers frowned upon, such as balls and receptions.

In 1801, President Thomas Jefferson appointed Madison as his secretary of state. Since both Jefferson and his vice president, Aaron Burr, were widowers, Dolley, as the wife of the highest-ranking Cabinet official, hosted presidential dinners and receptions. She carried out her duties with warmth, wit, and charm, characteristics that would continue after her husband was elected president in 1808. During the Madison presidency, Dolley produced a social whirlwind at the White House. The Executive Mansion became a nearly endless succession of dinner parties, lawn parties, luncheons, and dances. While she was always dressed in the most glamorous fashions of the day, she was known for having the talent to inject in the most formal occasion the informal gaiety of a country dance or a small tea party that allowed her guests, often highly partisan opponents, to socialize and find common ground.

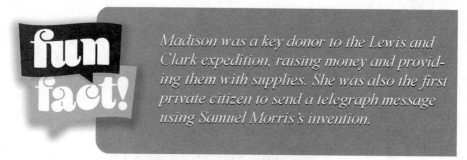

Madison was a key donor to the Lewis and Clark expedition, raising money and providing them with supplies. She was also the first private citizen to send a telegraph message using Samuel Morris's invention.

She became a heroine during the War of 1812. In August 1814, with her husband away at the front and British troops fast approaching the White House, she managed to save the famous Gilbert Stuart portrait of George Washington (though some believe it was her personal slave who saved the portrait) as well as other valuables before fleeing for safety in Virginia. The British burned the Executive Mansion, and it would not be fully restored until 1817 during James Monroe's presidency. After the British retreat, the Madisons moved to another Washington residence, the Octagon House. There, Dolley hosted several galas to celebrate the American victory over the British in 1815.

In 1817, after Madison's second term, the couple retired to his Virginia estate at Montpelier. James Madison died in 1836, and a year later, Dolley returned to Washington, where she lived for a time until Congress purchased her husband's papers to rescue her from dire poverty. With funds from Congress, she was able to resume her former role as the capital's most popular hostess. She died in Washington of a stroke at the age of eighty-one.

Claire McCardell (1905–1958)
Fashion Designer

Credited with creating American sportswear, Claire McCardell revolutionized and modernized what women wore. Breaking with the dominance of Parisian fashion and an age of stiff crinolines, corsets, girdles, and padded shoulders, McCardell helped to introduce an "American look," emphasizing freedom and flexibility in fashion and a casual, athletic, and unstructured look that began to define modern fashion.

McCardell grew up in Frederick, Maryland. Her father was a Maryland state senator and president of the Frederick County National Bank. As a child, she was nicknamed "Kick" for her ability to stand up to the boys in the neighborhood. She was fascinated by fashion from an early age and wanted to move to New York City to study fashion design at the age of sixteen. Her father convinced her to enroll in the home economics program at Hood College instead, but after two years, she moved to New York and entered Parsons (then known as the New York School of Fine and Applied Art). In 1927, McCardell continued her studies at the Parsons branch in Paris. After graduation, she worked odd jobs sketching at a fashionable dress shop, painting flowers on paper lampshades, and modeling for the B. Altman department store.

In the late 1930s, she began work as an assistant designer for Robert Turk, and, in 1932, after his death, McCardell was asked to finish his fall line for Turk's Townley Frocks. Not interested in copying European high fashion, McCardell sought inspiration in art and street fashion and began to introduce innovations such as sashes, string ties, and menswear details. She modernized the dirndl and pioneered matching separates. In 1938, she introduced the monastic dress, a simple, bias-cut tent dress with no seamed waist but with a versatile belt that could be adapted for any woman's figure. Sold exclusively by Best & Co., the dress sold out in a day. Townley went out of business trying to stop knockoffs, but it reopened in 1940 with the company's label, "Claire McCardell Clothes by Townley," making her one of the first American designers to have name recognition.

Among McCardell's honors are the Neiman-Marcus Award (1948) and the prestigious Coty American Fashion Critics Award (1943). She is credited with influencing such designers as Calvin Klein and Donna Karan.

During World War II, as other designers had to contend with limited availability of some materials, McCardell flourished under the restrictions, introducing denim, calico, and wool jersey, which were readily available. She popularized the ballet flat in response to the shortage of leather. She introduced a line of separates that made nine outfits out of five pieces. By 1955, McCardell was on the cover of *Time* magazine surrounded by models wearing her designs, which typified the American sportswear look she had popularized.

McCardell's life and work were cut short when she was diagnosed with terminal colon cancer in 1957. She completed her final collection from her hospital bed and checked out of the hospital to introduce her final runway show. She died at the age of fifty-two, and her family decided to close her label. In 1990, *Life* named her one of the one hundred most important Americans of the twentieth century.

Barbara McClintock (1902–1992)
Botonist, Cytogeneticist

Barbara McClintock's revolutionary work in the biology of heredity helped to transform the way we understand and make use of the essential building blocks of life to eliminate disease. As a female scientist, McClintock faced numerous obstacles for nearly three decades before the scientific community understood and accepted her groundbreaking research, and she gained the recognition she deserved.

McClintock was born in Hartford, Connecticut, and when she was six years old, her father, a physician, moved the family to Flatbush, Brooklyn, New York. As a young girl, she spent time roaming about rural areas and developed a love of nature that would last a lifetime. After high school, she attended Cornell University and became interested in the study of cells and chromosomes.

While earning her master's degree and doctorate from Cornell, McClintock began her study of the chromosomes of Indian corn (maize). In the 1930s, she proved that genetic information, the coded material that determines forms of life and function, was passed on at an early stage of cell division. This discovery would be recognized as one of the cornerstones of modern genetic research. Despite such an important discovery, McClintock struggled for funding for her research and a satisfactory faculty appointment largely because she was a woman. In 1941, she was offered a one-year position at the Cold Spring Harbor Laboratory on Long Island, New York. She would spend the remainder of her life there conducting the research that would eventually earn her widespread recognition.

Continuing her research on corn, McClintock noticed different-colored spots that did not belong on the green or yellow leaves of a particular plant and tried to account for this irregularity in the passing on of the genes controlling plant color. Eventually, she concluded that genetic material could shift unpredictably from one generation to the next, that genes "jumped" from one location on the chromosomes to another, producing unexpected results. McClintock's discovery challenged the accepted view of the

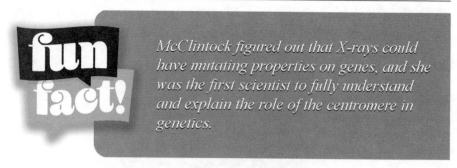

McClintock figured out that X-rays could have mutating properties on genes, and she was the first scientist to fully understand and explain the role of the centromere in genetics.

genetic process. Her colleagues ridiculed and dismissed her findings when she presented them at biology symposium in 1951. Nevertheless, McClintock continued her research with patience and determination.

In the 1970s, advancements in experiments by molecular biologists confirmed McClintock's conclusion from twenty years before. The scientific establishment finally understood that she had uncovered a fundamental law of genetics that helped pave the way for the breakthroughs to come in genetic engineering. In 1983, she became the first woman to be the sole recipient of a Nobel Prize in Physiology or Medicine.

McClintock died shortly after her ninetieth birthday, finally acknowledged as one the most influential geneticists and scientists of the twentieth century.

Margaret Mead (1901–1978)
Anthropologist, Educator

In 1928, twenty-seven-year-old anthropologist Margaret Mead published *Coming of Age in Samoa*, an account of her first field trip to the Pacific Islands. This ground-breaking work launched Mead's career as a pioneering researcher and helped establish her as one of the world's most celebrated social and cultural anthropologists and the most famous educator of the twentieth century.

Born and raised in Philadelphia, Margaret Mead was the oldest of the five children of her father, a professor of economics, and her mother, a sociologist and teacher. As a child, Mead was educated chiefly at home by her grandmother, later attending Barnard College and doing graduate work at Columbia, studying with the eminent anthropologist Franz Boas. In 1925, she set out to do fieldwork among the people of Polynesia, a daring act for a young woman of her time. Up until then, anthropology had largely been a male domain, but Mead brought to the science a woman's perspective and interest in the roles women play in social groups, subjects often ignored in previous re-search. For nine months, Mead lived in a tiny Samoan island village, learning the lan-guage and customs while observing the lifestyles of Samoan teenagers, especially their sexual practices. What she discovered and recorded in *Coming of Age in Samoa* challenged previous notions of so-called primitive peoples while contradicting some of the most deeply rooted notions concerning child rearing, mating practices, family relations, and gender assumptions. Mead helped to establish that behavior was not determined at birth but by cultural conditions that could be altered if better understood.

A second field trip produced *Growing Up in New Guinea* (1930), another commercial and critical success. Mead's subsequent studies of gender formation among three different cultures of New Guinea yielded what she considered her most important book, *Sex and Temperament in Three Primitive Societies* (1935). Mead demonstrated that gender roles were not universal and that temperament was determined by culture, not biology. Both men and women developed, in Mead's view, the personalities their society considered

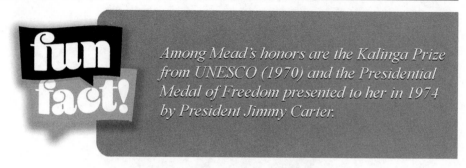

fun fact!

Among Mead's honors are the Kalinga Prize from UNESCO (1970) and the Presidential Medal of Freedom presented to her in 1974 by President Jimmy Carter.

acceptable for their sex. "It was exciting," Mead wrote in her autobiography, *Blackberry Winter* (1972), "to strip off the layers of culturally attributed expected behavior and to feel one knew at last who one was."

Mead would go on to write over forty books on a wide range of subjects, including education, science, religion, ecology, and feminism, while lecturing at colleges and universities worldwide and serving as a curator of ethnology at New York's American Museum of Natural History. Her influence in her field was enormous, but possibly, her greatest contribution was that she made anthropology accessible to the nonscientist. She invited millions of people to look with her at other cultures and, as she wrote, "to cherish the life of the world."

Maria Mitchell (1818–1889)
Astronomer

Considered America's first female professional astronomer, Maria Mitchell is also the first American scientist to discover a comet and the first faculty member to be hired by Vassar College when it was founded in 1861.

Mitchell, one of ten children, was born on Nantucket, an island off the coast of Massachusetts. Her Quaker parents encouraged her education, and her father, an amateur astronomer, stimulated her interest in the stars. She attended schools on Nantucket, including one run by her father. Mitchell assisted her father in his work rating chronometers for the Nantucket whaling fleet and encouraged her independent use of his telescope. From 1836 to 1856, she worked as a librarian and teacher at the Nantucket Atheneum and became a regular observer of the night skies.

In 1847, Mitchell established the orbit of a new comet, which became known as Miss Mitchell's Comet. Her discovery electrified the scientific community, gaining her a gold medal prize for her discovery from King Frederick VI of Denmark, and, in 1848, she became the first woman to be elected to the American Academy of Arts and Sciences. In 1850, she was elected to the American Association for the Advancement of Science. Leaving the Atheneum in 1856, Mitchell traveled throughout Europe meeting with other astronomers while she was also active in the antislavery and suffrage movements.

After the Civil War, Matthew Vassar recruited Mitchell to lend luster to Vassar's nine-member faculty. Mitchell and her widowed father moved into the Vassar Observatory, the first building of the college to be completed, equipped with a twelve-inch telescope, the third largest in the United States. As a teacher, Mitchell defied conventions by having her female students come out at night for classwork and celestial observations. Three of her students would later be included in the first list of Academic Men of Science in 1906.

Mitchell also was one of the founders of the American Association for the Advancement of Women (later the American Association of University Women) and served

A first cousin of Benjamin Franklin, Mitchell was ahead of her time on the issue of race. An abolitionist, she founded an integrated school in 1835 (something not done back then), and she even stopped wearing cotton clothing to protest slave labor in the South.

as its president in 1873. She was also elected vice president of one of the few mixed-gender professional associations at the time, the American Social Science Association. During the nation's centennial year in 1876, Mitchell delivered an important speech entitled "The Need for Women in Science."

Michell retired from Vassar in 1888 but continued her research in Lynn, Massachusetts. She died of brain disease at the age of seventy. She was one of three women elected to the Hall of Fame of Great Americans in 1905. Later astronomers honored her by naming a lunar crater on the moon the Maria Mitchell. New York's Metro North commuter railroad has a train named the *Maria Mitchell Comet*, and, in 2013, Google honored her with a doodle, showing her in cartoon form on top of a roof, gazing through a telescope at the heavens.

Toni Morrison (1931–2019)
Novelist

When novelist, essayist, editor, and teacher Toni Morrison was awarded the 1993 Nobel Prize in Literature, she became the first African American, and only the second American woman (after Pearl S. Buck), to be so honored. It was a remarkable achievement for a writer who did not publish her first book until she was thirty-nine. Her reputation today is secure as one of the most important American fiction writers, whose works dominate any listing of the most important achievements in the second half of the twentieth century and beyond.

Morrison was born Chloe Anthony Wolford in Lorain, Ohio, a child of the Great Depression. Her grandparents had been sharecroppers in the South, and their stories of the racial violence they faced made a strong impression on her as a young girl. In 1949, Morrison entered Howard University, where she majored in English and the classics and began to call herself Toni. After earning a master's degree from Cornell University in 1953, she began teaching, first at Texas Southern University in Houston and later at Howard. In 1958, she married Harold Morrison, a Jamaican architect, and they had two children.

After Morrison's marriage ended in divorce in 1965, she moved with her two children to New York City to become a senior editor at Random House and, to cope with the breakup of her marriage, she turned to writing. Morrison published her first novel, *The Bluest Eye*, in 1970. Her second, *Sula* (1975), was partly composed during her daily commute to work. Both works were praised for their poetic prose, emotional intensity, and original interpretation of the African American experience from the female perspective. Her third novel, *Song of Solomon* (1977), won the National Book Critics Award and allowed Morrison to devote herself full time to her writing career. A string of powerful novels followed, including the Pulitzer Prize-winning *Beloved* (1987), widely considered her masterpiece and one of the most humanly compelling explorations of the psychic cost and legacy of slavery ever written. "In *Beloved*," Morrison has stated, "I wanted to look at the ways in which slavery affected women specifically, particularly the

In addition to her award-winning novels for adults, Morrison also penned well-received children's books, including *The Big Box* (1999), *The Book of Mean People* (2002), *The Ant and the Grasshopper* (2003), and *Little Cloud and Lady Wind* (2010).

ways in which a slave woman could be a mother." In subsequent works, such as *Jazz* (1992), *Paradise* (1997), *Love* (2003), *A Mercy* (2008), *Home* (2012), and *God Help the Child* (2015), Morrison has accomplished the rare feat of producing works of dazzling and original poetic and narrative virtuosity and clear-eyed, challenging explorations of race and gender in American society that have appealed to a wide, popular audience. Devoted to the process of "re-membering," that is, restoring the physical and emotional realities of American history, Morrison's works serve as a kind of interior, heartfelt repossession of the American past and the nation's struggle for self-definition and liberation.

Carry Nation (1846–1911)
Temperance Activist

Although she is regarded today as something of a cartoon figure with a face that resembles the hatchet she used to smash up saloons, temperance crusader Carry Nation conduced a fierce rampage against what she called "bastions of male arrogance." Nation and her hatchet focused national attention on the abuses of alcohol and its devastating social and personal costs. She described herself as a "bulldog running along the feet of Jesus, barking at what He doesn't like" and approached her activism with a religious zeal.

Born Carrie Amelia Moore in Garrard, Kentucky (the spelling of her first name was changed later in life), she experienced childhood poverty, her mother's mental instability, and frequent bouts of ill health. Her education was intermittent, though she gained a teaching certificate from a state normal school. In 1867, she married a young physician, Charles Gloyd, whose hard drinking soon killed him, leaving Nation on her own to support a young child. In 1877, she married David Nation, a lawyer, journalist, and minister, and they eventually settled in Kansas.

Nation entered the temperance movement in 1890 when a U.S. Supreme Court decision weakened the Prohibition laws of Kansas. She joined the Women's Christian Temperance Union (WCTU), founded in 1874 by women "concerned about the problems alcohol was causing their families and society." In an era in which women lacked the same rights as men with little recourse if their husbands drank too much, the WCTU crusaded to raise awareness of the consequences of alcohol. In 1880, Kansas became the first state to adopt a constitutional provision banning the manufacture and sale of alcohol, and when the Supreme Court became in favor of the importation and sale of liquor from other states into Kansas, Nation considered that the Kansas saloons were illegally operating and that anyone could destroy them with impunity. Alone or accompanied by hymn-singing women, Nation would march into a saloon, sing, pray, and smash the bar's fixtures and stock with a hatchet. Jailed multiple times, she paid her fines from lecture tour fees and sales of souvenir hatchets. She also survived numerous physical assaults.

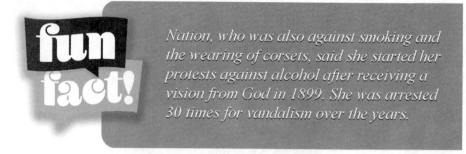

fun fact!

Nation, who was also against smoking and the wearing of corsets, said she started her protests against alcohol after receiving a vision from God in 1899. She was arrested 30 times for vandalism over the years.

Much in demand on the lecture circuit, Nation published newsletters—*The Smasher's Mail*, *The Hatchet*, and the *Home Defender*—and an autobiography, *The Use and Need of the Life of Carry A. Nation* (1904). She advocated other social reforms, including women's suffrage, and railed against tobacco, foreign food, the use of corsets, and skirts of improper length.

She divorced her husband in 1901, and Nation completed her last speaking tour in 1910, owing to failing health. She moved to a farm in Arkansas that she intended to turn into a school for Prohibition. She collapsed onstage in January 1911 during what would be her final speech. She died in a hospital in Leavenworth, Kansas, and was buried in an unmarked grave in Belton, Missouri. The WCTU would later erect a stone inscribed, "Faithful to the Cause of Prohibition, She Had Done What She Could." Nation never lived to see nationwide Prohibition in America, which was established with the Eighteenth Amendment in 1920. Although the remedy of Prohibition is considered a social policy failure (repealed in 1933), the cause that Nation crusaded to cure was real enough, and she deserves more consideration than that of a hatchet-wielding crank of popular memory for gaining national attention to a serious social problem.

Michelle Obama (1964–)
Attorney, First Lady

The first African American first lady of the United States, the wife of Barack Obama, the forty-fourth president of the United States from 2009 to 2017, Michelle Obama was a lawyer, a Chicago city administrator, and a community outreach worker, who has become one of the most admired contemporary American women.

Born Michelle LaVaughn Robinson in Chicago, Illinois, she was the daughter of a city water plant employee and a secretary at the Spiegel's catalog store. Her mother was a full-time homemaker until Michelle entered high school. She attended Bryn Mawr Elementary School before Whitney Young High School, Chicago's first magnet high school, established as a selective enrollment school. She followed her older brother, who graduated in 1983, to Princeton University, where she majored in sociology and minored in African American studies, graduating with a B.A. degree in 1985. She would say that being at Princeton was the first time she became more aware of her ethnicity and often felt "like a visitor on campus." She earned her law degree from Harvard Law School in 1988. She worked for the Harvard Legal Aid Bureau, assisting low-income tenants with housing cases, and participated in demonstrations advocating more minority teacher hiring. With her law degree, she is the third first lady (after Hillary Clinton and Laura Bush) with a postgraduate degree.

After law school, she worked as an associate in the Chicago branch of the law firm Sidley Austen. It was there, in 1989, that she met her future husband, Barack Obama, a summer intern to whom she was assigned as an adviser. After two years of dating, he proposed, and the couple married in 1992. Their two daughters, Malia and Natasha, were born in 1998 and 2001, respectively. In 1991, she decided to leave corporate law for a career in public service, first working as an assistant to Major Richard Daley, then the assistant commissioner of planning and development for the city of Chicago. In 1993, she became executive director for the Chicago office of Public Allies, a nonprofit leadership-training program that helped young adults develop skills for future careers in the public sector. In 1996, she joined the University of Chicago as associate dean of

Obama refused to date her future husband, Barack, until her brother played a game of basketball with him to see if he demonstrated good character and sportsmanship. When her brother gave her a good assessment of his opponent, she agreed to go out with the future president.

student services, developing the school's first community service program. In 2005, she was appointed as vice president for community and external affairs at the University of Chicago Medical Center.

In 2007, she reduced her own professional work to attend to family and campaign obligations during her husband's run for the Democratic presidential nomination. She faced the dual challenge on the campaign trail and in the White House as both an African American and the wife of an African American presidential candidate, a role never before experienced, and as a woman who came of age following the feminist movement of the 1970s, which would challenge previous conceptions of a politician's wife and first lady. Adept at campaigning, her openness and honesty helped to humanize the sometimes aloof and academic Barack Obama. She became known by staffers as "the closer" for her persuasiveness on the stump. As first lady, she involved herself in various causes, including supporting military families and ending childhood obesity. To promote healthy eating, she planted a vegetable garden on the White House's South Lawn. Despite multiple interests and experience as a lawyer and public servant, when people asked her to describe herself, she did not hesitate to say that first and foremost, she was the mother of her two daughters.

After leaving the White House, she published her memoir, *Becoming* (2018), which sold ten million copies in less than six months. She has invited comparisons with Jacqueline Kennedy for her sense of style and to Hillary Clinton for her political savvy and focus. Michelle Obama succeeded in a position no other American had done before as the first African American first lady while expanding the role of what a political wife should play and could become.

Sandra Day O'Connor (1930–)
Attorney, U.S. Supreme Court Justice

In 1981, Sandra Day O'Connor became the first woman to be appointed as an associate justice to the Supreme Court in its 191-year history. Born in El Paso, Texas, O'Connor grew up on a very large cattle ranch on the Arizona–New Mexico border. When she wasn't in school, she learned to fix fences, ride horses, brand cattle, shoot a gun, and repair machinery. These activities endowed her with self-confidence and independence while influencing her character and future judicial temperament. After graduating high school, she entered Stanford University at the age of sixteen and earned a degree in economics in 1950. She then remained at Stanford and received her law degree in 1952.

Despite having graduated third in a class of 102, she failed to win a position with law firms in San Francisco and Los Angeles because she was a woman; she received only one job offer—as a legal secretary. In 1952, she married her law school classmate John Jay O'Connor, and the couple worked as lawyers in Germany for three years. In 1957, they moved to Phoenix, Arizona, where O'Connor interrupted her law career for four years to raise their three sons. When O'Connor returned to work, she entered politics, serving first as an assistant state attorney general, then as a state senator, and later a county judge. In 1974, she was appointed to the Arizona Court of Appeals, where she earned a reputation for making decisions protecting the rights of women, the poor, and the mentally ill.

In 1981, President Ronald Reagan appointed O'Connor to the Supreme Court in part because of her experience in all three branches of government. Her appointment was widely condemned by conservatives, who called the nomination "a direct contradiction of the Republican platform to everything that candidate Reagan said and even President Reagan has said in regard to social issues." However, she was confirmed by the Senate with a vote of 99–0. O'Connor's service on the court since her appointment was consistent with her pledge when she confirmed "to do equal right to the poor and to the rich." She showed her independence on the court by voting at different times with both conservative and liberal justices on important cases such as abortion rights,

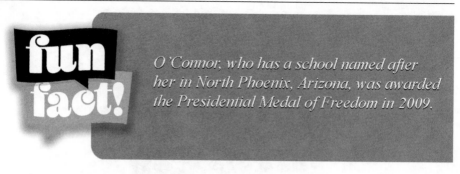

O'Connor, who has a school named after her in North Phoenix, Arizona, was awarded the Presidential Medal of Freedom in 2009.

affirmative action, and censorship. She was often the deciding swing vote in 5–4 decisions, which caused many to call O'Connor the most influential woman in America.

In 2004, O'Connor wrote the majority opinion in one of the most closely watched court cases in decades—the ruling that ordered the federal government to allow terrorist suspects held indefinitely to meet with counsel and to contest the charges against them in court.

In 2005, O'Connor announced her retirement to spend time with her husband, who was suffering from Alzheimer's disease. He died in 2009. In 2018, O'Connor announced her retirement from public life after disclosing that she had been diagnosed with the early stages of Alzheimer's-like dementia.

O'Connor's appointment to the court helped pave the way for other women to join the nation's most powerful judicial body. In 1993, President Clinton appointed Ruth Bader Ginsburg to become the second female justice; in 2009, President Obama appointed Sonia Sotomayor as the third and first Hispanic and Latinx justice and in 2010 the fourth, Elena Kagan.

Georgia O'Keeffe (1887–1986)
Painter

One of America's most renowned and influential artists, Georgia O'Keeffe was famous for the unique way in which she used light, color, and space in her paintings.

O'Keeffe was born in Sun Prairie, Wisconsin, the second of seven children. Gifted in art as a child, she later said that she knew by the age of ten that she would be an artist. She attended a convent school in Madison, Wisconsin, until 1902, when her family moved to Williamsburg, Virginia. There, O'Keeffe continued her education at Chatham, a girls' boarding school, where she was awarded a special art diploma upon her graduation. She went on to study art at the Art Institute of Chicago and the Art Students League in New York, supporting herself by working as an advertising illustrator and teacher.

In 1915, a friend showed O'Keeffe's drawings to Alfred Stieglitz, the well-known photographer and an important figure in the New York art world. He exhibited the drawings at his famous 291 Gallery and in 1917 sponsored the first of twenty one-woman shows for O'Keeffe. In 1924, Stieglitz and O'Keeffe were married.

O'Keeffe became the only woman in a group of modern artists known as the Stieglitz Circle. She was also the subject of some five hundred photographs Stieglitz took of her from 1917 to 1937. In the 1920s, O'Keeffe began to paint abstract and magnified representations of flowers, such as *Black Iris* (1926), which are favorites of many admirers of her works.

Beginning in 1939, O'Keeffe began spending her summers in Taos, New Mexico, where she gained new inspiration for her art from the rich, colorful expanses of the land and sky. In 1946, she had the first showing of a female artist ever held at the Museum of Modern Art in New York City. The same year, Stieglitz died, and O'Keeffe moved to New Mexico permanently.

She divided her time between her house in Abiquiu and a ranch outside of town that she had purchased in 1940. She lived simply, growing her own vegetables and grinding wheat flour by hand for bread. Her paintings of cow skulls and bones, adobe

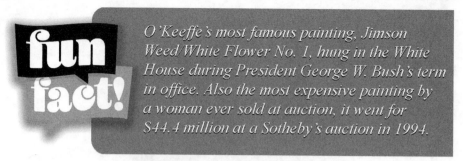

O'Keeffe's most famous painting, Jimson Weed/White Flower No. 1, hung in the White House during President George W. Bush's term in office. Also the most expensive painting by a woman ever sold at auction, it went for $44.4 million at a Sotheby's auction in 1994.

buildings, desert scenes, and her studies of Taos Pueblo, an Indian village, are among her most famous and critically acclaimed works.

In the 1960s, O'Keeffe had several major showings of her art in cities throughout the United States. In 1970, she was awarded a gold medal from the National Institute of Arts and Letters for her work, and in 1977, she received the Presidential Medal of Freedom. Nearly blind in her later years, O'Keeffe continued to paint and sculpt until her death at the age of ninety-eight.

Jacqueline Kennedy Onassis (1929–1994)
First Lady

Although first lady for just the one thousand days of the presidency of John F. Kennedy, Jacqueline Kennedy remains one of the most popular of all first ladies as well as one of the most admired modern women. She helped redefine the role of first lady with her style and grace. As the first first lady born in the twentieth century, she personified the new modern woman. As the grieving widow of a martyred president, she earned the respect and gratitude of a shocked nation as it struggled to cope with the tragedy of November 22, 1963. As a former first lady, she was called "the most intriguing woman in the world," earning admiration for her charitable work and for her second career as a book editor.

She was born Jacqueline Lee Bouvier in Southampton, New York, the daughter of a stockbroker father and a mother from a prominent New York banking family. After attending college at Vassar and George Washington University, she met John F. Kennedy while working as the "Inquiring Camera Girl," interviewing people and taking their photos for a daily column in the *Washington Times-Herald*. The couple were married in 1953, a year after Kennedy's election to the Senate. She slowly adjusted to her role as a senator's wife and actively participated in JFK's successful campaign for the presidency in 1960.

As first lady, she set fashion trends with her clothes, hairstyles, and famous pillbox hat that became a trademark. She directed a major restoration of the White House and gave the first televised tour of the Executive Mansion in 1962. She and the president also hosted numerous cultural events in the White House, featuring such noted artists as cellist Pablo Casals and violinist Isaac Stern. When she traveled with the president, she was so popular with the public that, during one trip to France, JFK jokingly identified himself as "the man who accompanied Jacqueline Kennedy to Paris."

She was riding with the president in the motorcade in Dallas, Texas, on November 22, 1963, when he was shot and fatally wounded by Lee Harvey Oswald. She supervised

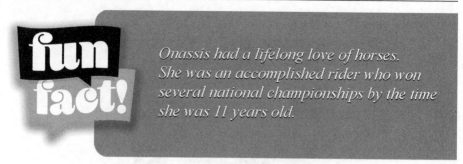

Onassis had a lifelong love of horses. She was an accomplished rider who won several national championships by the time she was 11 years old.

the arrangements for her husband's funeral and inspired a stunned and grieving nation with her strength and dignity. Her popularity continued undiminished after JFK's death, and polls continually ranked her as the most admired woman in the world.

In 1968, she shocked the country when she wed Aristotle Onassis, a wealthy Greek shipping magnate, with a profligate lifestyle and a reputation for womanizing. The subsequent newspaper and magazine photos showing "Jackie O.," as the press dubbed her, living a jet-set life on Onassis's ships and in the Greek islands added to the furor. After Onassis's death in 1974, she returned permanently to the United States, dividing her time between Manhattan, Martha's Vineyard, and the Kennedy Compound in Hyannis Port, Massachusetts. In 1975, she became a consulting editor at Viking Press, a position she held for two years before being hired at Doubleday as an editor. In addition to her work as an editor, she participated in cultural and architectural preservation, particularly in the campaign to renovate Grand Central Terminal in New York.

Jacqueline Kennedy Onassis died of cancer at the age of sixty-four and is buried next to President Kennedy at Arlington National Cemetery. She reflected on her life by saying, "I have been through a lot and have suffered a great deal. But I have had lots of happy moments as well. Every moment one lives is different from the other. The good, the bad, hardship, the joy, the tragedy, love and happiness are all interwoven into one single, indescribable whole that is called life. You cannot separate the good from the bad. And perhaps there is no need to do so, either."

Rosa Parks (1913–2005)
Civil Rights Activist

Called "the first lady of civil rights" and "the mother of the freedom movement," Rosa Parks made history in December 1955 when, returning home from her job as a seamstress at a Montgomery, Alabama, department store, she was ordered by the bus driver to relinquish her seat in the "colored section" to a white passenger when the whites-only section was filled. Parks's defiance challenged the policy of racial discrimination in the South and became the spark that ignited the modern civil rights movement in the United States. Parks became an international icon of resistance to racial segregation.

She was born Rosa Louise McCauley in Tuskegee, Alabama, the granddaughter of slaves. Her mother was a teacher in a one-room, rural schoolhouse, and her father was a carpenter. When she was ten, her family moved to Montgomery. She went to an industrial school for girls and later enrolled at Alabama State Teachers College for Negroes (now Alabama State University), but she was forced to withdraw after her grandmother became ill. In 1932, she married Raymond Parks, a barber and civil rights activist. The couple struggled during the Depression, contending with racial abuse and discriminatory "Jim Crow" laws, which enforced segregation throughout the South. She took what jobs she could get and eventually managed to get her high school diploma. Determined to work for racial equality, Parks joined the National Association for the Advancement of Colored People (NAACP) in 1943, becoming the chapter's secretary.

By the time Parks boarded the bus in 1955, she was an established organizer and leader in the civil rights movement in Alabama. Many have tried to diminish Parks's active resistance by depicting her as a seamstress who simply did not want to give up her seat because she was tired. "People always say that I didn't give up my seat because I was tired," she recalled. "But that isn't true. I was not tired physically, or no more tired than I usually was at the end of a working day. I was not old, although some people have an image of me as being old then. I was forty-two. No, the only tired I was, was tired of giving in." The bus driver called the police, and Parks was arrested for violating Montgomery's transportation laws. She was tried, found guilty, and fined. In protest,

Contrary to myth, Parks was not sitting in a whites-only seat in the bus nor were her feet too tired; she refused to give up her seat to a demanding white man because she was fed up. Parks's casket was lain in honor at the Capitol on October 24, 2005. Over 30,000 people paid their respects that day.

the black community, led by Reverend Martin Luther King Jr., responded with a citywide bus boycott that lasted 381 days. During that time, Parks appealed her conviction, and in December 1956, the U.S. Supreme Court upheld a federal district court ruling in her favor and declared the Montgomery segregated bus system unconstitutional. The bus boycott would become the model for a nonviolent campaign of sit-ins and protests that eventually brought segregation to an end throughout the South.

As a result of her arrest, both Parks and her husband lost their jobs. They were harassed and unable to find employment in Montgomery. They moved to Detroit, Michigan, in 1957, where Parks remained active in the civil rights movement. In 1965, she became an assistant to Congressman John Conyers and remained with him until she retired in 1988.

In 1980, widowed and without immediate family, she cofounded the Rosa L. Parks Scholarship Foundation for college-bound high school seniors, donating most of her speaking fees to the foundation. In 1992, she published *Rosa Parks: My Story* and a memoir, *Quiet Strength*, in 1995. She died of natural causes in Detroit at the age of ninety-two. Parks became the first woman to lie in honor in the rotunda of the U.S. Capitol. An estimated fifty thousand people paid their respects, and the event was broadcast on television. *Time* magazine named Parks one of the twenty most influential and iconic figures of the twentieth century. On the fiftieth anniversary of her arrest, President George W. Bush directed that a statue of Parks be placed in the U.S. Capitol's National Statuary Hall.

Nancy Pelosi (1940–)
Congresswoman, Speaker of the House of Representatives

As the first woman to serve as the speaker of the U.S. House of Representatives, Nancy Pelosi is second in the presidential line of succession, immediately after the vice president. She has served seventeen terms as a congresswoman, representing California's 12th, 5th, and 8th congressional districts. The first woman to lead her party in Congress, Pelosi has twice served as speaker (2007–2011 and 2019–present). She was the House minority leader (2003–2007 and 2011–2019) and House minority whip (2002–2003).

She was born Nancy Patricia D'Alesandro in Baltimore, Maryland. Her father, Thomas D'Alesandro Jr., was a New Deal Democrat and a Democratic congressman from Maryland as well as the mayor of Baltimore for twelve years. Pelosi's brother, Thomas D'Alesandro III, also was the mayor of Baltimore from 1967 to 1971. Pelosi helped her father at his campaign events and learned the value of social networking from her mother, who was active in politics and in organizing Democratic women. Pelosi majored in political science at Trinity College in Washington, D.C., graduating in 1962. The following year, she married Paul Pelosi, first moving to New York and then to San Francisco in 1969. While raising her family of five children, Pelosi slowly got into politics, volunteering for the Democratic Party, hosting parties, and helping with campaigns while gradually rising up in the party ranks, serving as California representative to the Democratic National Committee from 1976 to 1996 as well as the state and northern chair of the California Democratic Party.

In 1987, Pelosi won a special election for California's 8th District, which includes San Francisco. As a House member, she served on the Appropriations Committee and the Permanent Select Committee on Intelligence, becoming a strong supporter of increased funding for health research and for other health care and housing programs and initiatives. In 2001, Pelosi was elected House minority whip, the second-in-command to the minority leader and the first woman in U.S. history to hold the post. In 2001, Dick Gephardt resigned as minority leader to seek the Democratic nomination

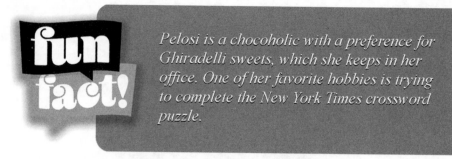

Pelosi is a chocoholic with a preference for Ghiradelli sweets, which she keeps in her office. One of her favorite hobbies is trying to complete the New York Times crossword puzzle.

in the 2004 presidential election, and Pelosi was elected to replace him, becoming the first woman to lead a major party in the House.

After the Democrats took control of the House in the 2006 midterm elections, Pelosi was the unanimous choice for speaker. Elected in 2007, Pelosi became the first woman, the first Californian, and the first Italian American speaker of the House. In her inaugural speech as speaker, she said: "This is a historic moment—for the Congress, and for the women of this country. It is a moment for which we have waited more than 200 years. Never losing faith, we waited though the many years of struggle to achieve our rights. But women weren't just waiting; women were working. Never losing faith, we worked to redeem the promise of America, that all men and women are created equal. For our daughters and granddaughters, today, we have broken the marble ceiling. For our daughters and our granddaughters, the sky is the limit, anything is possible for them."

During her first speakership, she blocked President George W. Bush's proposed changes to Social Security to allow workers to invest a portion of their withholding into stock and bond investments. She opposed the move to impeach President Bush for the invasion of Iraq, opposed the Iraq troop surge of 2007, and, most importantly, spearheaded the passage of President Obama's Affordable Health Care legislation during a two-month marathon session to craft the health care bill. For her successful efforts, President Obama called Pelosi "one of the best Speakers of the House the House of Representatives has ever had."

When the Democrats lost their majority in the House after the 2010 midterms, Pelosi served as House minority leader from 2011 to 2019. While blocking legislative victories by the GOP majority, Pelosi spearheaded a historic bipartisan agreement to strengthen Medicare, while her strength as a negotiator led to significant funding increases for key Democratic priorities such as an extension on expiring wind and solar renewable energy tax credits, an increase in spending to address the opioid epidemic, spending for medical research, and the largest single-year funding increase for childcare development block grants in the initiative's history. She was reelected to the speakership in January 2019, becoming the first person in more than sixty years to serve nonconsecutive terms in the post.

In some ways, Nancy Pelosi is the consummate political leader, a brilliant tactician and consensus builder who has managed to keep a diverse and contentious Democratic Party focused on achievable goals while withstanding withering attacks from the opposing party that would prefer that she fail. After Nancy Pelosi, few can question whether a woman has the capacity to lead at the highest level in politics and policy.

Frances Perkins (1880–1965)
Cabinet Secretary

Serving as the U.S. secretary of labor from 1933 to 1945, sociologist and workers' rights advocate Frances Perkins was the first woman to hold a Cabinet-level position as well as the second-longest-serving Cabinet member in American history. In her post, Perkins helped create jobs and training programs and helped establish child labor laws, maximum work hours, minimum wage standards, and unemployment insurance—all of which brought Americans relief from the economic devastation caused by the Great Depression while becoming standards for subsequent government public policy.

Perkins grew up in Worcester, Massachusetts, where her father ran a stationery store. She attended the Worcester Classical High School and then went on to Mount Holyoke College. After graduating in 1902, Perkins taught school in Chicago and volunteered at Jane Addams's Hull House, where she collected wages for workers who had been cheated by their employers. In 1910, Perkins earned a master's degree from the New York School of Philanthropy and then became executive secretary of the New York City Consumers' League, working for industrial reform and the improvement of sweatshop conditions. The following year, she witnessed the Triangle Shirtwaist Fire, in which more than 146 workers—most of them women and many of them young girls—perished because of the lack of access to fire escapes. This tragic event deeply affected Perkins, and she resolved to "spend my life fighting conditions that permit such a tragedy." While working for the New York Committee on Safety, she exposed employers who were jeopardizing the health and safety of their workers.

In 1917, Perkins became the first female member of the New York State Industrial Commission and, under Governors Al Smith and later Franklin D. Roosevelt, reorganized factory inspections, settled strikes, and established a reputation as one of the nation's leading experts on labor relations. As secretary of labor under FDR, Perkins played a major role in drafting legislation and developing programs that would become the foundation of Roosevelt's New Deal. These included the Federal Emergency Relief Administration to help states assist the unemployed; the Civilian Conservation Corps and

In 1935, Perkins was falsely accused of being a "Russian Jew" by anti-Semitic pamphleteer Robert Edward Edmondson and by the Pennsylvania Daughters of the American Revolution. Perkins was eventually vindicated after four long years.

the Public Works Administration to create jobs; and the Division of Labor Standards to improve working conditions.

During World War II, Perkins helped bring business and labor together in support of the war effort, creating the character of "Rosie the Riveter" to represent women who went to work in war industries. Rosie became a symbolic national heroine and helped pave the way for the greater acceptance of women in workplace after wartime.

After leaving the Cabinet, Perkins served in the Civil Service Commission. From 1957 until her death, she was a professor at Cornell University's School of Industrial and Labor Relations. She died in New York City at the age of eighty-five. As the first female member of a presidential Cabinet, Perkins faced considerable challenges to be taken seriously, but her accomplishments are remarkable: she is responsible for the adoption of Social Security, unemployment insurance, federal laws regulating child labor, and adoption of the federal minimum wage. Few other political figures, whether female or male, could claim such comparable accomplishments. In 1980, President Jimmy Carter renamed the headquarters of the U.S. Department of Labor in Washington, D.C., the Frances Perkins Building in her honor.

Jeannette Rankin (1880–1973)
Congresswoman

Politician and women's rights advocate Jeannette Rankin was the first woman to hold federal office in the United States. She was elected to the House of Representatives from Montana in 1916, four years before women won the right to vote nationwide. She remains the only woman ever to be elected to Congress from Montana.

Born near Missoula in Montana Territory, Rankin was the oldest of seven children. Her father was a successful rancher and lumber merchant, and her mother had been a schoolteacher before her marriage. Rankin was educated at public schools in Missoula and, in 1902, graduated with a BS degree in biology from the University of Montana. In 1908, Rankin went to New York to study at the New York School of Philanthropy. She briefly practiced social work in Montana and Washington and then entered the University of Washington.

Beginning in 1910, Rankin became active in the suffragist movement. She urged the Montana State Legislature to give women the right to vote, served as the field secretary for the National American Woman Suffrage Association, and lobbied for suffrage in fifteen states. In 1914, her efforts paid off when her home state granted women the right to vote.

In 1916, Rankin ran for Congress as a Republican and made history when she was elected as the first female U.S. representative. In 1917, Rankin, a lifelong pacifist and a member of the Woman's Peace Party, voted against America's entry into World War I. She was denounced for her vote by the press, the church, and fellow suffragists such as NAWSA president Carrie Chapman Catt, who believed that women should support the war effort to ensure their enfranchisement. Rankin spent the rest of her term sponsoring protective legislation for children and continued to work for passage of a federal suffrage amendment.

After making an unsuccessful attempt to become Montana's first female U.S. senator, Rankin returned to private life in 1919. She spent the next twenty years working on

*Rankin received numerous marriage pro-
posals by mail and a toothpaste company
wanted to feature her teeth in an advertise-
ment.*

behalf of numerous national and international peace organizations as well as continuing to push for passage of legislation designed to benefit women and children. In 1940, she won reelection to Congress, running as a Republican pacifist. On December 8, 1941, the day after the Japanese attack on Pearl Harbor, Rankin cast the single vote against U.S. entry into World War II. Because of her vote, Rankin lost any chance for reelection.

In the late 1960s, Rankin made news as she led the Jeanette Rankin Brigade, a group of feminists, pacifists, students, and other activists opposed to the Vietnam War. Well into her eighties, she demonstrated with the group in Washington, D.C., in January 1968. Shortly afterward, Rankin decided to run for Congress again, but failing health prevented her from beginning a campaign. She died in California at the age of ninety-two.

Rankin said in 1972, "If I am remembered for no other act, I want to be remembered as the only woman who ever voted to give women the right to vote." In 1985, a statue of Rankin with the inscription "I Cannot Vote For War" was installed in the U.S. Capitol's Statuary Hall. At its dedication, historian Joan Hoff-Wilson called Rankin "one of the most controversial and unique women in Montana and American political history."

Janet Reno (1938–2016)
U.S. Attorney General

The first woman ever to serve as U.S. attorney general, Janet Reno held the office during the Clinton Administration from 1993 to 2001 to become the second-longest-serving attorney general in U.S. history (two other women have been in the position since Reno: Loretta Lynch from 2015 to 2017 and Sally Yates, acting attorney general, from January 20, 2017, to January 30, 2017).

Born in Miami, Florida, Reno was the first of the four children of journalist parents. Her father, a Danish immigrant, wrote for the *Miami Herald* for forty-three years as a police reporter. Her mother was a reporter for the *Miami News* and built the Reno family home on the edge of Florida's Everglades. Reno as a girl loved canoeing, camping, and athletics and aspired to become a baseball player, a doctor, or a marine biologist. Instead, after earning a degree in chemistry from Cornell University in 1960, she enrolled at Harvard University Law school, one of only sixteen women in a class of five hundred, graduating in 1963.

From 1963 to 1971, Reno worked as a lawyer for two Miami law firms and in 1971 joined the staff of the Judiciary Committee of the Florida House of Representatives. In 1978, she was appointed state attorney for Dade County, the first woman ever named to the position of top prosecutor for a county in Florida. She held the position for fifteen years until her nomination by President Bill Clinton as U.S. attorney general in 1993. During her tenure, she had to contend with two explosive events: the deadly federal raid on the compound of a religious cult in Waco, Texas, in 1993 and the government's seizing of Elián González, a young, Cuban refugee at the center of an international custody battle. Under pressure and fierce criticism, Reno was praised for her integrity and willingness to accept responsibility. She was accused of protecting President Clinton when she refused to allow an independent counsel to investigate allegations of fundraising improprieties in the White House, and she was attacked by Clinton supporters for deciding to allow an independent inquiry into a failed Clinton land deal,

Reno was in a 2001 episode of Saturday Night Live in a skit with Will Ferrell called "Janet Reno's Dance Party." She also appeared in a Super Bowl XLI commercial as a guest in Chad Ochocinco's party. And she played herself in a 2013 episode of The Simpsons called "Dark Knight Court."

the Whitewater investigation, which expanded to encompass Clinton's sexual relationship with White House intern Monica Lewinsky and Clinton's impeachment.

After leaving office, she mounted an unsuccessful bid in Florida in 2002 to unseat Governor Jeb Bush, narrowly losing the Democratic primary. She followed the defeat by touring the country lecturing on issues related to the criminal justice system. She became a founding member of the board of directors for the Innocence Project, which assists prisoners who may be exonerated through DNA testing. In 2009 she received the prestigious Justice Award from the American Judicature Society.

In popular culture, Janet Reno was the butt of jokes about her height (6'1" tall)) and her perceived lack of traditional femininity. She never married and did not have children. She was diagnosed with Parkinson's disease in 1995, which caused her death in 2016. She was praised by President Barack Obama for her "intellect, integrity, and fierce commitment to justice."

Mary Lou Retton (1968–)
Gymnast

A gymnast who stunned judges and spectators with her superlative performances at the 1984 Summer Olympics in Los Angeles, Mary Lou Retton was born in Fairmont, West Virginia. When she was eight, Retton was inspired to take up gymnastics after watching television coverage of Romanian Nadia Comâneci and Russian Olga Korbut competing at the 1976 Summer Olympics in Montreal. With the support of her family, Retton moved to Houston to train under Romanians Béla and Márta Károlyi, who had coached Nadia Comâneci before their defection to the United States.

Retton soon began to win awards in competitions and in 1984 qualified for the Olympic Trials. Five weeks before the start of the Olympics, she underwent an operation for a knee injury; however, she recovered in time to compete. The competition for the all-around gold medal, which includes all four women's events, was intense—Retton was competing head-to-head with Ecaterina Szabo of Romania and was trailing with two events to go. Retton scored perfect 10s on both events (floor exercise and vault) and beat Szabo by 0.05 points, becoming the first American and the first female gymnast from outside Eastern Europe to win the individual all-around gold. In addition, she won two silver medals and two bronze medals. Her accomplishments and her exuberant personality made her a media star. She was named *Sports Illustrated*'s Sportswoman of the Year and was the first female athlete to appear on a Wheaties box.

In 1986, after winning the American Cup all-around competition for the third time, Retton retired from competitive gymnastics. She attended the University of Texas–Austin, appeared as herself in several movies, and captured many commercial endorsements. Retton is also a motivational speaker and commentator for televised gymnastics.

Retton's media appearances include Wheaties commercials and ads promoting Ronald Reagan for president. She had cameos in the movies Scrooged and Naked Gun 33 1/2 and was in an episode of Baywatch. She also hosted a fitness TV show called ABC Funfit and Mary Lou's Flip Flop Shop.

Condoleezza Rice (1954–)
Educator, National Security Adviser, U.S. Secretary of State

C ondoleezza Rice is the first African American woman to serve as the U.S. national security adviser as well as the first black woman to serve as U.S. secretary of state (the
second female secretary of state and second African American after Colin Powell), becoming
the highest ranking African American, female government official in U.S. history.

Rice was born in Birmingham, Alabama, the only child of a Presbyterian minister
and teacher. As a child, Rice was drawn to music and dreamed of becoming a concert
pianist. However, her love for international music would be transferred to her interest in
international affairs. She earned a bachelor's degree in political science from the University
of Denver in 1974, a master's degree from the University of Notre Dame in 1975, and a
Ph.D. from the University of Denver's Graduate School of International Studies in 1981.
From 1980 to 1981, Rice was a fellow at Stanford University's Arms Control and Disarm-
ament Program, a fellowship that led to her affiliation with Stanford, where she was
hired as a professor of political science in 1981. In 1993, Rice was promoted to Stanford's
provost, becoming the first African American woman to serve in that position.

Beginning in the 1980s, Rice began to spend time in Washington, D.C., working
as an international affairs fellow attached to the Joint Chiefs of Staff. In 1989, she
became director of Soviet and East European affairs with the National Security Council
and special assistant to President George H. W. Bush during the dissolution of the
Soviet Union and German reunification. In 2001, Rice was appointed national security
adviser by President George W. Bush, the first black woman (and woman) to hold the
post. In 2004, she became the first black woman to serve as U.S. secretary of state,
serving until 2009. Rice was associated during her tenure as secretary of state with the
concept of transformational diplomacy, the mission of building and sustaining democratic, well-governed states around the world.

After her service as secretary of state, Rice returned to Stanford as a political science
professor and senior fellow at the Hoover Institution in 2009. In 2012, Rice and South

Rice's given name comes from the musical phrase con dolcezza, which means "to play sweetly." She still plays piano with an amateur chamber music group. She also loves football and said her dream job would be commissioner of the NFL

Carolina businesswoman Darla Moore became the first women to become members of the Augusta National Golf Club, the notoriously all-male club that had repeatedly resisted admitting women. Also, in 2012, Rice addressed the Republican National Convention by stating, "I think my father thought I might be president of the United States. I think he would have been satisfied with secretary of state. I'm a foreign policy person and to have a chance to serve my country as the nation's chief diplomat at a time of peril and consequence, that was enough.... My future is with my students at Stanford and in public service on issues that I care about like education reform."

Sally Ride (1951–2012)
Astronaut, Physicist

In June 1983, astronaut Sally Ride became the first American woman in space when she spent six days in orbit as a flight engineer aboard the space shuttle *Challenger*. She was the third woman in space overall after two Soviet cosmonauts, Valentina Tereshkova (1963) and Svetlana Savitskaya (1982). She was also the youngest American astronaut in space at the age of thirty-two in 1983.

Born in Encino, California, Ride had dreamed of being an astronaut from childhood. Growing up, she was an outstanding athlete, and for a time, she had trouble choosing a career. Initially, she seemed headed for athletics as a nationally ranked tennis player. She attended Swarthmore College, then the University of California–Los Angeles before entering Stanford University as a junior, graduating with bachelor's degrees in English and physics in 1973. She remained at Stanford to earn a master's degree and a Ph.D. in physics in 1978, specializing in astrophysics. She was working at Stanford as a teaching assistant and researcher when she joined the astronaut program at NASA.

In 1978, NASA accepted only thirty-five astronaut candidates out of eight thousand applicants. For the first time, they selected six women, including Ride. She underwent an extensive year of training that included parachute jumping, water survival, gravity and weightlessness training, radio communications, and navigation. She also worked with the team that designed the fifty-foot remote mechanical arm that shuttle crews would use to deploy and retrieve satellites. On her 1983 flight aboard the *Challenger*, she took part in the deployment of two communications satellites and deployment and retrieval of the German-built shuttle pallet satellite. Part of Ride's job was to operate the robotic arm used to deploy and retrieve the satellite.

Ride returned to space aboard the *Challenger* in 1984 and helped to deploy the Earth Radiation Budget Satellite. Her fellow crewmember was Kathryn Sullivan, who would become the first American woman to walk in space. Ride was scheduled for a third flight aboard the *Challenger* in the summer of 1986, but that mission was canceled

Ride, who was ranked 18th in the United States as a juniors tennis player in 1969, was encouraged by tennis great Billie Jean King to go pro. Instead, Ride opted for science and earned a Ph.D. in physics. Ride was also the first openly LGBTQI astronaut.

when the spacecraft exploded shortly after takeoff in January 1986. Ride was the only astronaut selected as a member of the special commission to investigate the disaster and to recommend changes in the space program to prevent future accidents.

Ride left NASA in 1987 to resume her teaching career at Stanford's Center for International Security and Arms Control. Two years later, she became the director of the California Space Institute, a research center at the University of California. She also became a physics professor at the University of California–San Diego. From the mid-1990s until her death, Ride led two public outreach programs for NASA involving middle-school students. She was also president and CEO of Sally Ride Science, founded in 2001, to create science programming and publications for elementary and middle school students with a particular focus on attracting girls to science.

In 1982, Ride married fellow NASA astronaut Steve Hawley. They divorced in 1987. It was revealed after Ride's death that her partner of twenty-seven years was Tam O'Shaughnessy, a school psychologist at San Diego State University, whom Ride had met when both were aspiring tennis players. She died of pancreatic cancer at the age of sixty-one.

Eleanor Roosevelt (1884–1962)
First Lady

Historians have called Eleanor Roosevelt "the most liberated American woman of [the twentieth century]" and "the most influential woman of our times." To her husband, Franklin Delano Roosevelt, she was the "most extraordinarily interesting woman" he had ever known. She did not claim to be a feminist, yet she was the personification of the strong, independent, liberated woman. She used her influence as first lady and revered private citizen to advance the cause of human rights and, in doing so, became the conscience of the country and the most important public woman of the twentieth century.

Born in New York City into a distinguished and wealthy family, Anna Eleanor Roosevelt was the oldest of the three children of Elliott and Anna Hall Roosevelt. She was so shy and solemn as a child that her mother called her "Granny." By the age of ten, both her parents had died, and she went to live with her strict maternal grandmother. At fifteen, she enrolled at Allenswood, an English girls' school. There, she excelled at her studies, gained self-confidence, and began to develop an interest in social causes. After graduating in 1902, she returned home, where she made her debut into society. She also began to work at settlement houses and visit factories and sweatshops as a member of the National Consumers' League.

In 1905, she married her distant cousin, Franklin Roosevelt; her uncle, President Theodore Roosevelt, gave the bride away. Between 1906 and 1916, she and Franklin had six children. After he won election to the New York Senate in 1910, she worked hard to overcome her shyness so she could assist his rising political career. At the same time, she became active in groups such as the League of Women Voters and the Women's Trade Union League. Her public life expanded after her husband was stricken with polio in 1921. Beginning in 1932 with FDR's election as president and continuing throughout his twelve years in office, she traveled extensively, making speeches and meeting Americans from all walks of life, considerably expanding the role of the first lady. She would then report back to FDR on the conditions she found and the needs

fun fact!

Roosevelt once enjoyed riding in an airplane with famous aviator Amelia Earhart. The flight occurred in 1933, and Earhart took the first lady from Washington, D.C., to Baltimore, Maryland.

and concerns of the people she met. She was also a tireless advocate for bringing more women into government, for housing for the poorest Americans, and for full civil rights for minorities.

In 1933, she became the first first lady to hold a press conference. She also wrote a syndicated newspaper column, "My Day," and for a time hosted a radio show. In 1939, she publicly resigned from the Daughters of the American Revolution because the organization refused to allow African American singer Marian Anderson to perform at its Constitution Hall. After her husband's death in 1945, Roosevelt served as U.S. delegate to the newly formed United Nations and played a key role in drafting the Universal Declaration of Human Rights, which the UN adopted in 1948. Roosevelt also served as the first U.S. representative to the UN Commission on Human Rights, serving until 1953. Her last major official position was as chair for President John F. Kennedy's Commission on the Status of Women in 1961.

In 1960, Roosevelt was diagnosed with aplastic anemia after being struck by a car in New York City. In 1962, she was given steroids, which activated a dormant case of tuberculosis in her bone marrow. She died of cardiac failure in her Manhattan home at the age of seventy-eight. Harry S. Truman would call her the "First Lady of the World" for her human rights achievements, and at her funeral service, Adlai Stevenson asked, "What other single human being has touched and transformed the existence of so many?" He added that "she would rather light a candle than curse the darkness, and her glow has warmed the world."

Ileana Ros-Lehtinen (1952–)
Congresswoman

The first Cuban American and Latinx elected to the U.S. Congress, Ileana Ros-Lehtinen was the first Republican woman to be elected to the House of Representatives from Florida, representing Florida's 27th congressional district from 1989 to 2019. She would become the first Republican in the House to support same-sex marriage.

Born Ileana Ros y Adato in Havana, Cuba, she and her family left when Fidel Castro came to power when she was eight years old. They settled in Miami, and, after graduating from Southwest High School, she attended Miami-Dade Community College, earning her A.A. degree in 1972, a bachelor's degree in 1975, a master's degree in 1985, both from Florida International University, and, finally, a Ph.D. in education from the University of Miami in 2004.

She pursued a career as a teacher and later the principal of Eastern Academy in Hialeah, Florida, a school that she founded herself. She was elected to the Florida House of Representatives in 1982 and to the Florida Senate in 1986, the first Hispanic woman to serve in either body. In 1989, she became the first Hispanic woman to be elected to Congress. During her career in the House, she was an outspoken opponent of dictatorships, especially of Fidel Castro, based on her personal experience fleeing Cuba. She also has worked on behalf of women, particularly women in the military and women in domestic violence situations. She was the lead sponsor of the Violence Against Women Act, which provides resources to prosecute those who have committed acts of violence toward women. She broke with her party in 2012 to support marriage equality, becoming the first Republican in the House to do so, and was instrumental in passing marriage-equality legislation in 2015.

In 2017, Ros-Lehtinen announced that she would not be running for reelection in 2018. After a career lasting over thirty-five years, she stated, "It's been such a delight and a high honor to serve our community for so many years and help constituents every day of the week."

Ros-Lehtinen was dubbed la loba feroz (the ferocious wolf) by Cuban dictator Fidel Castro.

Susanna Rowson (1762–1824)
Novelist, Playwright, Poet

Author of the first best-selling novel in American history, Susanna Rowson was also a poet, playwright, actress, and educator who pioneered female education in America, opening and operating the Academy for Young Ladies in Boston in 1797, one of the first postprimary schools for girls in the country.

Rowson was born in Plymouth, England. Her father was a Royal Navy officer, who was posted to Boston. Following the death of her mother, Susanna joined him there in 1766. Her father remarried, and Susanna was largely self-educated at the family's home in Hull, Massachusetts. During the Revolution, Rowson's father remained loyal to the crown and was placed under house arrest and, in 1778, was deported with his family to England, where Susanna found work as a governess of the duchess of Devonshire. While working as a governess, Susanna began writing poetry, short stories, and novels, and the duchess helped Susanna publish her first novel, *Victoria*, in 1786, the same year that Susanna married William Rowson, a trumpeter in the Royal House Guards. He became bankrupt in 1792, and the couple turned to the theater to support themselves. Susanna continued to write, publishing a long poem, *A Trip to Parnassus*, in 1788 and five novels in rapid succession. She performed as a character actress in a traveling troupe and completed her first play, *Slaves in Algiers, or A Struggle for Freedom* (1794). It included the popular song "America, Commerce and Freedom," a tribute to her adopted country. Also in 1794, she published in America *Charlotte Temple*, a novel that had first appeared in England in 1791.

Charlotte Temple is a sentimental romance that tells the story of an English girl seduced by a dashing, British officer, who elopes with him after a promise of marriage and moves to New York, where he abandons her to die in childbirth. The novel struck a powerful chord with American readers, going through two hundred editions and read by an estimated half a million people, making it the biggest-selling novel in America until Harriet Beecher Stowe's *Uncle Tom's Cabin* (1852). Some were so moved by the plight of the heroine that they made a pilgrimage to her supposed burial place at

Rowson is also notable as the first woman editor of The Boston Weekly Magazine, a job she held from 1802 to 1805. Charlotte's Daughter; or, the Three Orphans (1828), a sequel to her best seller, was published posthumously.

New York's Trinity Churchyard. One of the central themes of *Charlotte Temple* was the need for better education for young women, which Rowson put into practice after moving back to Boston and opening the Academy for Young Ladies, serving as headmistress until 1822, two years before her death. The boarding school attracted the New England elite to its innovative curriculum, which emphasized not only the traditional female accomplishments such as music, drawing, and domestic economy but also subjects like mathematics and science, usually taught only to men. Rowson's fictional heroines are often conventional, passive victims of circumstances, but Rowson's own life in predominantly male occupations describes a very different course open to women.

Wilma Rudolph (1940–1994)
Track and Field Athlete

A world-record-holding track and field sprinter, Wilma Rudolph's story is one of the most inspiring in the history of American women's sports. Born in Saint Bethlehem, Tennessee, Wilma Glodean Rudolph was the twentieth of twenty-two children born to her father from two marriages. She was a sickly child who suffered from pneumonia, scarlet fever, and a bout with polio, and her doctor said she would never walk again. Through the intense effort she displayed while undergoing physical therapy and the support of her family, Rudolph overcame her illness and was able to regain strength in her legs and feet by the time she was twelve years old. In high school, she played basketball and ran track and was nicknamed "Skeeter" for her speed. Her outstanding athletic ability was recognized by Ed Temple, a legendary coach at Tennessee State University (TSU). She trained with the college team for the last two years of high school before attending TSU on an athletic scholarship in 1958.

Coached by Temple, the TSU Tigerbelles were among the top runners in the country. Five of them, including Rudolph, who was still in high school, qualified for the 1956 Summer Olympics in Melbourne. There, she was one of four Tigerbelles who won the bronze medal in the 4 × 100 relay. She continued to train and run at TSU with her eyes on the 1960 Summer Olympics in Rome. At the track and field trials, she set a world record in the 200-meter dash that stood for eight years. At the Olympics, she won a gold medal for the 100-meter dash (in a record time that was not credited because of wind speed) and then a gold medal for the 200-meter dash, setting the Olympic record. Finally, she and three other Tigerbelles repeated their gold medal win in the 4 × 100 relay, setting a new world record. Rudolph left the games with three gold medals, the most won by any American female athlete at that time.

In the 1960 Rome Olympics, the first to be televised worldwide, Rudolph's grace, speed, and beauty made her an international star and earned her the title of the "fastest woman in the world." After a post-Olympics European tour, Rudolph made a triumphant return to her hometown, now renamed Clarksville, with a parade and banquet which,

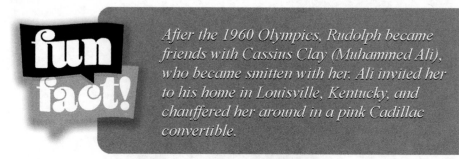

After the 1960 Olympics, Rudolph became friends with Cassius Clay (Muhammed Ali), who became smitten with her. Ali invited her to his home in Louisville, Kentucky, and chauffered her around in a pink Cadillac convertible.

as the result of Rudolph's insistence, was the first fully integrated municipal event in the city's history. Rudolph continued to race and win until her retirement from competitive racing in 1962. She graduated from TSU in 1963 with a degree in elementary education and returned to Clarksville to teach and coach at her old high school.

She spent the remainder of her life in various activities that promoted athletic development for American children, particularly those who would not otherwise have the opportunity to compete. She established and led the Wilma Rudolph Foundation, a nonprofit organization dedicated to promoting amateur athletics. Her autobiography, *Wilma: The Story of Wilma Rudolph*, was published in 1977. She also hosted a television show, served as a television sports commentator, and worked as a hospital executive. She died of brain cancer at the age of fifty-four at her home in Brentwood, Tennessee.

Florence Sabin (1871–1953)
Medical Researcher, Physician

A physician and medical researcher, Florence Sabin was one of the most influential American female scientists of her time. Her study of the lymphatic system made it possible to understand the origin of blood cells and blood vessels, and her research on tuberculosis led to better treatment of this widespread, often fatal, disease.

Florence Rena Sabin was born in the mining town of Central City, Colorado, the youngest daughter of a mining engineer. Her mother, a teacher, died when Sabin was four, and after attending boarding schools in Denver and Illinois, she was sent at the age of twelve to live with her grandparents in Vermont. She attended Vermont Academy and Smith College, where she graduated with a B.S. degree in 1893. She went on to study medicine at Johns Hopkins University, and while she was a student there, she constructed accurate models of the brain that were later used as teaching aids in several medical schools.

During her medical school years, Sabin was active in the Baltimore women's suffrage movement, sometimes speaking in public on behalf of the cause. In 1900, she became the first woman to receive a medical degree from Johns Hopkins. She interned at Johns Hopkins Hospital and then turned to teaching and research on the lymphatic system. In 1917, Sabin became the first woman at Johns Hopkins to attain the position of full professor.

From 1924 to 1926, Sabin served as president of the American Association of Anatomists, and in 1925, she became the first woman to be elected to the prestigious National Academy of Science. That same year, she accepted an appointment at New York City's Rockefeller Institute (later Rockefeller University), an institution dedicated to scientific research. She became the first female member of the institute and directed a team of researchers in groundbreaking work on the biological causes of tuberculosis.

Sabin retired from the Rockefeller Institute in 1938 and returned to Colorado, where the governor appointed her chair of a state subcommittee on public health. As a

Sabin's biography Franklin Pain Mall: The Story of a Mind is a tribute to Dr. Franklin P. Mall, the anatomy professor at Johns Hopkins who became her mentor and for whom she worked for fifteen years.

result of Sabin's work, Colorado passed the Sabin Health Bill, which led to a massive drop in the death rate from tuberculosis.

At the age of seventy-six, Sabin was appointed manager of Denver's Department of Health and Welfare. She served in that position for five years and then retired to care for her ailing sister. Sabin died of a heart attack in Denver in 1953. A bronze statue of Florence Sabin, shown sitting at her microscope, is in the Statuary Hall in the Capitol Building in Washington, D.C.

Sacagawea (c. 1786–c. 1812)
Frontier Guide

Sacajawea is famous for her participation in one of the most important expeditions in American history. From 1805 to 1806, she traveled with Meriwether Lewis and William Clark on their historic journey to explore the vast new territory acquired by the United States through the Louisiana Purchase, which covered thousands of miles from North Dakota to the Pacific Ocean. She played a central role in establishing contact with the Native American tribes the expedition encountered and providing invaluable assistance guiding them to the Pacific and back.

A member of the Lemhi band of the Shoshone, or Snake, Native American tribe, Sacagawea grew up in what is present-day central Idaho. When she was thirteen, a Hidatsa band of Indians captured her in a tribal battle and traded and gambled her away to Touissaint Charbonneau, a French-Canadian trapper living with the Hidatsas. She became his wife and lived with him in a village near the Missouri River in present-day North Dakota. When Lewis and Clark stopped at the village on their way west, Sacagawea and her infant son, Jean-Baptiste, went with them.

Sacagawea proved to be an invaluable member of the party as they traveled across the Great Plains and the Rocky Mountains to the Pacific Northwest and back. She led the explorers through Mandan and Shoshone villages and, acting as interpreter with her husband, helped Lewis and Clark avoid hostilities. During the journey, she reunited with her native tribe, the Lemhi Shoshones, and was overjoyed to learn that her brother had become the Lemhi chief. She convinced the Lemhi to provide the explorers with horses and to guide them across the Continental Divide. During the journey, Sacagawea gathered firewood, cooked, washed clothes, and made moccasins. She showed, Clark later reported, "equal fortitude and resolution" when, on one occasion, she saved valuable mapping instruments and records after one of the expedition's boats overturned during a storm. When the expedition neared the Pacific Coast, Sacagawea asked to be shown the "great water," where she hoped to see a "monstrous fish." Lewis and Clark

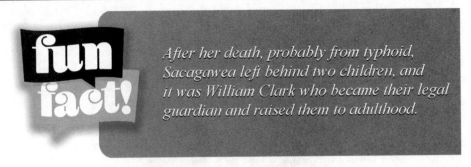

After her death, probably from typhoid, Sacagawea left behind two children, and it was William Clark who became their legal guardian and raised them to adulthood.

canoed with Sacagawea and Charbonneau downriver to the Pacific Ocean. There, they saw the remains of beached whales.

The members of the expedition were greeted with great acclaim when they returned to St. Louis, Missouri, on September 23, 1806. William Clark tried to help Sacagawea, Charbonneau, and their son settle there, but she became homesick for her native lands, and Charbonneau wished to return to fur trapping. In 1811, they moved to Fort Manuel on the Missouri River, on the present-day border of North and South Dakota. Sacagawea reportedly died from a fever in December 1812.

The National American Woman Suffrage Association in the early twentieth century adopted her as a symbol of women's worth and independence. In 2000, the U.S. Mint issued the Sacagawea dollar coin in her honor depicting Sacagawea and her son. In 2003, an eleven-foot-tall bronze statue of Sacagawea was unveiled in Statuary Hall in the Capitol Rotunda in Washington, D.C., becoming the first Native American woman so honored in Statuary Hall.

Deborah Sampson (1760–1827)
Soldier

Called America's first female soldier, Deborah Sampson became a hero of the American Revolution when she disguised herself as a man and joined the Continental Army. She was the only woman to earn a full military pension for her participation in the Revolutionary Army.

Sampson was born in Plympton, Massachusetts. Her mother was the great-granddaughter of William Bradford, governor of Plymouth Colony. After her father abandoned the family, Sampson was raised in different households and, at the age of ten, was bound out as an indentured servant to a farmer with a large family. At eighteen, Sampson, who was self-educated, worked as a teacher and as a weaver.

In 1782, Sampson disguised herself as a man named Robert Shurtleff and joined the Fourth Massachusetts Regiment. At West Point, New York, she was given the dangerous assignment of scouting for British troop movements in Manhattan. Sampson and two sergeants led about thirty infantrymen on a raid of a Tory home that resulted in the capture of fifteen men. At the Siege of Yorktown, Sampson dug trenches and helped storm a British redoubt. For over two years, her gender escaped detection. When shot in the left thigh, she extracted the pistol ball herself to protect her identity. However, when she became ill during an epidemic, she was taken to a hospital, where she lost consciousness, and her identity was revealed when her doctor removed her clothes to treat her. Instead of revealing his discovery to Army authorities, the doctor kept her secret and took her to his house, where his wife and daughters nursed her.

After receiving an honorable discharge in 1783, Sampson returned to Massachusetts, where she married, had three children, and lived the life of a typical farmer's wife. She received a military pension from the State of Massachusetts. The story of her life, *The Female Review; or, Memoirs of an American Young Lady*, appeared in 1797, and in 1802, Sampson began a yearlong lecture tour about her experiences—the first woman in America to do so—dressing in full military regalia.

The doctor who kept Sampson's secret had a daughter who fell in love with her, thinking she was a man. Sampson had to tell the truth, thus revealing her gender. Much later, after leaving the service, Sampson was encouraged by Paul Revere to tell her story on the lecture circuit, which she did to earn needed money.

Four years after death at the age of sixty-six, her husband petitioned Congress for pay as the spouse of a soldier. Even though they were not married at the time of her service, he was awarded payment in 1837 because, as the committee declared, the history of the American Revolution "furnished no other similar example of female heroism, fidelity, and courage."

Margaret Sanger (1879–1966)
Birth Control Activist

The founder of the Planned Parenthood Federation of America, Margaret Sanger devoted her life to providing women with information on birth control and fighting for the legal right to practice contraception. Sanger popularized the term "birth control" and opened the first birth control clinic in the United States.

Born Margaret Higgins in Corning, New York, Sanger was the sixth of eleven children. She saw how difficult life was for her hardworking mother, who had endured eighteen pregnancies and died of tuberculosis at the age of fifty. In 1900, after graduating from Claverack College, a secondary school in the Catskill Mountains, Sanger entered the nursing program at White Plains Hospital in New York, where she completed two years of practical nursing training.

In 1902, she married architect William Sanger, and the couple had three children. They divorced in 1920, and Sanger married oil manufacturer J. Noah Slee, although she retained Sanger's surname for the rest of her life. In 1910, Sanger began working as a midwife and visiting nurse on the Lower East Side of New York City. In this poverty-stricken neighborhood, she confronted the sickness, misery, and helplessness that many young mothers faced trying to care for their children. Childbirth in the slums was a risky experience that all too often led to serious health problems for mother and baby. However, it was against the law for anyone, including doctors, to give out birth control information. Sanger came to believe that the ability to control family size was crucial to ending the cycle of women's poverty.

Sanger began a crusade to help women receive information on family planning. In 1914, she traveled to Europe to investigate birth control techniques there. When she returned to New York, she published her findings in a monthly magazine, *The Woman Rebel*, which ceased publication when Sanger was charged with sending obscene materials through the mail and fined. In 1916 in Brooklyn, New York, Sanger opened the country's first birth control clinic, dispensing contraceptives and providing birth

Although she was, of course, for family planning and contraception, Sanger was against abortion. On the other hand, she was in favor of eugenics, although not in the traditional sense of birthing superior children for the benefit of the state but, rather, for economic reasons.

control advice. The clinic gave out copies of Sanger's pamphlet "What Every Girl Should Know." Ten days after opening, the police closed the clinic, which had already been visited by five hundred women. Sanger was arrested and jailed for thirty days. Her arrest drew extensive media attention and several affluent supporters. She appealed her conviction, and although she lost, the courts ruled that physicians could prescribe contraceptives to women for medical reasons. This exception allowed Sanger to open another clinic in 1923, staffed by female doctors and social workers. It became the model for over three hundred clinics established by Sanger throughout the country. In 1937, largely due to her efforts, the American Medical Association recognized contraception as a subject that should be taught in medical schools. In 1942, Sanger organized her clinics into the Planned Parenthood Federation of America.

Sanger retired in 1942 and moved to Tucson, Arizona. She remained a passionate advocate for birth control and women's rights. In the 1950s, Sanger convinced philanthropist and feminist Katherine McCormick to fund research into a female-controlled contraceptive, which led to the development of the first birth control pill in 1960. Sanger lived long enough to see the Supreme Court in *Griswold v. Connecticut* rule in 1965 that birth control was legal for married couples. She died in a nursing home in Tucson at the age of eighty-six. Between 1953 and 1963, Sanger was nominated for the Nobel Peace Prize thirty-one times, but she was never awarded the prize.

Bessie Smith (1894–1937)
Singer

Bessie Smith is one of the most important figures in the history of American music. By successfully blending African and Western styles of music, she helped transform the folk tradition of the blues into an indigenous American art form with worldwide impact. Few contemporary singers of pop, jazz, or blues have not been influenced by her. An electrifying performer, she expressively and emotionally verbalized actual life. As music critic Carl van Vechten summarizes: "This was no actress, no imitator of women's woes; there was no pretense. It was the real thing."

Bessie Smith was born into a large, poor family in Chattanooga, Tennessee. Her father was a Baptist preacher who died soon after she was born; her mother died when Smith was nine, and her oldest sister became head of the family. Smith soon went to work singing on street corners for tips. She won a job as a dancer in a minstrel show, and while touring with the troupe, she met blues legend Ma Rainey, who became a life-long friend and influence on Smith's singing style.

In 1913, Smith moved to Atlanta to become a headliner at a local club but continued to tour rural areas, performing in dance halls, cabarets, and camp meetings with F. S. Walcott's Rabbit Foot Minstrels and other traveling shows. In 1920, she formed her own troupe with herself as the star. Her rich contralto and commanding stage presence projected emotional depths never heard onstage before. Her material was drawn from vernacular African American oral tradition. As one critic observed, "More than any other singer, she set the blues tradition in terms of style and quality. She not only gave a special musical aura to this tradition but her own singing and accompaniments of the many jazz artists who assisted her in her recordings placed her firmly in the broader jazz tradition."

Smith's recording sessions of the mid-1920s produced some of the finest work of her career. Smith used her impressive range and skill to turn her voice into another instrument in classics such as "Weeping Willow Blues," "The Bye Bye Blues," and "St.

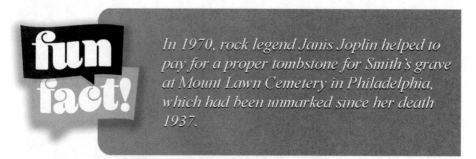

In 1970, rock legend Janis Joplin helped to pay for a proper tombstone for Smith's grave at Mount Lawn Cemetery in Philadelphia, which had been unmarked since her death 1937.

Louis Blues." Her material emphasized the daily plight of African Americans, including poverty, bootlegging, unemployment, eviction, and sexual betrayal. During the Depression, Smith's fortunes declined, as they did for many black performers, with venues closing and the record industry collapsing. A final recording session in 1933 produced the classic "Nobody Knows You When You're Down and Out." Smith continued to perform on tour until her death in an automobile accident in 1937. John Hammond incorrectly reported that Smith had died because an all-white hospital refused to admit her. She was in fact taken to an all-black hospital in Clarksdale, Mississippi, where she died from massive injuries sustained in the accident.

Smith was a great original whose life epitomized the excesses of the Roaring Twenties but whose music reflected the experience of African Americans with deep empathy and emotion. As Ralph Ellison declared, "Bessie Smith might have been a 'blues queen' to the society at large, but within the tighter Negro community where the blues were part of a total way of life, and major expression of an attitude toward life, she was a priestess, a celebrant who affirmed the values of the group and man's ability to deal with chaos."

Elizabeth Cady Stanton (1815–1902)
Suffragist

One of the most prominent figures in the fight for women's rights in the nineteenth century, Elizabeth Cady Stanton was heading the campaign to gain equality for American women and worked to gain for women the right to vote.

Born in Johnstown, New York, where her father was a prominent attorney, Stanton learned about her father's cases when she was young and overheard stories of married women who, because of the laws of the times, could not own property, sue for divorce, or retain custody of their children after a divorce. These injustices so angered the young Stanton that she threatened to cut those specific laws from her father's law books.

After graduating from Emma Willard's Troy Female Academy, she studied law with her father and became involved with the abolitionist movement. In 1840, she met antislavery activist Henry Stanton, and they married that year. During their marriage, they had six children, one of whom, Harriot Stanton Blatch, become one of the early twentieth century's most noted women's activists. On their honeymoon, the Stantons attended the World Anti-Slavery Convention in London, where Stanton met Lucretia Mott, one of the delegates. Stanton became determined to fight for women's rights after learning that women delegates would not be allowed to speak at the convention.

In 1848, Stanton and Mott organized the first women's rights convention in Seneca Falls, New York. A highlight of the convention was Stanton's Declaration of Rights and Sentiments, modeled on the Declaration of Independence, in which Stanton stated, "We hold these truths to be self-evident, that all men and women are created equal" and called for property rights for women, equal pay for equal work, and the first public demand for the vote for women. The convention would become the first great event in American women's history, and the Declaration of Rights and Sentiments became the founding document of the women's movement.

In 1851, Stanton met Susan B. Anthony at an antislavery lecture. The two women joined forces in the interest of women's rights, temperance, and abolition of slavery. During

Although she supported the 13th Amendment, Stanton was against the 15th Amendment that granted the vote without regard to "race, color, or previous condition of servitude" because she wanted a better amendment that granted voting rights to all adults without any restrictions to race or sex.

the Civil War, they formed the Women's Loyal National League to support the 13th Amendment ending slavery. In 1869, they founded the National Woman Suffrage Association to lobby for a constitutional amendment giving women the right to vote. They also collaborated on the first volume of the *History of Woman Suffrage* and, although neither lived to see ratification in 1920 of the 19th Amendment, granting women the right to vote, Stanton rightly believed that they had laid the groundwork for such an amendment.

When Elizabeth Cady Stanton died in 1902, she was recognized as the founding figure of the American women's rights movement.

Gloria Steinem (1934–)
Journalist, Women's Rights Activist

A feminist, journalist, and social and political activist, Gloria Steinem is perhaps the most famous—and iconic—figure in the history of second-wave feminism and the women's liberation movement that began in the late 1960s. Nationally recognized as a leader of the feminist movement as well as its spokeswoman, Steinem continues to be an influential advocate for women's rights, gender equality, and social justice.

Gloria Marie Steinem was born in Toledo, Ohio, the younger of the two daughters of Ruth and Leo Steinem. Her paternal grandmother, Pauline Perlmutter Steinem, had been a suffragist and a National American Woman Suffrage Association (NAWSA) delegate to the 1908 International Council of Women as well as the first woman to be elected to the Toledo Board of Education. Steinem's father was an itinerant antiques dealer, and the family lived and traveled around the country in a house trailer. Steinem's mother, who had suffered a severe mental breakdown before Gloria was born, spent long periods in and out of sanatoriums for the mentally ill. When the Steinems separated in 1944, Leo Steinem went to California to find work, and ten-year-old Gloria stayed with her mother in Toledo. Steinem's older sister, Susanne, was attending Smith College at the time. Steinem's parents divorced in 1946. Steinem later traced her commitment to social and political equality for women back to her experiences with her mother, attributing Ruth Steinem's inability to hold a job and the apathy of doctors regarding her mental illness to a basic hostility and bias toward women.

Steinem attended high school in Toledo and Washington, D.C., where she graduated from Western High School while living with her sister, who was working there and in New York City as a gemologist. After graduating Phi Beta Kappa from Smith College in 1956, Steinem went to India on a two-year scholarship. There, she participated in nonviolent protests against the present Indian government and briefly clerked for the Chief Justice of India's Supreme Court. In 1960, she began working as a writer and journalist in New York City with writing positions at the satire magazine *Help!* and at *Esquire* magazine, for which she researched and wrote an article in 1962 on the dilemmas of

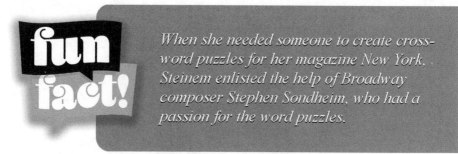

When she needed someone to create cross-word puzzles for her magazine New York, Steinem enlisted the help of Broadway composer Stephen Sondheim, who had a passion for the word puzzles.

women forced to choose between a career and marriage. In 1963, Steinem went under-cover for the arts and entertainment magazine *Show* as a Playboy Bunny waitress at New York's Playboy Club. The article Steinem wrote for the magazine revealed the sex-ually exploitive and underpaid conditions under which women worked at Playboy clubs and was published under the title "A Bunny's Tale." The article featured a photo of Steinem in her bunny outfit. The image caused Steinem to briefly lose assignments because, as she later observed, "I had now become a Bunny—and it didn't matter why." In 1968, after doing freelance work, which included an interview with Beatles member John Lennon and writing for the 1965 season of the satirical TV revue series *That Was the Week That Was*, she obtained a job as an editor and writer at the newly formed *New York* magazine. The following year, while working at *New York*, she covered an abortion speak-out in Greenwich Village, at which she shared her story of the abortion she had had in London at the age of twenty-two. Steinem credited the event as the catalyst that sparked her determination to become an active feminist.

Throughout her long career as an activist, Steinem has been involved in numerous initiatives on behalf of women. In 1969, she wrote an article for *New York* titled "After Black Power, Women's Liberation," which brought her to the forefront of the women's liberation movement. The following year, she testified before the Senate Judiciary Com-mittee in favor of the Equal Rights Amendment (ERA) and wrote an article for *Time* magazine on a vision for gender equality titled "What Would It Be Like If Women Win." In 1971, she cofounded the National Women's Political Caucus and, as the NWPC's convener, delivered a speech called "Address to the Women of America," which defined the organization's goals and stated in part, "We are talking about a society in which there will be no roles other than those chosen or those earned. We are really talking about humanism." The WPC continues to support gender equality as well as proequality, female candidates for public office. Another organization Steinem cofounded in 1971 was the Women's Action Alliance, which promotes nonsexist, mul-tiracial children's education. In 1972, Steinem became the first woman to speak at the National Press Club, cofounded *Ms.* magazine, which remains a premier source of articles on issues concerning women, and helped establish the Ms. Foundation for Women. In 1977, she became an associate of the Women's Institute for Freedom of the Press (WIFP) and cofounded Voters for Choice, a prochoice political action committee.

In 1984, Steinem protested against South African apartheid at the South African embassy and was arrested along with several members of Congress and civil rights activists for disorderly conduct. In the 1990s, she helped established Take Our Daughters to Work Day, the first national effort to empower girls to learn about career opportunities. In 1992, she cofounded Choice USA, a nonprofit organization that provides support to younger women lobbying for reproductive rights. In 2005, she joined with actor Jane Fonda and writer and activist Robin Morgan to found the Women's Media Center to promote positive images of women and to encourage and support the diverse perspectives of women in the media. She has spoken out and written about female genital mutilation, feminist theory, pornography, same-sex marriage, and transgender rights.

Steinem has been the recipient of numerous honors and awards, including the Presidential Medal of Freedom, awarded to her in 2013. She has been the subject of three biographies, has produced and been featured in TV documentaries, and was the main character in *Female Force: Gloria Steinem*, a 2013 comic book created by Melissa Seymour. She is also the author of several books, including *Outrageous Acts and Everyday Rebellions* (1983); *Marilyn: Norma Jean* (with George Barris, 1986); *Revolution from Within* (1992); and *My Life on the Road* (2015). She contributed the piece "The Media and the Movement: A User's Guide" to Robin Morgan's 2003 anthology *Sisterhood is Forever: The Women's Anthology for a New Millennium*.

In 2000, Steinem, who had eschewed marriage when she was younger because of her commitment to activism as well as marriage laws that were unfavorable to women, was married for the first time to entrepreneur and activist David Bale, the father of actor Christian Bale. The wedding was performed at the Oklahoma home of Steinem's friend, Wilma Mankiller, the first female principal chief of the Cherokee Nation. Sadly, David Bale died three years later of brain lymphoma.

Steinem has approached aging with equilibrium, asserting that it represents a new phase of life that has freed her from the "demands of gender." She is clearly not finished with the demands of activism nor is she any less a subject of interest. On January 21, 2017, the day after the inauguration of Donald Trump as president, Steinem, who had endorsed Hillary Clinton, was an honorary cochair of and speaker at the Women's March on Washington to protest Trump's presidency. In 2018, the play *Gloria: A Life*, written by Emily Mann and directed by Tony Award winner Diane Paulus, opened at the Daryl Roth Theatre in New York City. Posters for the production feature the words "History. Her Story. Our Story."

Harriet Beecher Stowe (1811–1896)
Novelist

The author of the most read and most controversial novel of the nineteenth century, Harriet Beecher Stowe produced in *Uncle Tom's Cabin* (1852) the first great American literary phenomenon: only the Bible sold more copies in nineteenth-century America, and the novel became the first American work of literature that achieved worldwide cultural saturation. It is the first great social purpose or political novel in America that served to coalesce (and polarize) attitudes toward race that could be considered a contributing factor in the outbreak of the American Civil War. Few writers, either male or female, have ever been as forceful or as influential as Harriet Beecher Stowe.

Stowe was born in Litchfield, Connecticut, the daughter of Lyman Beecher, one of the best-known clergymen of his day. She attended the Hartford Female Seminary, run by her older sister Catherine, where she received an education in the classics, languages, and mathematics, subjects usually reserved for male students. In 1832, she joined her father, who had become the president of Cincinnati's Lane Theological Seminary. There, she met Calvin Ellis Stowe, a widower and professor at the seminary. They married in 1836 and raised seven children together. It was across the border in Kentucky that Stowe would view the impact of slavery directly. She also listened to the stories of the fugitive slaves who sheltered at the Stowe home after escaping to the North on the Underground Railroad.

In 1850, Stowe moved with her family to Brunswick, Maine, where her husband was teaching at Bowdoin College. When the U.S. Congress passed the Fugitive Slave Law mandating the return of escaped slaves in the North, Stowe became determined to write a story about the problem of slavery, stating, "I feel now that the time is come when even a woman or a child who can speak a word for freedom and humanity is bound to speak ... I hope every woman who can write will not be silent." The first installment of *Uncle Tom's Cabin* appeared in serial form in *The National Era* newspaper from June 1851 to April 1852 and in book form in March 1852. In less than a year, the novel had sold an unprecedented three hundred thousand copies. Stowe's ability to

Her 1852 anti-slavery novel *Uncle Tom's Cabin* was so widely read and so influential that when she met President Abraham Lincoln in 1862 during the Civil War, he said, "So this is the little lady who made this big war."

dramatize the emotional and physical effects of slavery on individuals, so much more effective than any previous abolitionist tract, electrified readers, exciting great adulation in the North and virulent attack in the South as well as praise from around the world. Thomas Macaulay in England declared her novel "the most valuable addition America has made to English literature." Tolstoy considered it the highest achievement ever of moral art. Dramatizations, without Stowe's authorization, flooded the stage, and it has been estimated that between 1853 and 1930, it never ceased to be performed.

Stowe answered critics who charged her with exaggeration and invention of the plight of her characters in *A Key to Uncle Tom's Cabin* (1853), which documented the abuses she had dramatized. Stowe would take up the cause of slavery again in *Dred: A Tale of the Great Dismal Swamp* (1856) before retreating from overtly political subjects in novels that drew on her memories of childhood in New England, including *The Minister's Wooing* (1859), *The Pearl of Orr's Island* (1862), and *Old Town Folks* (1869). She would continue to publish novels, stories, articles, and essays into the 1890s.

Maria Tallchief (1925–2013)
Ballet Dancer

Considered America's first major prima ballerina, Maria Tallchief was also the first Native American to hold that rank. In a field that featured excellent dancers, *The New York Times* called her "one of most brilliant American ballerinas of the twentieth century."

Elizabeth Marie Tallchief, known as "Betty Marie" to her family and friends, was born in Fairfax, Oklahoma, and grew up on the Osage reservation. Her father, Alexander, was a member of the Osage Nation, who had inherited oil revenues, and he was a wealthy man as a result; her mother, Ruth, was of Scottish and Irish descent. Tallchief had five siblings, three of whom were from her father's first marriage. As young children, Tallchief's Osage grandmother frequently took her and her sister, Marjorie, to ceremonial tribal dances, and Tallchief and her sister, an accomplished ballerina in her own right, studied ballet from an early age. In 1933, the family went to Los Angeles in an attempt to secure acting work for the children in Hollywood musicals. At the age of twelve, Tallchief began studying with Bronislava Nijinska, a sister of the celebrated Russian ballet dancer Vaslav Nijinsky, and David Lichine, a student of famed Russian ballerina Anna Pavlova. At the age of fifteen, she danced her first solo performance at the Hollywood Bowl in a piece staged by Madame Nijinska, *Chopin Concerto*. She danced her first pas de deaux for choreographer Ada Broadbent and attracted the interest of prima ballerina Mia Slavenska, who arranged for her to audition for Serge Denham, director of the famous Ballet Russe de Monte Carlo. Denham was impressed, but Tallchief's audition did not result in a position with the company.

Tallchief graduated from Beverly Hills High School in 1942 and won a bit part in a Judy Garland MGM movie musical called *Presenting Lily Mars*. However, she did not find the experience to be a gratifying one. Instead, at the age of seventeen, she left for New York City with a family friend, Russian American ballerina and teacher Tatiana Riabouchhinska, as her chaperone. In New York, Tallchief was eventually taken on as an apprentice dancer with the Ballet Russe and while touring in Canada with the company made her first performance in the ballet *Gaite Parisienne*. After the Canadian tour,

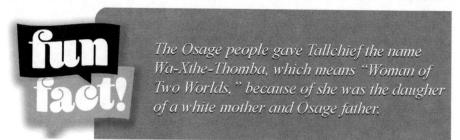

fun fact!

The Osage people gave Tallchief the name Wa-Xthe-Thomba, which means "Woman of Two Worlds," because of she was the daugher of a white mother and Osage father.

Tallchief was offered a place in the troupe when one of the dancers left due to pregnancy. When Madame Nijinska arrived at the Ballet Russe as a choreographer, she cast Tallchief as the understudy to the first ballerina in *Chopin Concerto*. During rehearsals for Agnes de Mille's ballet *Rodeo, or The Courting at Burnt Ranch*, de Mille suggested that Tallchief change her name to suggest a more European image. Proud of her heritage, a name change was a sensitive topic for Tallchief, so she compromised with the name by which she became known.

In 1944, well-known choreographer George Balanchine arrived at the Ballet Russe to stage a new ballet, *Song of Norway*. Impressed with Tallchief, he cast her as the lead ballerina's understudy. In 1946, Balanchine and Tallchief married and moved to Paris, where Tallchief became the first American ballerina to debut at the Paris Opera and was the first to appear with the Paris Opera Ballet at the Bolshoi Theatre in Moscow. She became the company's ranking soloist, and upon the couple's return to New York, she quickly became the prima ballerina of Balanchine's New York City Ballet, which opened in 1948. Balanchine created many roles especially for Tallchief, including the lead in composer Igor Stravinsky's *The Firebird* in 1949, a technically difficult role that launched Tallchief to the top of her profession. Although her marriage to Balanchine ended in 1952, Tallchief remained with the company until 1960, when she joined the American Ballet Theatre. In 1958, she created the lead role in Balanchine's *Gounod Symphony* before leaving the company to have her only child with her third husband, Chicago businessman Henry Paschen, to whom she was married from 1956 until his death in 2004.

In the 1950s and 1960s, Tallchief made guest appearances in films and on television. By the time of her retirement from dancing in 1966, she had appeared with ballet companies around the world during her career. She relocated to Chicago with her husband and from 1973 to 1979 served as the director of ballet for the Lyric Opera Company of Chicago and founded and taught at the company's ballet school. In 1981, with her sister, Marjorie, she founded the Chicago City Ballet and served as its coartistic director until its demise in 1987. In 1996, Tallchief received a Kennedy Center Honor for lifetime achievement, and in 1999, she was awarded the National Medal of the Arts by the National Endowment of the Arts. The Metropolitan Museum of Art held a special tribute to Tallchief in 2006, which was attended by the ballerina. In 2018, she was one of the first inductees into the National Native American Hall of Fame.

Amy Tan (1952–)
Essayist, Novelist, Short Story Author

A novelist, short-story writer, and essayist, Amy Tan is a critically acclaimed and widely read contemporary chronicler of the Chinese American experience, particularly the lives and conflicts of women, which she explored in her best-selling novel *The Joy Luck Club* (1989).

Born and raised in Oakland, California, Tan was expected to become a physician by her Chinese-born parents. Tan majored in English at San Jose State in California, and, after graduate work at the University of California–Berkeley, she began her career as a technical writer. She turned to fiction as a distraction from the demands of her work, inspired from reading Louise Erdrich's novel of Native American family life, *Love Medicine*.

Tan's hobby resulted in *The Joy Luck Club*, which linked stories told by four Chinese, immigrant women and their four American-born daughters, who struggle to bridge the generational and cultural gap. The novel stayed on the *New York Times* best-seller list for nine months. One reviewer observed that the book "is that rare find, a first novel that you keep thinking about, keep telling your friends about long after you've finished reading it." In 1993, Tan coauthored the screenplay for the film version, the first major movie to treat the Chinese American experience. Tan's follow-up, *The Kitchen God's Wife* (1991), concerns a daughter who learns of her mother's Chinese past. *The Hundred Secret Senses* (1995) focuses on the relationship between two sisters. Tan's fourth novel, *The Bonesetter's Daughter* (2001), returns to the theme of the cultural clash between a Chinese mother and her American-born daughter. *Saving Fish from Drowning* (2005) examines American tourists visiting China and Burma, while *The Valley of Amazement* (2013) returns to mother–daughter relations set among the courtesans of Shanghai in the early twentieth century. In 2017, Tan published *Where the Past Begins*, a memoir that recounts her childhood, her relationship with her mother, and her evolution as a writer.

Tan's achievement over a productive career has been to demonstrate the power exerted by cultural heritage and the search for some kind of constructive synthesis between

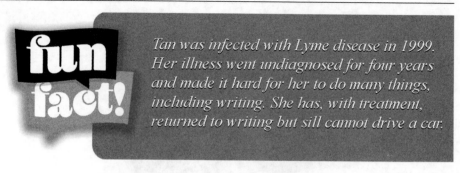

fun fact!

Tan was infected with Lyme disease in 1999. Her illness went undiagnosed for four years and made it hard for her to do many things, including writing. She has, with treatment, returned to writing but sill cannot drive a car.

the past and the present, between generations, and between languages as well as the roles that can limit us but can adapt to suit experience.

Ida M. Tarbell (1857–1944)
Journalist

A journalist, biographer, and historian, Ida Tarbell was a pioneering figure of investigative journalism. The leading muckraking journalist during the Progressive Era of the early twentieth century, Tarbell's famous critical study *The History of the Standard Oil Company* (1902) is one of the great landmarks in journalism history. Its exposé of the shady business practices of John D. Rockefeller, America's richest figure, would help bring about the dissolution of the Standard Oil monopoly in 1911, when the Supreme Court ruled that the company was in violation of the Sherman Antitrust Act.

Born in a log cabin in Erie County, Pennsylvania, Tarbell was educated at Allegheny College and taught briefly before becoming an editor for the Chautauqua Literary and Scientific Circle from 1883 to 1891. She next traveled to Paris to research a projected biography of a female leader of the French Revolution, Madame Marie-Jeanne Roland. Tarbell enrolled at the Sorbonne and supported herself by writing articles about Parisian life for American magazines. She failed to complete her biography of Roland but, after her return to America in 1894, began a biographical series on Napoleon. A series of popular works on Abraham Lincoln followed. In 1899, she was hired to work as an editor for *McClure's* magazine, where she set out to expose the practices of John D. Rockefeller's Standard Oil Company. Tarbell's father had worked in the Pennsylvania oil fields, and she was compelled to undertake her investigation by the conviction that her father had been victimized by the company's practices. Originally serialized in nineteen parts beginning in 1902 in *McClure's*, Tarbell's *The History of the Standard Oil Company* was published in book form in 1904. Tarbell's exposé created a sensation and provoked a public outcry at the practices of Standard Oil that Tarbell had so meticulously documented and was praised for its monumental scope and careful documentation. One reviewer from the *Economic Journal* declared, "it is difficult to write about Miss Tarbell's remarkable achievement without using language approaching the edge of hyperbole. So careful is she in her facts, so sane in her judgments, that she seems to have reached the high-water mark of industrial history."

TRAILBLAZING WOMEN!

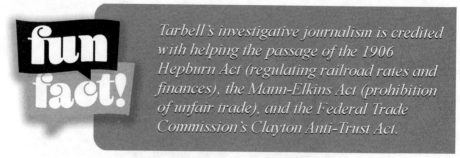

Tarbell's investigative journalism is credited with helping the passage of the 1906 Hepburn Act (regulating railroad rates and finances), the Mann-Elkins Act (prohibition of unfair trade), and the Federal Trade Commission's Clayton Anti-Trust Act.

Tarbell's work ushered in the era of muckraking journalism, and her powerful investigative reporting would be followed by such important works as Lincoln Steffens's *The Shame of the Cities* (1904) on urban political machines; Upton Sinclair's *The Jungle* (1906) on the U.S. meat-packing industry; and Edwin Markham's *Children in Bondage* (1914) on child labor. In 1906, Tarbell helped to launch the *American Magazine*, writing a series of investigative articles on tariffs and their impact, which became the book *The Tariff in Our Times* (1911). As in her work on Standard Oil, Tarbell was able to make complex topics understandable to the general reader. She would lecture widely and serve on several presidential panels addressing industrial and social issues through the early 1920s.

A contrarian in regard to women's rights, Tarbell rose to the pinnacle of male-dominated journalism and was outspoken in asserting women's rights, but she opposed women's suffrage, alienated by the more militant aspects of movement. She instead recommended that women should embrace home and family life as a proper sphere for women and that the drive for suffrage was "a misguided war on men." She collected her essays on women in *The Business of Being a Woman* (1912). Tarbell completed her autobiography, *All in a Day's Work*, in 1939 when she was eighty-two. She was working on another book, *Life after Eighty*, when she died in 1946 at the age of eighty-six.

Mary Church Terrell (1863–1954)
Civil Rights Activist, Women's Rights Activist

The cofounder and first president of the National Association of Colored Women, Mary Church Terrell was a pioneering civil rights advocate, educator, author, and lecturer on women's suffrage and rights for African American women.

The daughter of former slaves, Terrell was born in Memphis, Tennessee. Her father was a successful businessman who became one of the South's first African American millionaires. Terrell attended Antioch College Model School in Yellow Springs, Ohio, for elementary and secondary school before entering Oberlin College, where she became one of the first African American women to graduate, earning both her bachelor's and master's degrees. She spent two years teaching at Wilberforce College, a historically black college in Ohio, before moving to Washington, D.C., where she joined the faculty teaching Latin at the M Street Colored High School (now Dunbar High School). When she married Robert Heberton Terrell, chairman of the school's language department, she was forced to resign since married women could not work as teachers.

In 1892, Terrell learned that Thomas Moss, a close friend from Memphis, had been lynched, and after Terrell and Frederick Douglass's appeal to President Benjamin Harrison failed to elicit a public condemnation, she formed the Colored Women's League in Washington to address social problems facing black communities. Four years later, Terrell helped create the National Association of Colored Women with its motto, "Lifting as We Climb." She served as president from 1896 to 1901, becoming a well-known speaker and writer. She supported the women's suffrage movement, even though some tried to exclude black women from the cause. She was the author of scholarly articles, poems, and short stories on race and gender and in 1940 produced her autobiography, *A Colored Woman in a White World*, chronicling her struggle with both gender and racial discrimination.

After World War II, Terrell fought to end legal segregation in Washington, D.C., and she lived to see the Supreme Court rule that segregation in public schools was unconstitutional. She died two months after that decision at the age of ninety.

Terrell was a cofounder of the College Alumnae Club, which is known today as the National Association of University Women.

Sojourner Truth (c. 1797–1883)
Abolitionist, Women's Rights Activist

An illiterate ex-slave and preacher, Sojourner Truth became one of the nineteenth century's most important African Americans in both the abolitionist and women's movements and one of the most inspiring American women in U.S. history.

Born on a farm in the Hudson River Valley area of New York, Truth was the ninth child of slaves James and Betsey Bomefree. Her slave name was Isabella, and as a child, she was sold to several owners in the area. At fourteen, she married an older slave named Thomas. The couple had five children, although Truth later claimed to have borne thirteen children. In 1826, a year before New York State law abolished slavery, she ran away from her owner and found refuge with a Quaker family, the Van Wageners, whose name she took. While working for them, she discovered that her son had been illegally sold into slavery in Alabama. She went to court in Kingston, New York, and successfully sued for his return.

In the early 1830s, Truth moved to New York City, where she worked as a domestic servant and joined the Magdelene Society, a Methodist missionary organization. In 1843, Truth experienced a calling to become a wandering preacher, changing her name to Sojourner Truth, left home with a quarter and a new dress, and began to travel throughout New York and Connecticut, preaching and singing at camp meetings and churches. She visited Northampton, Massachusetts, where she met abolitionist leader William Lloyd Garrison, who persuaded her to publish her life story. *The Narrative of Sojourner Truth* (1850) was one of the first accounts of the life of a woman slave. The book exposed the evils of slavery and became a powerful weapon in the abolitionist cause. Truth became dedicated to the movement, and she traveled widely on the anti-slavery circuit, often with Frederick Douglass, who was, like Truth, a former slave.

In 1850, Truth took up the cause of women's rights and began to lecture at women's suffrage meetings. She saw black emancipation and women's rights as issues that were inextricably linked, but her audiences often rejected the notion of mixing what they

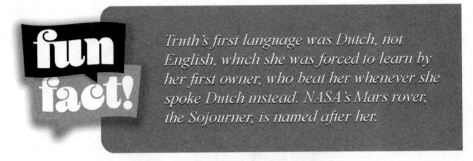

Truth's first language was Dutch, not English, which she was forced to learn by her first owner, who beat her whenever she spoke Dutch instead. NASA's Mars rover, the Sojourner, is named after her.

considered to be separate issues. In 1851, at the Women's Convention in Akron, Ohio, she delivered what has come to be called the "Ain't I a Woman?" speech, one of the most famous addresses in the history of the American women's movement. In it, Truth asked, "And ain't I a woman? Look at me! Look at my arm! I have ploughed and planted, and gathered into barns, and no man could head me! And ain't I a woman? I could work as much and eat as much as a man—when I could it—and bear the lash as well! And ain't I a woman? I have borne thirteen children, and seen 'em sold off to slavery, and when I cried out with my mother's grief, none but Jesus heard me! And ain't I a woman?" As later scholars Avtar Brah and Ann Phoenix have stated, Truth's speech "deconstructs every single major truth-claim about gender in a patriarchal slave social formation" while asking her audience to compare their expectations of gender with her actual experiences.

In the 1850s, Truth settled in Battle Creek, Michigan. During the Civil War, she urged African Americans to fight for the Union, and she worked tirelessly on behalf of freed slaves. In 1864, President Lincoln received her at the White House. After the war, she worked for the Freedman's Relief Association, leading an unsuccessful campaign to obtain land grants for the settlement of African Americans in the West. She died at her home in Battle Creek after a long life in which she fought with evangelical fervor for the rights of African Americans and women, "disrupting," as scholar Nell Painter has put it, "assumptions about race, class, and gender in American society."

Harriet Tubman (1820–1913)
Abolitionist, Social Activist

Known as the "Moses of her people," Harriet Tubman escaped from slavery at the age of twenty-nine and then spent years as the first woman "conductor" on the Underground Railroad helping others achieve the same freedom she had gained. She was also a nurse, a Union spy during the Civil War, and a women's suffrage supporter. She is considered the first African American woman to serve in the military and remains one of the most inspirational figures in American history.

Born Araminta Ross, the daughter of parents who had been brought from Africa in chains, Tubman had eight siblings. By the age of five, her owners rented her out to neighbors as a domestic servant and later as a field hand. At the age of twelve, she intervened to keep her master from beating an enslaved man who tried to escape. She was hit in the head with a two-pound weight, leaving her with a lifetime of severe headaches and narcolepsy. Although not legally allowed to marry, she entered a marital union with John Tubman, a free black man, in 1844, taking his last name and dubbing herself Harriet.

In 1849, after her master died, Tubman feared that she would be sold away from her family, and she fled to Philadelphia. Later, she went even farther north to Ontario, Canada. Although now free, Tubman said that her heart was still "down in the old cabin quarters, with the old folk and my brothers and sisters." Over the next ten years, she made nineteen trips to the South to lead others, including her aged parents and her sister and brothers, to freedom. Her success made her a target, and slave owners placed a $40,000 reward for her capture or death. Proud that she never "lost a passenger," Tubman was personally responsible for leading more than three hundred slaves to freedom along the Underground Railroad—the network of safe houses where abolitionists assisted runaway slaves in their journey out of bondage.

Because of Tubman's expert knowledge of the towns and transportation routes in the South, she worked during the Civil War as a Union spy and scout. Often transforming

When Tubman drifted into sleep because of her narcolepsy, she considered her dreams to be religious visions, and her beliefs were a big reason for the work she did freeing slaves. Later, she had brain surgery to fix the problem, but she refused anasthesia during the procedure.

herself into an aged woman, Tubman would travel behind enemy lines and learn from the enslaved population about Confederate troop movements and supply lines. She also became a respected guerilla operative and nurse to black and white soldiers stricken with infection and disease.

After the war, she helped to establish schools for freedmen in North Carolina as well as the Harriet Tubman Home for Indigent Aged Negroes on twenty-five acres of land she purchased adjacent to her home in Auburn, New York. She joined Elizabeth Cady Stanton and Susan B. Anthony in their campaign for women's suffrage. In 1895, thirty years after the end of the Civil War, the government granted Tubman a pension of twenty dollars a month in recognition for her unpaid war work. She remained active in the cause of black women's rights serving as a delegate to the first convention of the National Federation of Afro-American Women in 1896. She spent her final years in poverty, dying of pneumonia at the age of ninety-three. She was buried with military honors in Auburn, New York.

In 2016, the U.S. Treasury announced that Tubman's image would replace that of former president and slave owner Andrew Jackson on the twenty-dollar bill. The new bill was expected to enter circulation sometime after 2020. However, U.S. Treasury Secretary Steven Mnuchin reported that no change will take place before 2024, saying, "Right now we have a lot more important issues to focus on."

Karen Uhlenbeck (1942–)
Mathematician

In 2019, Karen Uhlenbeck became the first woman ever to be awarded one of mathematics's highest awards, the Abel Prize, "for her pioneering achievements in geometric partial differential equations, gauge theory, and integrable systems, and for the fundamental impact of her work on analysis, geometry, and mathematical physics." Royal Society Fellow Jim Al-Khalili has called Uhlenbeck's achievements "the most important advances in mathematics in the last 40 years."

Uhlenbeck's father was an engineer, and her mother was an artist. As a child, Uhlenbeck loved reading, which led to an interest in science. "We lived in the country," she recalled, "so there wasn't a whole lot to do. I was particularly interested in reading about science." She entered the University of Michigan intending to study physics, but she changed to mathematics, gaining her B.S. degree in 1964. She continued her studies at the Courant Institute at New York University. She received a master's degree in 1966 and a Ph.D. in 1968 from Brandeis University.

After graduation, she could only find temporary jobs at MIT and at Berkeley. As she recalls, "I was told ... that people did not hire women, that women were supposed to go home and have babies." Her husband, biophysicist Olke C. Uhlenbeck, was offered positions at MIT, Stanford, and Princeton, but nepotism rules did not allow her to be hired there as well. Finally, she took a position at the University of Illinois–Urbana-Champaign, and her husband followed her. She remained there from 1971 to 1976 before being promoted to full professor at the University of Illinois–Chicago. In 1983, she was awarded the MacArthur Prize Fellowship and moved to the University of Chicago. In 1988, she became the Sid W. Richardson Foundation regents chair in mathematics at the University of Texas, where she worked for more than twenty-five years. She left Texas to become a visiting senior research scholar at Princeton University as well as visiting associate at the Institute for Advanced Study.

Uhlenbeck has described her mathematical interests in this way: "I work on partial differential equations which were originally derived from the need to describe things

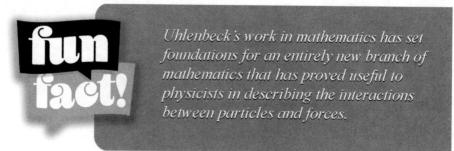

Uhlenbeck's work in mathematics has set foundations for an entirely new branch of mathematics that has proved useful to physicists in describing the interactions between particles and forces.

like electromagnetism but have undergone a century of change in which they are used in a much more technical fashion to look at the shapes of space. Mathematicians look at imaginary spaces constructed by scientists examining other problems. I started out my mathematics career by working on Palais' modern formulation of a very useful classical theory, the calculus of variations. I decided Einstein's general relativity was too hard but managed to learn a lot about geometry of space time. I did some very technical work in partial differential equations, made an unsuccessful pass at shock waves, worked in scale invariant variational problems, made a poor stab at three-dimensional manifold topology, learned gauge field theory and then some about applications to four dimensional manifolds, and have recently been working n equations with algebraic infinite symmetries." She would help formulate the mathematical underpinning to techniques widely used by physicists in quantum field theory to describe fundamental interactions between particles and forces. She also helped pioneer the field of geometric analysis. As fellow mathematician Sun-Yung Alice Chang has stated, "She did things nobody thought about doing, and after she did, she laid the foundations of a branch of mathematics."

Throughout her career, Uhlenbeck has been a strong advocate for gender equality in science and mathematics. She is one of the founders of the Park City Mathematics Institute at the Institute of Advanced Study at Princeton, which aims to train young researchers and promote mutual understanding of the interests and challenges of mathematics. She is also the cofounder of the institute's Women and Mathematics Program created in 1993 to recruit and empower women to lead in mathematics research. "I am aware of the fact that I am a role model for young women in mathematics," Uhlenbeck has said. "It's hard to be a role model, however, because what you really need to do is show students how imperfect people can be and still succeed.... I may be a wonderful mathematician and famous because of it, but I'm also very human."

Madame C. J. Walker (1867–1919)
Entrepreneur

America's first black self-made millionaire, Madame C. J. Walker was the child of former slaves who attained her success by creating and marketing an innovative line of beauty products and hair-care techniques to African American women. Through her Walker System of hair care, she built a company that defined a new role for African American entrepreneurs.

Born Sarah Breedlove on a cotton plantation in Louisiana, she was orphaned at six, married at fourteen, and a mother and widow at twenty. After her husband's death in an accident, she moved to St. Louis, where she worked as a washerwoman and part-time sales agent for a manufacturer of hair products.

In 1905, she conceived her own formula for a preparation to improve the appearance of African American women's hair consisting of a shampoo, followed by the application of her Wonderful Hair Grower, a medicated pomade to combat dandruff and prevent hair loss. The final part of her hair-care system consisted of applying light oil on the hair and then straightening it with a heated metal comb. In 1906, she moved to Denver and married Charles Walker, a sales agent for a newspaper. Together, they began a successful mail-order business selling her preparations as well as demonstrating her methods door-to-door. She also began to call herself "madame" to add prestige to the company.

In 1910, Walker transferred her operations to Indianapolis and opened a manufacturing plant there that would eventually employ three thousand to five thousand workers and become the country's largest African American-owned business. Walker's agents trained at beauty colleges and schools founded by Walker and made house calls to demonstrate and sell the company's products. Dressed in the Walker uniform—white shirtwaists tucked into long, black skirts—and carrying black satchels containing hair preparations and hairdressing apparatus, the Walker agents became familiar figures in African American communities throughout the United States.

Walker and her husband divorced in 1912 over disagreements about control and the direction of the company. In 1916, she moved her headquarters to Harlem in New

Walker's mansion, an Italian-style home designed by Vertner Tandy, New York's first registered black architect, was built next door to John D. Rockefeller's home. It has 34 rooms comprising 20,000 square feet. In 2018, it was purchased by the New Voices Foundation.

York City, and the business continued to thrive. By 1919, it had become the largest and most lucrative black-owned enterprise in the United States.

After having amassed a considerable fortune, Walker became a committed philanthropist, who made sizable contributions to the programs of the NAACP, the National Conference on Lynching, and homes for the aged in St. Louis and Indianapolis. She sponsored scholarships for young women at the Tuskegee Institute and led fundraising drives on behalf of noted educator Mary McLeod Bethune's Daytona Educational Training School. When Walker died in 1919, she left an estate worth $2 million, two-thirds of which went to charities, educational institutions, and African American civic organizations.

Barbara Walters (1929–)
Broadcast Journalist

A pioneer for women in broadcasting, Barbara Walters was the first woman to host *The Today Show* and the first to coanchor a network evening news program. She is particularly renowned for her effective, in-depth interviews with world-renowned figures.

Walters was born in Boston, Massachusetts, one of the three children of Dena and Lou Walters. She attended schools in Boston, New York City, and Miami Beach, where her father operated a series of nightclubs. After her graduation from the Birch Wathen School in New York City in 1947, she attended Sarah Lawrence College, where she earned a bachelor's degree in English in 1951. She worked as a secretary for a small New York advertising agency for a year and then obtained a job with the local NBC station working in the publicity department and writing press releases. In 1953, she began producing a 15-minute children's show, *Ask the Camera*, and also produced a talk show hosted by gossip columnist Igor Cassini, known in the trade as "Cholly Knickerbocker." She left the show after a brief office romance with her married boss, Ted Cott, which resulted in Cott stalking her and challenging one of her dates to a fistfight on the street. She moved to WPIX, where she produced the short-lived talk show *The Eloise McElhone Show*. In 1955, she became a writer on *The Morning Show* at CBS.

In 1955, Walters married business executive Robert Henry Katz; the marriage ended in 1957. The second of Walters's three husbands was theater producer and owner Lee Guber, whom she married in 1963. The couple adopted a daughter, Jacqueline, and divorced in 1976. Walters' third husband was Merv Adelson, CEO of Lorimar Productions. The marriage lasted from 1981 to 1984; they remarried in 1986 and divorced again in 1992.

After stints as a publicist with the Tex McCrary public relations firm and as a writer for *Redbook* magazine, Walters's career began in earnest when she joined NBC's popular morning program *The Today Show* in 1961. In an era when women were seen as decorative presences on television and not considered capable of reporting "hard

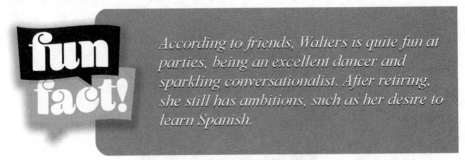

According to friends, Walters is quite fun at parties, being an excellent dancer and sparkling conversationalist. After retiring, she still has ambitions, such as her desire to learn Spanish.

news," Walters rose to become the program's regular "Today Girl," handling lighter assignments and providing the weather forecast. However, within a year, the assertive Walters had become a reporter-at-large, developing, writing, and editing her segments and interviews. In 1966, she became the show's first female host, cohosting first with Hugh Downs and then with Tom Brokaw from 1966 until 1976, when ABC hired her as the first female coanchor for a network evening news program. Walters's stint at the ABC evening news was marked by a difficult relationship with her cohost, Harry Reasoner, and ended in 1978. The following year, she began a twenty-five-year association with the ABC newsmagazine *20/20*, which she cohosted with Hugh Downs. In 1997, Walters cocreated and co-executive produced *The View*, a daytime talk-and-interview show aimed at female viewers with an audience featuring a panel of women in the entertainment industry discussing social and political issues. Walters cohosted the show until 2014, although she intermittently returned as a guest cohost afterward.

Walters became additionally famous for her in-depth series of what are sometimes known as "scoop interviews" beginning in 1977, when she jointly interviewed Egyptian President Anwar el-Sadat and Israeli Prime Minster Menachem Begin in the wake of the historic Camp David Accords. She would go on to interview a long list of luminaries ranging from world leaders to superstars in the entertainment, sports, and publishing industries. However, according to Walters, her most inspirational interview was with Robert Smithdas, a deaf and blind man dedicated to improving the lives of other sight- and hearing-impaired people.

In the second decade of the twenty-first century, Walters continued to host such shows as *20/20* and the documentary series *American Scandals* and to conduct interviews. Her last interview was with presidential candidate Donald Trump for ABC News in 2015.

Walters' published works include *How to Talk to Anyone about Practically Everything* (1970) and *Audition: A Memoir* (2008).

Randi Weingarten (1957–)
Educator, Labor Leader

A labor leader and educator, Randi Weingarten is the current president of the American Federation of Teachers (AFT) and the former president of the United Federation of Teachers (UFT). Weingarten became the first openly gay individual to be elected president of a national American labor union.

Born in New York City, Weingarten grew up in Rockland County, New York, and developed an early interest in labor unions and politics when her mother—a teacher—went on strike. Weingarten attended Cornell University and then the Cardozo School of Law. In 1986, she became counsel to the then president of the United Federation of Teachers, representing the union in several important cases and, by the early 1990s, was the union's chief contract negotiator. From 1991 to 1997, Weingarten also taught history at Clara Barton High School in Crown Heights, Brooklyn. She was elected the union's assistant secretary in 1995, treasurer in 1997, and finally president in 1998, a position she held for twelve years before becoming president of the American Federation of Teachers in 2008.

As president of the UFT, Weingarten fought for higher salaries and better training for teachers as well as merit pay. As president of the AFT, she has worked to put educational reform on the national agenda, to change how teachers are evaluated, and to improve access for all students. Weingarten has long advocated a "bottom up" approach to education reform that takes into account the views and needs of teachers and their students. Worried about the consequence of certain market-based proposals that she fears will result in the "eventual elimination of public education altogether," Weingarten sees the role of private, charter schools as complementing, rather than competing with, public schools. "Charter schools should be laboratories for innovation and creative ideas," she has asserted, "that can be scaled up so they can enrich communities."

Often a lightning rod for the contentious issues surrounding education in America, Weingarten has been a tireless advocate for teachers' rights and responsibilities as well as one of the nation's most effective contemporary labor leaders.

Weingarten announced publicly in 2007 that she is a lesbian, and in 2018 she married Rabbi Sharon Kleinbaum.

Ida B. Wells-Barnett (1862–1931)
Civil Rights Activist

Journalist, lecturer, and social activist Ida Wells-Barnett was an outspoken advocate for civil and economic rights for African Americans and women. She is perhaps best known for her fearless antilynching crusade in the 1890s and as one of the founders of the National Association for the Advancement of Colored People (NAACP).

Born into slavery in Mississippi six months before Abraham Lincoln signed the Emancipation Proclamation, Wells-Barnett was educated at a high school and industrial school for freed blacks. Her parents, who were socially active in Reconstruction Era politics, instilled in her the importance of education. She enrolled at Shaw University (now Rust College) in Mississippi, a traditionally black college that her father helped to start; however, she had to drop out at the age of sixteen when both her parents and one of her siblings died in a yellow fever outbreak, leaving her to care for her six siblings. She continued her education for a time at Fisk University in Nashville and passed her teaching examination before going to work teaching at a rural school.

In 1884, when she was traveling from Memphis to Nashville, having purchased a first-class ticket, she was ordered by the train crew to move to the car for African Americans. She refused and, when forcibly removed from the train, bit one of the men on the hand. She sued the railroad, winning a $500 settlement that was later overturned by the Tennessee Supreme Court. The injustice she felt drove her to journalism, and she began writing a weekly column for some of the small, black-owned newspapers then springing up in the South and East at the time. She would eventually become a full-time journalist and acquire a financial interest in the weekly newspaper the *Memphis Free Speech and Headlight.*

She also worked as a teacher in a segregated public school in Memphis and became a vocal critic of the conditions there. In 1891, she was fired from her job for her attacks. In 1892, a lynching in Memphis of three of her friends who were falsely accused of raping three white women drove her to denounce the lynchings as motivated not under

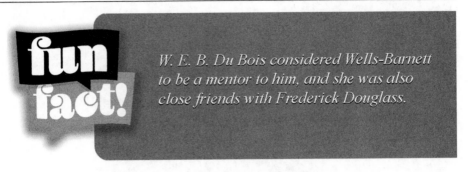

fun fact!

W. E. B. Du Bois considered Wells-Barnett to be a mentor to him, and she was also close friends with Frederick Douglass.

the familiar pretext of defending Southern, white womanhood but because the victims, grocery store owners, had been successful in competing with white shopkeepers. Wells-Barnett's exhaustive research into lynchings across the country confirmed her assertion that the violence aimed at African Americans was an attempt to enforce the repression of blacks in America. As a result of her vocal antilynching campaign, a white mob destroyed her newspaper's offices, and she received death threats. She left Memphis for New York but continued to write in-depth reports on lynchings in America. She also began to travel across the country to lecture and gain support for her campaign against lynching, founding antilynching societies and black women's clubs wherever she went.

In 1893, she moved to Chicago, where she wrote for the *Chicago Conservator*, established by lawyer Ferdinand Barnett, whom she married in 1895. In the same year, she published *A Red Record,* her three-year statistical study of lynchings in America. Wells-Barnett was also active in the struggle for civil rights for African Americans and women. She participated in the 1910 meeting that led to the formation of the NAACP. She also founded the Negro Fellowship League to assist African Americans who had migrated from the South to cities in the North. In 1913, she helped to form the Alpha Suffrage Club, believed to be the first black women's suffrage organization.

During World War I, the U.S. government placed Wells-Barnett under surveillance, labeling her a dangerous "race agitator." She continued her activism undeterred. In the 1920s, she fought for African American workers' rights, and in the 1930s, she made an unsuccessful bid for a seat in the Illinois Senate. She died of kidney disease at the age of sixty-eight. Her memoir, *Crusade for Justice,* that was left unfinished was posthumously published in 1970.

Regarded as the most famous African American woman of her era, Ida Wells-Barnett has been a much-admired precursor figure of the civil rights and women's movements of the 1960s and 1970s.

Gladys West (1930–)
Mathematician

A frican American mathematician Gladys West was instrumental in the creation of the Global Positioning System (GPS). One of the so-called Hidden Figures, women who were innovators in the early Air Force space program, West programmed a computer to deliver calculations for a geodetic Earth model and participated in the astronomical study that proved in the early 1960s the regularity of Pluto's motion relative to Neptune.

West was born in Dinwiddie County, Virginia, to a farming family of sharecroppers. Resisting her fate to work in the fields, West learned that the top two students in her class would be awarded scholarships to Virginia State College, and she managed to graduate as the class valedictorian. She studied mathematics at Virginia State College and, after graduation, taught for two years before returning to school for her master's degree. She would eventually receive a doctorate in 2018 from Virginia Tech.

In 1956, she became the second black woman ever hired to work at the U.S. Naval Weapons Laboratory Dahlgren Division as a mathematician. She would remain there for forty-two years. She worked among a small group of women on computing for the U.S. military before the age of reliance on computers. West participated in research on Pluto's motion and analyzing data from satellites to calculate Earth's shape. Describing her role in the development of the Global Positioning System, Captain Godfrey Weekes, commanding officer of the Naval Surface Warfare Center, stated, "She rose through the ranks, worked on the satellite geodesy and contributed to the accuracy of GPS and the measurement of satellite data."

After retiring in 1998, West was inducted into the U.S. Air Force Hall of Fame in 2018, one of the Air Force Space Command's highest honors. West, who married in 1957 and had three children, lives in King George County, Virginia. She has said that she prefers a paper map over use of the GPS, which she helped to create.

West not only earned her Ph.D. when she was in her eighties, but she also completed her advanced degree after she suffered a stroke.

Phillis Wheatley (c. 1753–1784)
Poet

The first published African American, female poet and, after Anne Bradstreet, the second published American female poet, Phillis Wheatley, with the 1773 publication of her book *Poems on Various Subjects*, also became the first African American to publish a book and the first to attempt to make a living from her writing.

Born in West Africa, she was sold into slavery at the age of seven, transported to the American colonies, and purchased by the Wheatley family in Boston, who provided her surname; her given name comes from the slave ship she arrived in, *The Phillis*. The Wheatleys' eighteen-year-old daughter, Mary, taught her to read and write and encouraged her verse writing. She was freed in 1773, shortly after her book of poems was published in England. Wheatley married a freed black grocer in 1778, enduring the deaths of two infant daughters and the imprisonment of her husband for debt. She failed to find a publisher or patron for a second poetry collection and was forced to support her infant son as a scullery maid in a boardinghouse. She died at the age of thirty-one.

Wheatley's first published poem, "An Elegiac Poem, on the Death of That Celebrated Divine, and Eminent Servant of Jesus Christ, the Reverend and Learned George Whitfield," a tribute to the leading minister of the religious revivalist movement of the 1740s and 1750s, known as the Great Awakening, at the age of fourteen, earned her the attention of Boston's literary elite and established her as a prodigy. Some doubted that a female African slave could have been the author, and Wheatley was forced in 1772 to defend her authorship in court, where a group of Boston luminaries, including Thomas Hutchinson, the governor, concluded that she had indeed written the poems attributed to her. Their attestation was included as the preface to her collection, published in England. Included is "On Being Brought from Africa to America," in which she recalls, "Twas mercy brought me from my Pagan land. / Taught my benighted soul to understand / That there's a God, that there's a Saviour too: / Once I redemption neither sought nor knew." Wheatley's classicism (she mastered Greek and Latin), expressed in her allusions, poetic forms, and subjects (mainly religious), is remarkable

Wheatley, unlike most slaves, was provided an education at an early age. She learned Latin, Greek, astronomy, geography, and other subjects, and she started writing at the age of fourteen.

for a woman of her time, making her one of the earliest and most accomplished American female writers.

Laura Ingalls Wilder (1867–1957)
Novelist

L aura Ingalls Wilder is best known for her eight-volume *Little House* children's book series, published between 1932 and 1943, based on her own experiences of frontier life. Regarded as a children's literature classic, Wilder's works are unique in that they reflect their author's progress from childhood, through adolescence, and on to married life, "growing up" in language and style as Wilder's own experiences matured.

Wilder was born in the Big Woods region of Wisconsin, the second of five children. When she was two years old, the family settled in 1869 in the Indian country of Kansas, near current-day Independence, Kansas. In 1871, they were on the move again back to Wisconsin and then on to Minnesota and South Dakota, where, at the age of fifteen, she began teaching in a one-room schoolhouse while attending high school. She married Almanzo Wilder in 1885 and gave birth to her daughter, Rose, in 1886. Almanzo's illness from diphtheria left him partially paralyzed, and a fire destroyed their South Dakota home. In 1894, the Wilders moved to Mansfield, Missouri, settling in a log cabin on an undeveloped property that eventually became a prosperous poultry, dairy, and fruit farm. Wilder's writing career began in 1911 with articles and columns in the *Missouri Ruralist*. A regular feature, "As a Farm Woman Thinks" found a receptive audience for Wilder's domestic subject, and she was encouraged by her daughter to develop her writing talents.

After the stock market crash of 1929 wiped out the family's investments, Wilder was prompted to earn additional income by recasting her memories of childhood into a book called *Pioneer Girl*. Her publisher encouraged her to develop and expand her story into a series, and the first book, *Little House in the Big Woods*, appeared in 1932, followed by *Farmer Boy* (1933), *Little House on the Prairie* (1935), *On the Banks of Plum Creek* (1937), *By the Shores of Silver Lake* (1939), *The Long Winter* (1940), *Little Town on the Prairie* (1941), and *These Happy Golden Years* (1943). A ninth volume, *The First Four Years*, which chronicles Laura and Alamanzo's early married life, was published posthumously in 1971. Each of the *Little House* books chronicles portions of Wilder's experiences,

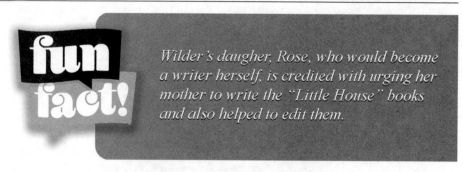

Wilder's daugher, Rose, who would become a writer herself, is credited with urging her mother to write the "Little House" books and also helped to edit them.

somewhat altered from the particulars of Wilder's actual biographical chronology. They achieved great success due to their intimate portrayals of frontier and family life.

Despite her popularity and acclaim for her classic series, controversy has clouded Wilder's legacy. One issue has been the extent to which her daughter, Rose Wilder Lane, was responsible for the production of her mother's books and whether she was in fact a coauthor. More recently, the American Library Association's lifetime achievement award, the Laura Ingalls Wilder Medal, was renamed the Children's Literature Legacy Award in 2018 due to charges of racist language and bias against Native Americans and African Americans in Wilder's books.

Oprah Winfrey (1954–)
Actress, Media Executive, Television Host

Oprah Winfrey is a show business phenomenon—an Academy Award-nominated actress, a dedicated philanthropist, and a one-woman media empire. One of the world's wealthiest entertainers, she is most famous for her long-running talk show *The Oprah Winfrey Show*, but her forays into producing and publishing have further enhanced her status as a savvy businesswoman and multitalented artist.

She was born Orpah Gail Winfrey in Kosciusko, Mississippi (she changed her birth name to Oprah because that was the way most people spelled and pronounced it). Born to an unmarried teenage mother, she grew up under difficult circumstances, primarily with her mother in Milwaukee and her father in Nashville. She graduated with honors from East Nashville High School and won a scholarship to Tennessee State University, from which she graduated in 1976.

Winfrey's media career began in high school, when she started working for a local radio station. By the age of nineteen, she was a coanchor for the evening news on Nashville's WLAC-TV. After college graduation, she was hired as a reporter and coanchor for Baltimore's WJZ-TV. Her personality and interests led her to work in the talk show format first in Baltimore and then in 1983 in Chicago. Her success in Chicago led to her own show, *The Oprah Winfrey Show*, an immediate hit, which began broadcasting nationally in 1986. For twenty-five years, her show had top ratings and had an enormous influence on U.S. culture. For example, a book selected for Oprah's Book Club would become an immediate best-seller.

Winfrey also began a screen acting career in the 1980s, and her work has included roles in *The Color Purple* (1985), for which she received an Oscar nomination, and *Beloved* (1998). In 1999, she produced the Emmy Award-winning TV movie *Tuesdays with Morrie*. Other starring or feature roles include *The Butler* (2013), *Selma* (2014), *The Immortal Life of Henrietta Lacks* (2017), and *A Wrinkle in Time* (2018). She has also served as a producer for such productions as *Their Eyes Were Watching God* (2005), *Queen Sugar* (2016), and *Love Is* (2018).

As a child, Winfrey suffered rape at the hands of family members and, when she was 14, gave birth to a son who died in infancy. She turned her life around at age 19, when she became the first black woman (and the youngest at the station) to anchor at Nashville's WTVF-TV.

In 2011, Winfrey started her own TV network, the Oprah Winfrey Network (OWN). She has gone on to pursue many other ventures in film (her production company Harpo Films), online media (with Apple), radio (Oprah Radio), and publishing (*O magazine*). By 2003, she was the first black, female billionaire and is one of the wealthiest self-made women in the United States.

Winfrey has consistently been among the top philanthropists in the United States. In 1998, she created the Oprah's Angel Network, which supported projects and provided grants to organizations around the world. She especially focused on South Africa, where she established the Oprah Winfrey Leadership Academy for Girls. She has won numerous awards for her professional and charitable work, including the U.S. Presidential Medal of Freedom in 2013.

Sarah Winnemucca (c. 1844–1891)
Educator

A Native American educator, lecturer, and tribal leader, Sarah Winnemucca is known for her book *Life Among the Piutes: Their Wrongs and Claims* (1883), the first known autobiography written by a Native American woman, which has been described by anthropologist Omer Steward as "one of the most enduring ethnohistorical books written by an American Indian."

A granddaughter of Truckee and daughter of Winnemucca, both Northern Paiute chiefs, she was born in northwestern Nevada but lived in central California, where she developed an aptitude for languages, learning English, Spanish, and several Native American dialects. She returned to Nevada in 1857, where she lived briefly with a white family, who called her Sarah. During the Paiute War of 1860, she lost several family members and decided to offer her language skills as an interpreter for the Bureau of Indian Affairs. She went with her tribe when it was relocated to the Malheur Reservation in Oregon in 1872 to help free her father when he was taken hostage by the Bannocks.

In 1879, Winnemucca lectured on plight of her tribe, and her cause attracted the attention of President Rutherford B. Hayes, whose commitment to help was never kept. Winnemucca taught at a reservation school in Washington Territory and traveled to the East Coast on lecture tours to arouse public opinion on behalf of her people. The success and sales of *Life Among the Piutes* led to a petition campaign with Congress passing a relief bill in 1884, but it did not change the economic status of the tribe. Winnemucca then returned to teaching at a Paiute school near Lovelock, Nevada.

A tireless advocate on behalf of her people, Winnemucca would become one of the earliest Native American women to educate white America to the tragedy that had befallen the Paiutes and other western Indian tribes.

Winnemucca's original given name was Thocmetony, which means "Shell Flower." She had an early hatred for white people, who killed many of her people.

Susan Wojcicki (1968–)
Company Executive

The CEO of YouTube, a subsidiary of Alphabet, Inc., the parent company of Google, Susan Wojcicki was born in Santa Clara, California, one of the three daughters of parents who are both educators. Wojcicki's sister Janet is an anthropologist and epidemiologist, while her sister Anne is the founder of the DNA testing company 23andMe. Susan Wojcicki attended Gunn High School in Palo Alto and earned a B.A. degree from Harvard in 1990, where she took her first computer science class and decided to pursue a career in technology. She received an M.S. degree in economics from the University of California–Santa Cruz in 1993 and an M.B.A. degree from the University of California– Los Angeles in 1998.

In 1998, Wojcicki rented out garage space in her Menlo Park home to Larry Page and Sergey Brin, founders of the newly incorporated Google Inc., who briefly used it as the company's first headquarters. Wojcicki became Google employee number sixteen and the company's first marketing manager the following year. During her years at Google, she helped the company grow with the development and acquisition of a variety of products, including its acquisition of YouTube in 2006 and the video website's integration into Google. She has been the CEO of YouTube since February 2014 and has guided its growth through international marketing and new applications to approximately two billion monthly users. As a result of YouTube's financial and media success, Wojcicki consistently ranks high on the lists of Most Powerful Women in such publications as *Forbes* and *Fortune* magazines.

In addition to her position at YouTube, Wojcicki serves on the boards of several organizations and is an advocate for better working environments for women and educational opportunities in computer science for girls.

Wojcicki, who is also responsible for spear-heading Google's AdSense and for the original marketing of its search engine, is a dedicated mother of five children.

Victoria Woodhull (1838–1927)
Suffragist

Women's suffrage leader Victoria Woodhull is most (in)famous for being the first woman to run for president of the United States (in 1872), but other details of her extraordinary life make Woodhull one of the most exceptional women of hers or any era. She worked for a time as a traveling clairvoyant; she and her sister were the first female brokers on Wall Street; she was the first woman to start a weekly newspaper and the first woman to address a congressional committee (in 1871); she spent election day 1872 in jail; she was a proponent of free love who declared to her lecture audiences: "I want the love of you all, promiscuously." She broke with fellow suffragist leaders Elizabeth Cady Stanton and Susan B. Anthony, who warned British suffrage leaders that she was "lewd and indecent."

Born Victoria Claflin in the rural town of Homer, Ohio, she was one of ten children. Her mother was illiterate, and her father was a con man and snake oil salesman. Woodhull did not start elementary school until she turned eight and then attended off and on for only three years before ending her formal education by marrying at the age of fifteen. As a child with a purported gift for communicating with the dead, her father put her to work telling fortunes and contacting spirits as a traveling medical clairvoyant.

In 1868, Woodhull and her sister moved to New York City, where they met the recently widowed Cornelius Vanderbilt, who was interested in spiritualism and set them up in a stockbrokerage firm, Woodhull, Claflin, & Company, which opened in 1870 and was quite successful. With the profits, Woodhull founded *Woodhull and Claflin Weekly*, a women's rights and reform newspaper that espoused legalized prostitution and dress reform as well as the utopian social system called Pantarchy, a theory rejecting conventional marriage and advocating free love and communal management of children and property. The *Weekly* would publish the first English-language version of Karl Marx and Friedrich Engels's *Communist Manifesto*.

Woodhull attended a suffrage convention in 1869 and was converted to the cause. She convinced a Massachusetts congressman to invite her to testify before the House Ju-

Woodhull spent election day 1872 in jail, after being accused of libel and sending obscene materials (her newspaper) through the mail. She would be found not guilty, but was harshly criticized by author Harriet Beecher Stowe and cartoonist Thomas Nash, who called her "Mrs. Satan."

diciary Committee in 1871 to present a petition to pass "enabling legislation" of voting rights for women. Her notoriety gained her the acceptance of suffrage leaders, and she was invited by Susan B. Anthony into the National Woman Suffrage Association. Woodhull would soon, however, join with a dissident group, the National Radical Reformers, who broke from the NWSA in 1872 to form the Equal Rights Party, who nominated Woodhull for the presidency with Frederick Douglass as vice president, although he never acknowledged the nomination. A few days before the election, Woodhull was arrested for "publishing an obscene newspaper" and jailed but acquitted on a technicality six months later. In jail on Election Day, Woodhull was prevented from attempting to vote as she intended. Her name appeared in ballots in some states, but no record exists of how many votes she received because they apparently were not counted. Woodhull would try unsuccessfully to gain nominations for the presidency again in 1884 and 1892.

In 1876 after Cornelius Vanderbilt's death, his son paid Woodhull and her sister to leave the country, and they moved to England, where Woodhull met her third husband, a wealthy banker, and would reside there until her death in 1927. She devoted her later years to running a new newspaper, preserving the English home of George Washington's ancestors, running a village school, and being a champion of education reform.

Victoria Claflin Woodhull Blood Martin died at her English home at the age of eighty-eight, a woman of great contradictions and accomplishments who broke seemingly every restriction for women of her time.

Chien-Shiung Wu (1912–1997)
Physicist

C hinese American experimental physicist Chien-Shiung Wu was a pioneer in the research of radioactivity. A member of the Manhattan Project, which developed the first atomic weapons, she is best known for the Wu experiment, which contradicted the law of conservation of parity. This discovery would earn her colleagues, Tsung-Dao Lee and Chen-Ning Yang, the 1957 Nobel Prize in Physics and Wu, whose contribution was not acknowledged at the time, the inaugural Wolf Prize in Physics in 1978. Her accomplishments in experimental physics earned her the accolades the "Chinese Madame Curie," the "First Lady of Physics," and the "Queen of Nuclear Research."

Born in a small town near Shanghai, Wu attended a school started by her father, who believed in education for girls and challenged the prevailing belief at the time in China. After attending a boarding school and serving as a schoolteacher from 1930 to 1934, Wu studied at the National Central University (later Nanjing University) first in mathematics and later in physics. After graduation, she did graduate work in physics at Zhejiang University. Urged to earn a Ph.D. abroad, Wu was accepted at the University of Michigan and departed for the United States in 1936. Arriving in San Francisco, she was shown the Radiation Laboratory at the University of California–Berkeley, and she enrolled there instead. She completed her Ph.D. in 1940. She married Luke Yuan, a fellow physicist, in 1942.

Unable to find a desired research position at a university, Wu became a physics instructor at Princeton University and Smith College. In 1944, she joined the Manhattan Project at the Substitute Alloy Materials Lab at Columbia University, focusing on radiation detectors. She would be instrumental in diagnosing the problem that shut down the first nuclear reactor by helping to identify poisoning by xenon-135 as the cause. After the war, she was offered a position at Columbia and began to study beta decay, which occurs when the nucleus of one element changes into another element, and was the first to confirm Enrico Fermi's theory of beta decay. In 1956, she was asked by theoretical physicists Tsung Dao Lee and Chen Ning Yang to devise an experiment to prove their

When influential physicist Wu married fellow physicist Luke Chia-Liu Yuan in 1942, she did not take her husband's name, a cultural custom in China but an unusual decision in the United States at the time. She even corrected students who mistakenly called her Professor Yuan.

theory of the law of conservation of parity, which held that all objects and their mirror images behave the same way. Wu's experiment using radioactive cobalt at near-absolute zero temperatures proved that identical nuclear particles do not always act alike. This discovery of parity violation was a major contribution to high-energy physics. Wu's book, *Beta Decay* (1965), is still a standard reference for nuclear physicists.

Wu continued making significant scientific contributions throughout her life, including helping to answer important biological questions about blood and sickle cell anemia. She became the first woman to serve as president of the American Physical Society. Her honors include the National Medal of Science, the Comstock Prize, and the first honorary doctorate awarded to a woman at Princeton University. Wu retired in 1981 and died in New York City at the age of eighty-four after suffering a stroke. According to her wishes, her ashes were buried in the courtyard of the school her father founded and from which Wu's academic and research career was launched.

Rosalyn Sussman Yalow (1921–2011)
Medical Physicist

Medical physicist and cowinner of the 1977 Nobel Prize in Physiology or Medicine, Rosalyn Sussman Yalow was the second woman (after Gerty Cori) and the first American-born woman to be awarded a Nobel Prize in Physiology or Medicine. Yalow was the first to apply nuclear physics to medicine, developing radioimmunoassay, a method of detecting minute quantities of biologically active substances that the Nobel Prize committee credited as "the most valuable advance in basic clinical research" up to that time. For her work, Yalow was called the "Madame Curie of the Bronx."

Yalow was born in New York's South Bronx to parents from an Eastern European immigrant background, who insisted that Yalow and her brother get the education that had been denied to them. Yalow would credit her father for instilling in her the idea that girls could do anything that boys could do. A chemistry teacher at Walton High School got her excited about chemistry, but when she attended Hunter College, she switched her emphasis to physics. As a woman in physics, Yalow faced the challenge of being accepted for graduate work. Because she could type, she obtained a position as a secretary for a leading biochemist at Columbia University's College of Physicians and Surgeons after taking stenography at a business school. As Yalow recalled, "This position was supposed to provide an entry for me into graduate course, via the backdoor." However, after only a few months in her position, she received a teaching assistantship in physics at the University of Illinois, where she earned her Ph.D. in 1945. From 1946 to 1950, she returned to Hunter to teach physics while becoming a consultant in nuclear physics at the Bronx Veterans Administration Hospital. She would work there as a research physicist and assistant chief of the radioisotope service from 1950 to 1970.

Partnering with fellow physicist Solomon A. Berson, Yalow used radioactive isotopes to analyze blood for thyroid deficiencies, for the distribution of globin and serum proteins, and to study the relationship between hormones and insulin. Their work eventually led to the development of the diagnostic process RIA that was first used to study and analyze diabetes. It is now one of the most commonly used ways to screen human

Along with thirteen other scientists, Yalow filed briefs with the California Supreme Court in 1995 asserting that, counter to complaints of home owners against San Diego Gas & Electric, there was no evidence of a link between electromagnetic fields from power lines and cancer.

blood and tissue. It made possible such practical applications as the screening of blood in blood banks for hepatitis and the determination of effective dosage levels of drugs and antibiotics.

In 1970, Yalow was appointed chief of the Nuclear Medicine Service (formerly the Radioisotope Section) at the Veterans Administration Hospital. In 1976, she became the first female recipient of the Albert Lasker Basic Medical Research Award and, in 1979, became a distinguished professor at large at the Albert Einstein College of Medicine at Yeshiva University. In 1985, she accepted the position of Solomon A. Berson distinguished professor at large (named for her former partner) at the Mount Sinai School of Medicine.

After publishing more than five hundred research papers and being honored for her achievement with the National Medal of Science in 1988, Yalow, at the age of seventy-one, retired in 1992 to become senior medical investigator emerita at the VA Hospital, still working in her lab several days a week. "I am a scientist," she remarked, "because I love investigation. Even after the Nobel Prize, the biggest thrill is to go to my laboratory and hope that one day I will know something that nobody ever knew before. There are few days when it happens, but the dream is still there. That's what it means to be a scientist."

Kristi Yamaguchi (1971–)
Figure Skater

An Olympic champion figure skater, Kristine Tsuya Yamaguchi was born in Hayward, California, and grew up in Fremont. She began taking skating and ballet lessons as a child as physical therapy to correct her clubfeet. Yamaguchi began her competitive career as both a singles skater and a pairs skater, skating with another champion singles skater, Rudy Galindo. The pair won the junior U.S. title in 1986 and 1988 and the senior pairs title in 1989 and 1990.

In women's singles, Yamaguchi won her first major international gold medal at the 1990 Goodwill Games and went on to win the 1991 World Championship. She won the U.S. championship in 1992, assuring her a spot in the 1992 Winter Olympics in Albertville. In a close competition, she won the gold in women's singles and later that year again won the World Championship. She then turned professional and began touring with Stars on Ice, which she continued to do for years. She also competed on the professional skating circuit.

In 1996, Yamaguchi established the Always Dream Foundation to support the hopes and dreams of children with a special focus on early childhood literacy. She has created a women's active-wear clothing line, worked as a broadcast skating analyst, and written several books, including three children's books. In 1997, she published *Figure Skating for Dummies*, which includes a forward by skater Scott Hamilton.

A member of the U.S. Figure Skating Hall of Fame and World Skating Hall of Fame, Yamaguchi won the 2008 Dancing with the Stars competition, and in 2011 her children's book Dream Big, Little Pig, was Number 2 on the New York Times bestseller list.

Babe Didrikson Zaharias (1911–1956)
Golfer

Considered the most outstanding female athlete in the first half of the twentieth century and possibly of any century, Babe Didrikson Zaharias was a phenomenon: a champion in basketball, track and field, and golf, also excelling in baseball, tennis, and swimming. "My goal," she once declared, "was to be the greatest athlete that ever lived." Her tenacious pursuit of that goal would change women's sports forever.

Born Mildred Didrikson, she was the child of Norwegian immigrants who settled in Beaumont, Texas. Didrikson showed remarkable athletic gifts at an early age, surpassing any child—girl or boy—in her town and received the nickname "Babe" after the great baseball star Babe Ruth, the era's reigning sports hero.

Didrikson's first organized sport was basketball, which she played in high school and on a semiprofessional team. She next took up track and field and in 1932 entered the Amateur Athletic Union women's national championship. Competing as an individual against several teams of athletes, she won six events, broke four women's world records, and won the championship, scoring twice as many points as the second-place team. Two weeks later, as a member of the U.S. team at the Summer Olympics in Los Angeles, Didrikson shattered world records in the javelin throw and the 8-meter hurdles, winning gold medals in both events. The following day, she won a silver medal in the high jump.

Despite her success, few opportunities existed for a female amateur athlete in the 1930s, and Didrikson turned professional, performing in exhibitions and on the vaudeville circuit more as a curiosity than as a respected athlete. In 1934, Didrikson followed a suggestion that she take up golf, a game that she had previously played infrequently. In 1938, while trying to qualify for a men's tournament in Los Angeles, she met and married George Zaharias, a professional wrestler.

In the 1940s, Didrikson starred on the golf course. She won the Western Open in 1940, 1944, and 1945 and, after reclaiming her amateur status, captured the 1946 National Amateur title; in 1947, she became the first U.S. woman to win the British

Never one to give up, Zaharias won her third U.S. Open and four other golf tournaments in 1954 while wearing a colostomy bag. She is still considered the greatest women's golfer of all time, winning 82 tournaments between 1933 and 1953.

Women's Amateur Tournament. In 1947, she turned professional again and went on to win thirty-four pro tournaments over the next several years, including three U.S. Open titles. She also helped to form the Ladies Professional Golf Association, which attracted more women to professional sports. Despite being diagnosed with cancer, Didrikson continued to compete in the 1950s, winning the U.S. Open and the All American Open in 1954. She died of cancer two years later.

In 1982, a poll taken of some of America's leading sports experts to name the ten most outstanding and influential American sports figures ranked Didrikson second behind only her namesake, Babe Ruth.

BIBLIOGRAPHY

Banner, Lois W. *American Beauty*. Los Angeles: Figueroa Press, 2006.

Berkin, Carol. *Revolutionary Mothers: Women and the Struggle for America's Independence*. New York: Vintage Books, 2006.

Bracken, Jeanne Munn, ed. *Women in the American Revolution*. Auburndale: History Compass, LLC, 2009.

Brumberg, Joan. *The Body Project: An Intimate History of American Girls*. New York: Random House, 1997.

Charleyboy, Lisa, and Mary Beth Leatherdale, eds. *#NotYourPrincess: Voices of Native American Women*. Toronto: Annick Press, 2017.

Clifford, Geraldine J. *Those Good Gertrudes: A Social History of Women Teachers in America*. Baltimore: Johns Hopkins University Press, 2014.

Collins, Gail. *When Everything Changed: The Amazing Journey of American Women from 1960 to the Present*. Boston: Little, Brown, 2014.

Felder, Deborah G. *The American Women's Almanac: 500 Years of Making History*. Canton: Visible Ink Press, 2020.

Frazer, Coral Celeste. *Vote!: Women's Fight for Access to the Ballot Box*. Minneapolis: Lerner Publishing Group, 2019.

Friedan, Betty. *The Feminine Mystique*. New York: W.W. Norton, 1963.

Goldmith, Connie. *Women in the Military: From Sergeants to Fighter Pilots*. Minneapolis: Lerner Publishing Group, 2019.

Gordon, Linda Perlman. *Woman's Body, Woman's Right: Birth Control in America*. New York: Penguin Books, 1990.

Haskell, Molly. *From Reverence to Rape: The Treatment of Women in the Movies*. 3rd ed. Chicago: University of Chicago Press, 2016.

Hine, Darlene, and Kathleen Thompson. *A Shining Thread of Hope: The History of Black Women in America*. New York: Broadway Books, 1998.

Kass-Simon, G., Patricia Farnes, and Deborah Nash, eds. *Women of Science: Righting the Record*. Bloomington: Indiana University Press, 1990.

Kessler-Harris, Alice. *Out to Work: A History of Wage-Earning Women in the United States*. 20th ed. New York: Oxford University Press, 2003.

Lerner, Gerda, ed. *Black Women in White America: A Documentary History*. New York: Vintage Books, 1992.

Ling, Huping. *Surviving on the Gold Mountain: A History of Chinese American Women and Their Lives*. Albany: SUNY Press, 1998.

Mays, Dorothy A. *Women in Early America: Struggle, Survival, and Freedom in a New World*. Santa Barbara: ABC-CLIO, 2004.

Moon, Danelle. *Daily Life of Women During the Civil Rights Era*. Santa Barbara: ABC-CLIO, 2011.

Raphael, June Diane, and Kate Black. *Represent: The Women's Guide to Running for Office and Changing the World*. New York: Workman Publishing Company, 2019.

Rossiter, Margaret W. *Women Scientists in America: Forging a New World since 1972*. Baltimore: Johns Hopkins University Press, 2012.

Rubinstein, Charlotte Streifer. *American Women Artists: From Indian Times to the Present*. New York: Avon Books, 1982.

Ruiz, Vicki L. *From Out of the Shadows: Mexican Women in Twentieth Century America*. New York: Oxford University Press, 2008.

Schultz, Jaime. *Qualifying Times: Points of Change in U.S. Women's Sports*. Urbana: University of Illinois Press, 2014.

Showalter, Elaine. *The Vintage Book of American Women Writers*. New York: Random House, 2011.

Weiss, Elaine. *The Woman's Hour: The Great Fight to Win the Vote*. New York: Viking Press, 2018.